Post-Apocalyptic
Patriarchy

Post-Apocalyptic Patriarchy

American Television and Gendered Visions of Survival

CARLEN LAVIGNE

McFarland & Company, Inc., Publishers

Jefferson, North Carolina

LIBRARY OF CONGRESS CATALOGUING-IN-PUBLICATION DATA

Names: Lavigne, Carlen, 1976– author.
Title: Post-apocalyptic patriarchy : American television and gendered visions of survival / Carlen Lavigne.
Description: Jefferson, North Carolina : McFarland & Company, Inc., Publishers, 2018. | Includes bibliographical references and index.
Identifiers: LCCN 2018035671 | ISBN 9780786499069 (softcover : acid free paper) ∞
Subjects: LCSH: Apocalyptic television programs—United States—History—21st century. | Western television programs—United States—History—21st century. | Patriarchy on television. | Sex role on television. | Race on television.
Classification: LCC PN1992.8.A67 L38 2018 | DDC 791.43/655—dc23
LC record available at https://lccn.loc.gov/2018035671

BRITISH LIBRARY CATALOGUING DATA ARE AVAILABLE

ISBN (print) 978-0-7864-9906-9
ISBN (ebook) 978-1-4766-3445-6

Front cover images © 2018 iStock

Printed in the United States of America

McFarland & Company, Inc., Publishers
  Box 611, Jefferson, North Carolina 28640
  www.mcfarlandpub.com

Acknowledgments

FUNDING FROM THE RED DEER COLLEGE professional development committee made this research possible. I am grateful as well for the institutional support provided by Jane MacNeil and Torben Andersen, and the professional support of my communications studies colleagues Cindy Brooks, Trish Campbell, Adrienne Orr, Kathy Pallister, and Dan Whiteside. My shenanigans are routinely endured by a multitude of other people at RDC, including Nancy Batty, Jenna Butler, Laura and Roger Davis, Heather Marcovitch, Stéphane Perreault, Jamie Prowse-Turner, Elaine Spencer, and Larry Steinbrenner.

Percy Walton and Todd Harper graciously wrote the external letters that supported my initial sabbatical project.

The Banff Centre for Arts and Creativity kindly provided me with a week-long writing residency that allowed me to finish the manuscript's first draft in the soothing shadow of the Rockies.

Thanks as well as to the anonymous reviewers who provided feedback on the manuscript in progress, and to Nikki Streeper for her kind assistance with the index.

Perennial and sincere thanks to my parents, James and Elizabeth Lavigne, as well as to Erica, Pedro, Elsa, Mila, and Davi Pereira. I couldn't do any of this without you. Additional gratitude goes to friends who have offered me their time, encouragement, and crash space (physical and/or mental): Gwen Larouche and Milks Milks, José Pou and Sarah Picard, Theresa Campbell, Andy and Linds Colven, Holly Ellingwood, Kim Horne, Diana Knapton, Jim and Margaret Martens, Elaine and Chris Parker, Anne Price, Mike Prince, Andrea Principe, Dave Principe, Susan Richter, Cindy See, Jennifer Terry, and Matt Webber.

Also, thanks to coffee, and to the cat. I'm just saying.

Table of Contents

Preface

"THE DEVIL HAS COME TO TOWN and it is the end of days" (Thompson 1). Granted, this study of American post-apocalyptic television is less concerned with religious harbingers and more concerned with the glut of world-ending programs that appeared on American (and international) screens between 2001 and 2016. It examines recent series that engage with a variety of doomsday scenarios—whether we are warring with alien forces, with nature, with science, or with ourselves—and details how this particular iteration of a long-standing genre represents current cultural moments, most notably the ambitions and fears of a dominant (white, hetero, cis male) group in flux. Whether the apocalypse comes by nuclear blast, rogue artificial intelligence, pandemic, outer space invasion, or zombie uprising, there's a TV show for that.

Within this volume's analysis, the category of "television" is focused but not pure—one cannot study *The Walking Dead* (AMC, 2010–), for example, without acknowledging its origins as a graphic series, the ways in which it has spread to other media such as video games, board games, Hallowe'en costumes, and even lottery scratch cards, or the debt it owes to earlier zombie texts like Romero's *Night of the Living Dead* (1968). *Defiance* (Syfy, 2013–15) was created as both a television series and a video game, released simultaneously. *Falling Skies* (TNT, 2011–15) is a television series and a video game that owes much of its invasion imagery to Wells's 1897 novel (and Welles's 1938 radio broadcast) *The War of the Worlds.* No television series exists in a cultural vacuum; further, our concepts of "television" are changing, as media companies like Netflix and Amazon are beginning to produce series for web streaming, and as international filming locations, casts, and co-productions (like the Sky/NBC *You, Me, and the Apocalypse,* 2015/2016) complicate attempts to situate series as being quintessentially or uniquely "American."

However, while broad examinations of Western culture and the post-apocalypse have been ably produced—Heather Urbanski's *Plagues, Apocalypses*

1

and Bug-Eyed Monsters as one example—a close reading of a sampling of post-apocalyptic texts still has much to reveal, even when the rules defining that sampling are, by necessity, arbitrary. This volume is essentially a series of case studies, each drawn from network or cable television series produced (or co-produced) by American companies at the beginnings of the twenty-first century.

The reasoning here is twofold. First, "even as it gets reconfigured in the digital era, television is still America's dominant mass medium, impacting nearly everyone" (Thompson and Mittell 5); while it may be evolving into new formats and platforms, television at this point is still the mass medium that most effectively insinuates itself into our everyday lives, whether audiences are watching network airings, binging shows on Netflix, or pirating torrents online. Viewing habits may be slowly shifting, but the average American is still watching five hours of television per day (Koblin).

Second, to narrow the field to a manageable amount of material, it is most effective to focus on one particular series of cultural productions. American television does not have a monopoly on the end times—the BBC, for example, has recently given us *Survivors* (2008–10), *Outcasts* (2010), and *In the Flesh* (2013–14), while Canada's Showcase aired *Continuum* (2012–15). However, focusing on series from one national market provides the clearest look at a specific national cultural psyche, and focusing on American television also arguably details series that have the greatest international, intercultural reach. American television has also been most clearly marked by twenty-first century Western anxieties like the post–9/11 war on terror, and analyzing its productions offers a window to a precise era of social and political change.

This study focuses specifically on the *post*-apocalypse—that is, series wherein the disaster has already occurred and survivors are left to pick up the pieces, as opposed to pre-apocalypses where protagonists are seeking to avert or prepare for catastrophe. Examining these specific post-apocalyptic scenarios allows us to address two important questions: first, how do such catastrophes speak to the fears of the present moment? How do fictional disaster scenarios reflect—either directly or metaphorically—contemporary events and concerns, from the war on terror to financial recession and the aftermath of disasters like Hurricane Katrina?

Admittedly, these initial questions could also be answered by examining pre-apocalyptic threat scenarios. The post-apocalypse, however, lends itself to additional analysis: if society as we know it does end, what happens after? One of the advantages of post-apocalyptic fiction is its potential for escaping the constrictions of current societal structures and positing different ways of being. The analyses presented here concentrate on stories which explicitly take place on a shattered Earth, where there's nothing left to do but rebuild human society. There is a potential clean slate: what will this society look like? Who will have power? Can speculative post-apocalyptic societies be formed without falling back to sexism, racism, ageism, ableism, or other conflicts of our time?

A close examination of American television series produced in the early twenty-first century reveals a deep cauldron filled with a multitude of anxieties, and further reveals a distinct sense of nostalgic wish fulfillment, particularly a desire to return to a mythical American frontier where the white male cowboy (or soldier, or police officer, or FBI agent) can take the lead in fighting off the bad guys, protecting the homestead, and crafting a new world order based heavily on the old. It is never the argument of this volume that such themes are new, or limited exclusively to the post-apocalyptic genre; certainly the white male lead can be found across both Western television and wider popular culture, and the glorification of the cowboy or the soldier has long been a part of the American mythos. The patterns occurring in post-apocalyptic television are strongly marked, however, and repetitive.

The ensuing chapters break down recently televised examples of four common post-apocalyptic scenarios: nuclear devastation, alien invasion, pandemic, and the rise of the shambling undead. In part, this borrows from Urbanski's "nightmare model," in which speculative fiction is a mirror held to cultural anxieties. Scenarios are situated in terms of wider contemporary fears regarding nuclear warfare, immigration and the foreign Other, global viral outbreaks, and the morass of concerns that has led to the recent popularity of the zombie uprising. Each series will be analyzed in terms of its major themes and their relation to twenty-first-century American cultural contexts; each will also be discussed in terms of its approaches to gender, race, and sexuality in the end times. Further chapters examine a post-apocalyptic comedy, and also discuss *post*-post-apocalyptic scenarios in which the descendants of original survivors live in futures farther flung from the initial traumatic event. The concluding section sums up overall findings, attempts to delve into some of the smaller trends running through the respective case studies, and discusses some of the contextual issues involving the television industry—whether series' ratings and longevity (or lack thereof) are relevant issues, or whether the state of American post-apocalyptic television may be more indicative of the television production industry than of specific audience preferences.

These analyses do not follow a strict format or analytical framework, but a general emphasis on critical lenses of gender, race, and sexuality is maintained throughout. Each chapter of free-form essays explores the particulars of each individual program while ultimately returning to the same major questions. The end result reveals significant patterns running through a variety of American post-apocalyptic genre programming. Admittedly, there are limitations to any academic approach—including, here, both the arbitrary lines defining series worthy of study, and the inevitable, flexible subjectivity of my own readings. In the ensuing chapters, I have tried to indicate larger contexts and incorporate the viewpoints of scholars and critics working from a number of different, often-marginalized perspectives. It is my hope that the close readings presented in this book will complement wider research about our international cultural love affairs with disaster—not just the recent popularity of post-apocalyptic television, but also films, games, comic books, and novels. In examining Hollywood's apparent desire to preserve the patriarchy above all else, I will further present an American television industry reacting to both recent world disasters (or the looming threats thereof) and ongoing advances in the feminist, civil rights, and queer rights movements—all of which threaten traditional hegemonic structures. In re-establishing patriarchal norms, the post-apocalypse looks a lot like the pre-apocalypse; after the disaster, we can return to yesterday.

Introduction

IT'S THE TWENTY-FIRST CENTURY, and the world is ending.

It isn't ending only once, or for any specific reason; it's ending over and over again, in popular culture from television to film to video games, to novels, board games, comic books, and zombie walks. It is the topic of CDC emergency scenarios and survivalist discussion boards. Our doomsday scenarios are prolific, whether we die by nuclear Armageddon, worldwide pandemic, alien invasion, zombie uprising, or supernatural event.

Images of worldwide destruction are not new, whether they are being traced back to Biblical notions of "apocalypse," medieval plague fiction, or more recent cultural products like Romero's zombie film oeuvre or the 1950s horror movies depicting death by giant monster or alien ship. After all, "it has become a cultural truism that levels and types of cultural anxiety can often be tracked by the kind of monsters that a given culture produces for entertainment purposes" (Simpson 38). However, recent years have seen a glut of doomsday scenarios in American popular culture. In film, Hollywood is revisiting old franchises through remakes like *War of the Worlds* (2005) and *The Day the Earth Stood Still* (2008). Throwback properties are receiving new installments such as *Terminator: Genisys* (2015) or *Land of the Dead* (2005), *Diary of the Dead* (2007), and *Survival of the Dead* (2009). We're also seeing new entries like *28 Days Later* (2002), *The Day After Tomorrow* (2004), *2012* (2009), or the *Resident Evil* series (2002–16). The world just keeps ending. Television has been much the same: post-apocalyptic television series produced by American networks since the year 2000 include *Jeremiah* (Showtime, 2002–04), *Battlestar Galactica* (Sci-Fi, 2005–09), *Jericho* (CBS, 2006–08), *The Walking Dead* (AMC, 2010–), *Falling Skies* (TNT, 2011–15), *Revolution* (NBC, 2012–14), *Defiance* (Syfy, 2013–15), *The Leftovers* (HBO, 2014–17), *The 100* (The CW, 2014–), *The Last Ship* (TNT, 2014–), *Z Nation* (Syfy, 2014–), *Wayward Pines* (Fox, 2015–16), *Zoo* (CBS, 2015–17), *Fear the*

Walking Dead (AMC, 2015–), *The Last Man on Earth* (Fox, 2015–), *Into the Badlands* (AMC, 2015–), *Aftermath* (Syfy, 2016), and *Colony* (USA, 2016–). Moreover, if fictional heroes are not trying to survive in a devastated world, they may be trying to prevent its demise in the first place. Time travelers attempt to avert future catastrophe in *Terminator: The Sarah Connor Chronicles* (Fox, 2008–09) and *12 Monkeys* (Syfy, 2015–). Scientists fight pandemics with biochemistry on *Helix* (Syfy, 2014–15) and quarantine on *Containment* (The CW, 2016). Other plucky heroes battle the invading forces of the unknown on *V* (ABC, 2009–11), *The Strain* (FX, 2014–), and *Extant* (CBS, 2014–15). In these lists too, we see remakes, revisitations, and new properties. The cultural ubiquity of such apocalypse stories is marked:

> Late–twentieth-century American culture is not monolithic, and for that reason it is all the more striking to see the conclusive social cataclysm repeated in so many related forms, and with so much pleasure. It requires a concerted effort for a fiction *not* to portray the end of the world [Berger 31, original emphasis].

The case studies herein are organized as an examination of several of the major fears currently saturating American culture; programs such as *Jericho*, *The Last Ship*, or *Falling Skies* incorporate worries—both longstanding and bitingly contemporary—about nuclear disaster, bioweaponry, computers and surveillance run amok, or mutating viruses. From this perspective, many of these series are distinct from each other in terms of the real fears and fictional remedies they address: *Jericho* combines twentieth-century nuclear panic with uncertainties surrounding the post–9/11 war on terror, situating the hope for salvation in small-town Midwestern America; *The Last Ship* skims over viral pandemic fears to instead act as a recruitment tool for the U.S. Navy, implicitly advocating military discipline and traditional institutions of the American government as the key to survival; and *Falling Skies* calls to American nationalism, offering Revolutionary War history and frontier patriotism as a solution to a society under siege from the invading Other. These are only three examples of series that, on one level, deal with a number of possible apocalypses in a number of related but still separate ways; in such detail, each program's borders are defined. A morass of cultural and social anxieties offers variations on potentially limitless material.

On another level, however, the case studies in this book all begin to look the same. A repetitive scenario develops: a heterosexual, cisgender white man rises to become a leader in a shattered landscape. He is often a former soldier or government agent; he often becomes some version of a cowboy in a new, crumbling wild frontier. As the series readings accumulate, it becomes apparent that post-apocalyptic television is part of the ongoing, pervasive trends in science fiction film that "record and mirror the white man's vision of future life … in which he has assigned himself centrality" (Omolade, cited in Helford

3). Women, non-white characters, queer characters, and all those whose identities cross over and between those groups are sidelined in favor of the straight white male lead. But this lingering patriarchy goes unacknowledged; in a post-apocalyptic world, it is often implied (or more than implied), there is no time or space for sexism, racism, homophobia, or other types of systemic discrimination. As such, the devastated landscape is presented as a meritocracy—post-feminist, post-racial, post-everything—in which the struggling hero claims leadership simply because he is the best person for the job. He is *needed*. He has the experience, the gumption, and the innate ability to survive.

This re-casts post-apocalyptic television as something more ominous. When considering each type of apocalypse individually—nuclear explosion, pandemic, etc.—it is possible to view these series as a type of disaster-training manual or emergency scenario (Manjikian 125), or an expression of the differing anxieties, threats, and traumas of this specific time period. In such readings, the envisioned catastrophe represents an "absence of security" (Manjikian 43)—a fictional representation of real-world terrors. When considering the genre as a whole, however, it becomes apparent that these series serve primarily to address one group's fears; they are hegemonic dream-fictions in which the political and social movements of the twentieth century are wiped from the Earth, and the straight white male hero can assume precedence without fear of challenge or criticism (Nilges). In other words, despite the global collapse, the security of the cultural status quo is, in fact, reinstated. The end of the world becomes reassuring to those who are most afraid that the society in which they claim and maintain power is in danger. In such narratives, the forces that threaten that society (feminism, civil and queer rights movements, etc.) are safely eliminated.

This invokes more traditionally religious apocalypses, in the teachings of multiple faiths, which signify "an end of one thing and a new beginning of another" (Holba and Hart xviii). In such scenarios, the end times bring about change, but that change serves as a cleansing and a renewal:

> Apocalyptic literature has traditionally been written to comfort people whose lives are, or who perceive their lives to be, overwhelmed by historical or social disruption. Its purpose is to exhort its readers to maintain faith in the midst of trying times and to assure them that they will ultimately be rewarded for their faithfulness and that their enemies will be vanquished [Rosen xii].

If such apocalypses have historically been the "province of the weak and disenfranchised" (Manjikian 2), they are undergoing a shift wherein they now provide reassurance to the rich and powerful who "expect to feel safe and are therefore particularly surprised when [they] are not" (Manjikian 4). Post-apocalyptic American television sends the message that if those in power—

specifically, heterosexual white men—are feeling frightened or threatened, the end of the world will simply remove any barriers to their greatness.

There are, then, two separate readings at work here. The post-apocalyptic series in this book are contemporary in that they are markedly influenced by post–9/11 anxieties and the recent realities of the war on terror, and accompanying anxieties about globalization and the Other. But they are also part of a much older, much broader patriarchal discourse that "has historically functioned to oppress the 'other' (e.g., women, homosexuals, people of colour)" (Hassler-Forest 36)—in Western science fiction, popular culture, or mainstream culture in general. In fact, they are particularly and oppressively conservative—emblematic of a heterosexual white male patriarchy struggling against a rising tide of the voices it has marginalized. Recent post-apocalyptic American television series are not singularly sexist, racist, or heteronormative, but they are overwhelmingly and noticeably so, steadily reinforcing gender binaries, glorifying the masculine, and excluding those whose presence might be disruptive to this myth.

— 1 —

Nuclear Attack
or Nanite Apocalypse?
The New Wild West

ALL TELEVISION PROGRAMS EXAMINED in this volume are post–9/11 texts. Indeed, the recent prevalence of televised apocalypses may be in part explained by the same cultural anxieties manifested on the cover of the *London Daily Mail* on September 12, 2001, superimposing the headline "APOCALYPSE!" over a photograph of a World Trade Center tower collapsing in New York City (Rosen xiv). The subsequent glut of post-apocalyptic television, particularly but not exclusively in the United States, may suggest a desire for disaster narratives that replicate the trauma of terrorist attack without revisiting the actual events in detail (Walliss and Aston 55); such stories may allow audiences to explore (and re-explore) alternate "scenarios where science, technology and the government are, at best, powerless against the apocalyptic forces, and at worst willingly complicit with them" (57). The CBS series *Jericho* (2006–08) and NBC's *Revolution* (2012–14) are both symptomatic, incorporating both conspiracy themes and the persistent need to unravel the mystery behind a devastating national event. *Jericho* harks to twentieth-century nuclear paranoia; *Revolution* incorporates the specter of nuclear devastation but also centers twenty-first-century issues such as nanotechnology, artificial intelligence, and bioweaponry. Both series feature an America whose political, technological, communications and transportation infrastructures have catastrophically failed, where humanity survives in rural enclaves, and where multiple factions now compete to become the new United States government. Each sets the stage for major themes that recur throughout the contemporary post-apocalyptic genre: the return to a new wild west, the glorification of military and law enforcement figures, and the associated emphasis on masculine and masculinized leadership.

9

Both *Jericho* and *Revolution* incorporate dusty American heroes, small towns, and determined settlers in a new type of wild west frontier. These series' use of frontier imagery situates them within a multitude of U.S. cultural texts—radio and television series including *The Lone Ranger* (WXYZ, 1933–54; ABC, 1949–57), *Gunsmoke* (CBS, 1955–75), or *Bonanza* (NBC, 1959–73), or films like *The Man Who Shot Liberty Valance* (1962) or *The Good, The Bad and the Ugly* (1966), but also nineteenth-century penny dreadful novels, more recent graphic novels, video games, lunch boxes, children's toys, and any number of other cultural artifacts. The cowboy inhabits American language from political speeches (from leaders such as Theodore Roosevelt and John F. Kennedy) to common vernacular like "riding shotgun" or "straight shooter" (O'Connor and Rollins 1). The figure of the cowboy has been foundational not only in popular culture but in models of ideal masculine behavior (Wright 8); indeed, "American culture would be almost unimaginable without the West as a touchstone of national identity" (O'Connor and Rollins 2).

But if "the Western hero ... has held a traditional place as one of America's oldest and most basic popular heroes" (Parks 3), post-apocalyptic television has marked a specific resurgence of western imagery. Its dystopias signify a post–9/11 America in which images of explosive catastrophe and terrorist attack represent trauma and danger, but the frontier myth is concurrently and reassuringly associated with nostalgia and the promise of safety. Wild west imagery has historically been envisioned in opposition to the apocalypse; Patrick B. Sharp has observed of texts like David Brin's *The Postman* (1982), "American popular culture is still strewn with images of frontiersman and pioneer families fighting against a post-apocalyptic wasteland, trying desperately to reestablish 'American' communities and values" ("Space" 155). Susan Faludi suggests the post–9/11 resurgence of the western, particularly televised reruns of classic films, as a search for security and familiarity:

> We reacted to our trauma ... not by interrogating it but by cocooning ourselves in the celluloid chrysalis of the baby boom's childhood. In the male version of that reverie, some nameless reflex had returned us to that 1950s Hollywood badlands where conquest and triumph played and replayed in an infinite loop [4].

The popularity of the cowboy in catastrophe invokes the wild frontier and a return to the small town, and merges also with the comforting figure of the soldier; in the post-apocalypse, they are seldom distinguishable figures. The series in this analysis are replete with protagonists who rely on military experience or some variant—former police officers, former FBI agents, former secret service. They are men (almost always men) who already know how to use both their guns and their fists. This expertise in gunplay, combat and tactics may be the hallmark of the gritty, independent protagonist, or it may come wrapped in brotherhood and the American flag, but it is nearly omnipresent.

The post-apocalypse contains multiple versions of the soldier archetype, and there is a clear overlap between military or law enforcement skills and survival in the new wild west.

Such military imagery is also a mainstay of American popular culture, from films like *All Quiet on the Western Front* (1930), *The Dirty Dozen* (1967), or *Inglourious Basterds* (2009), to television programs like *M*A*S*H* (1972–83) or *Band of Brothers* (2001), or the books that inspired them—or board games, or G.I. Joe toys, or plastic guns, or Civil War reenactment societies. The perennial popularity of action movies and war games also factors into any analysis of violence and masculinity in American media. Again, however, post–9/11 America saw a resurgence in pro-military rhetoric—the success of films like *Black Hawk Down* (2001), *The Hurt Locker* (2008), and *American Sniper* (2014), but also the resurgence of camouflage and other military-inspired fashion (Faludi 137–8; Martin and Steuter 154–55), and literal cultural signs like "Support Our Troops"–type ribbon campaigns (Lilley et al.). The involvement of American troops in Iraq and Afghanistan, continued conflicts in the Middle East, and the ever-present specter of terrorist attack have ensured that military action remains in the public consciousness. Again, both *Jericho* and *Revolution* reflect this, though their premieres are a decade apart.

Importantly, these paradigms—masculinist stereotypes associated with both the wild west and the American military—are inherently regressive with regard to issues such as gender, race and sexuality; they are both associated with patriarchal myths that advance heterosexual white men as heroes and natural leaders. Post-apocalyptic texts incorporating these ideas explore anxieties about the breakdown of civilization while simultaneously reinscribing the straight white male privilege at its root. Such catastrophic societal reboots do away with the complications that late twentieth-century advances in feminism, queer activism, or the civil rights movement have presented to the historical status quo. These speculative futures essentially wipe the slate clean—a "secular cleansing" (Curtis 7)—and offer fantasy environments in which the straight white male can return to a position of unquestioned dominance (Nilges 31). This holds particularly true in the imagery of the new American western frontier—a frontier that obviates the "unjust and inhumane" history of actual historical colonial expansion and instead creates new, guilt-free spaces for the propagation of white patriarchal ideologies (Oldring 12). Series like *Jericho* and *Revolution* are typical of the post–9/11 western, in which characters may contend with a loss of civilization, but this new world order has forced them back into reliance on traditionally masculine abilities such as wilderness survival and combat skills—thus providing straight white male protagonists an environment in which, John Wayne–like, they can flourish anew.

Jericho

One of the earlier entries in the most recent wave of post-apocalyptic American television, *Jericho* focuses on Jake Green (Skeet Ulrich), a former soldier who returns to his small Kansas hometown of Jericho just as nuclear bombs detonate in 23 major American cities. The disaster destroys the U.S. government and leaves the town residents struggling to survive as they are faced with radioactive fallout, crop shortages, electrical blackouts, refugee crises, and assault from neighboring communities. Jake must work to help keep order and save the town, becoming a leader to protect those he loves. The series is specifically situated at the turn of the century, balancing the vestiges of twentieth-century Cold War nuclear paranoia with contemporary post–9/11 trauma.

Jericho relies in large part on the threat of nuclear apocalypse that has loomed over American culture at least since H.G. Wells first coined the term "atomic bomb" in his 1914 work *The World Set Free* (Sharp "Space" 151), and most evocatively since the World War II U.S. bombing of Hiroshima (see also Urbanski 27). Perhaps the best-known incarnations of this anxiety are the giant monster movies of the 1950s (e.g., *THEM!* in the U.S., 1954; or *Godzilla* in Japan, 1954), in which radiation causes the mutation of otherwise innocent creatures who then attack the human race (Donovan). Nuclear fears—also linked to metaphoric horrors such as alien invasions or zombie narratives—have since been more explicitly included in popular novels (e.g., *A Canticle for Leibowitz*, 1960; *The Road*, 2007), films (e.g., *The Day the Earth Caught Fire*, 1961; *WarGames*, 1983; *The Terminator*, 1984), and television programs (e.g., *A Day Called "X,"* 1957; *The Day After*, 1983; or *24*, 2001–10). Considering the dissolution of the Soviet Union and the scattering of its nuclear arsenal in the 1990s, continuing contemporary fears about nuclear programs in countries such as North Korea (e.g., Kelly, Worland) and Iran (e.g., Rubio), and the recent threat of nuclear meltdown after the 2011 earthquake in Fukushima, Japan, nuclear energy and weaponry have remained timely topics through the end of the twentieth century and into the twenty-first.[1] *Jericho* plays to these concerns.

But *Jericho* was also produced less than five years after 9/11, and its narratives are clearly inflected by those events; it seems no coincidence that the bombings that decimate major American cities are referred to within the series as the "September attacks." This is what distinguishes *Jericho* as the inaugural case study in this text; it is an early example of a twenty-first-century post-apocalypse clearly informed by post–9/11 culture. The town residents, reeling from the unexpected assault on their urban centers and government systems, speculate about potential terrorist villains such as North Korea or Iran (1.15, "Semper Fidelis"), and the rumor is that New York City still survives because "after 9/11, they got pretty good at security" (1.07, "Long Live the Mayor"). *Jericho* also hinges on conspiracy plot lines as characters unravel the mystery behind the American forces that secretly orchestrated the attack, evoking comparison to 9/11 "truther" theories that insist the September 11 attacks were the result of an inside plot by the U.S. government.[2]

Jericho subsequently situates military combat and tactical skills as the keys to post-apocalyptic survival. Jake is a former military contractor and pilot who worked in the Middle East; he idolizes his deceased grandfather, a retired U.S. Army Ranger who regaled him with stories of World War II heroism. His father Johnston (Gerald McRaney) is also a retired Ranger. The links between the Green military men, Jericho's militia, and World War II history are explicit; in the season 1 finale, Jake responds to New Bern's demands for surrender with the simple statement "Nuts," a direct reference to General Anthony McAuliffe's message of defiance to the Germans at the 1944 Battle of the Bulge (1.22, "Why We Fight").[3] These consistent callbacks to Jake and Johnston's military experience, as well as the direct comparison of Jericho's season 1 "last stand" with a famous World War II battle, suggest that in a catastrophic emergency, small-town American values and culture will only survive with the protection of noble-minded men with guns (and, in this case, a tank). Such military nostalgia is symptomatic of an American trauma reaction in which "political commentators and analysis fall back to historical links with Pearl Harbor as the last attack on American soil and revisit World War II (not Vietnam or the Gulf War, interestingly) to remind the public of its own resiliency" (Kakoudaki 111). Salvation for the town of Jericho comes through the actions of trained, brave, and male American soldiers—evoking a "support our troops" mentality situated in a long history of American war propaganda, but noticeable once more at the dawning of the Iraq War.

As a post–9/11 text, *Jericho* is additionally deeply marked by American western tradition, providing a variation on the lone-gunslinger-comes-to-town narrative; Jake returns to his hometown as a taciturn stranger, long absent under mysterious circumstances, who must demonstrate his leadership skills and combat prowess to earn a position of community respect before he leads the town's militia defense against outside denizens of the newly lawless frontier. The series does not evoke a specific period in American history so much as the general image of determined men with rifles defending their homesteads against the untamed world outside; its homage to the aesthetic of Midwest American independence is evoked by armed men on horseback (e.g., 1.15, "Semper Fidelis") and the town's use of the Gadsden flag, featuring a Revolutionary War–era snake with the motto "don't tread on me" (Whitten; 2.02, "Condor"). *Jericho*'s debt to the western genre is perhaps even more apparent in season 2, which sees Jake formally established as the new town sheriff—a "key figure" in the western mythos (O'Connor and Rollins 20). He then works to preserve his small community against an authoritarian, unelected American government closely tied to the new megacorporate railway company Jennings & Rall—railway companies being noted foes of cowboys and the open frontier (Slotkin 19; Hewitson 166). Here, *Jericho*'s archetypes call to populist suspicions of big government (Slotkin 22–3) and are steeped in the same wild west lore on which the American colonial dream was founded.

These contextual influences work together to explain *Jericho*'s socially and politically regressive themes. Multiple aspects of the series—its ties to nuclear paranoia and colonial nostalgia, military images and history, and the wild west mythos—set the stage for its gender-stereotyped, white-centered, heteronormative story.

Women in the Pantry, Men in the Field

The influences of *Jericho*'s major paradigms are most apparent when examining the strict gender roles enforced in the series. First, the back story of nuclear disaster implicitly harks back to mid–twentieth-century American government pamphlets that sought to instruct citizens terrified of potential nuclear catastrophe. Such publications promised that in the event of nuclear attack, it was still possible for Americans to survive and thrive using things from "Grandma's Pantry"—in essence, by returning to survival skills preserved from colonial settler times. This reassuring narrative reinforced the association of women with the domestic sphere, while reasserting men as protectors and providers for the family (Sharp *Savage Perils*; see also Faludi 282, Coleman 42). If promises of "Grandma's Pantry" and the resilience of the American settler were the solution to post–World War II nuclear trauma, this same promise is inherent in *Jericho*, where survival in the face of catastrophic nuclear attack is dependent on the men who take charge and the women who support them.

Jericho's frequent use of military imagery also invokes strict gender divisions, symptomatic of post–9/11 rhetoric in which twenty-first-century news and lifestyle commentaries were frequently marked by the desire for more masculine men and more feminine women. This return to traditional gender roles would presumably shore up America. In such narratives, feminism was cast as a "treasonous" weakening of the men whose heroism was vital to the country (Faludi 22–3):

> Of all the peculiar responses our culture manifested to 9/11, perhaps none was more incongruous than the desire to rein in a liberated female population. In some murky fashion, women's independence had become implicated in our nation's failure to protect itself. And, conversely, the need to remedy that failure somehow required a distaff cor-

rection, a discounting of female opinions, a demeaning of the female voice, and a general shrinkage of the female profile [Faludi 21].

This included fears that women would weaken the military (26)—a set of institutions long associated with masculine prowess. Post–9/11 media called for a return of America's masculine heroism and military might, positioning women as a hindrance to the masculinity of its soldiers.

In compliance with both of these conservative paradigms, the gender division between public and domestic spheres is evident in *Jericho*, where all political, military, and paramilitary forces are marked as intrinsically male. The two successive mayors of Jericho, Johnston Green and Gray Anderson (Michael Gaston), are men; so is deputy mayor Eric Green (Kenneth Mitchell); so is former FBI agent Robert Hawkins (Lennie James); so are the police; so are the soldiers. The decimated United States becomes divided into six territories as six men war for the presidency (1.13, "Black Jack"). The mastermind behind the attacks, Valente (Daniel Benzali), is male, as is the mysterious "John Smith" (Xander Berkeley). Jonah Prowse (James Remar) runs an all-male road gang just outside Jericho and Phil Constantino (Timothy Omundson) has recruited the men of nearby town New Bern as the army that supports his dictatorship. There is one female police officer who appears in the pilot, and one female soldier who appears in season 2 (2.02, "Condor"); there is also a single female Marine who turns out to be a fraud (1.15, "Semper Fidelis"). Apart from these brief and rather dismal exceptions, any figures of authority, or any figures occupying traditionally "masculine" roles, are male. It is not unusual to see scenes in which the men of Jericho gather grimly in an office or station in order to debate with each other regarding the future of the town and the best manner of dealing with the latest crisis (e.g., 1.17, "One Man's Terrorist"; 1.19, "Casus Belli"; 1.21, "Coalition of the Willing"). The lines between public and private are firmly drawn.

Further, *Jericho* is a western, and westerns are fundamentally patriarchal power fantasies (Hassler-Forest 345) in which "women are most closely associated with civilization and domestication—the taming of the frontier wilderness and the wildness of the men who have made it their home" (Coleman 42). It is unsurprising, then, that women's roles in *Jericho* are visibly skewed to the traditional and nurturing, reinscribing hegemonic notions of the domestic feminine. Female characters include Emily Sullivan (Ashley Scott), a school teacher and Jake's love interest; Heather Lisinski (Sprague Grayden), also a school teacher; Gail Green (Pamela Reed), a retired nurse and wife of Johnston Green/mother to Jake and Eric; Mimi Clark (Alicia Coppola), an IRS employee; Bonnie Richmond (Shoshanna Stern), a farm girl; Mary Bailey (Clare Carey), a bar owner and Eric's mistress; April Green (Darby Stanchfield), the local doctor/Eric's wife; Skylar Stevens (Candace Bailey), a wealthy teenager left orphaned in the disaster, and Darcy Hawkins (April Parker-

Jones), Robert's wife and mother to their two children. There are frequently and consistently women present, but they are nurturers, dependents, and love interests.

Some of the women occupy particularly stereotypical roles. In the gendered figures of the American frontier, the "schoolmarm-civilizer" archetype is embodied by the pure and gracious woman who is the love of the wild west cowboy (O'Connor and Rollins 15); elementary teacher Emily fills this space. Emily is the one who comforts Jake in times of crisis or injury (1.22, "Why We Fight"; 2.06, "Sedition") and the one whose love he earns by establishing his place of moral responsibility in the community (1.22, "Why We Fight"; see Wright 152), but he is certain to remind her that loving him is dangerous: "Look, you shouldn't be near me. You're a school teacher, kid. A *school teacher*" (1.21, "Coalition of the Willing"; emphasis as vocalized). Mary Bailey, who runs the town bar and engages in an illicit affair with the married Eric Green, also invites comparison to stereotypes of the prostitutes or women of "loose morals" associated with western saloons (see O'Connor and Rollins 1; Coleman 33).

Mostly, however, westerns are simply stories about men; women are wholly secondary, except as rewards or as damsels in distress. In such stories, "women should not be competitive with men. Rather, they should provide a loving, supportive refuge" (Wright 144). If one method of culturally privileging masculinity is "putting women down, both by excluding them from the public sphere and by the quotidian put-downs in speech and behaviors that organize the daily life of the American man" (Kimmel 191), then we see this reflected in *Jericho*. One quite common pattern in series episodes involves a man asking a woman to leave a conversation so he can talk to another man. An incomplete list of examples includes:

> "Darcy, I'm gonna need a minute alone with Mr. Anderson" [1.08, "Rogue River"].
>
> "Hey, sweetie. Do you mind giving me and my man here a little privacy?" [1.11, "Vox Populi"].
>
> "Uh, sweetie, will you ... will you give us a moment to talk?" [1.12, "The Day Before"].
>
> "April, can we have a minute?" [1.14, "Heart of Winter"].

The same patterns are not true in other gender configurations. On the single occasion that Darcy Hawkins asks her young son to leave a room so she can talk to the deputy sheriff (1.19, "Casus Belli"), she inadvertently equates the positioning of women in other scenes with children or innocents who either need protection or whose input would be tangential to discussions of serious import. As the women of *Jericho* are consistently sidelined from political and tactical discussion, it becomes apparent how the series can casually incorporate dialogue such as "women and children first" (1.03, "Four

Horsemen"), "You squealed like a little girl" (1.14, "Heart of Winter"), "Women are from Venus and men are wrong" (1.19, "Casus Belli"), or "We just need some more manpower to show people there's still law and order in the town" (1.04, "Walls of Jericho").

On one notable occasion, Major Beck (Esai Morales) dismisses a male soldier so he can speak with Heather (2.01, "Reconstruction"). Heather's rare but recurring inclusion in men's discussions marks her as "the exception"; she is also a school teacher, but her specialty is science. As one of the few female characters who is neither a love interest nor a male character's immediate family member, she occupies a more independent position and is associated with masculine logic. She is the token female character whose mechanical expertise startles Jake (1.02, "Fallout"), and who can be secondarily included in Jake and Hawkins's spy craft (2.04, "Oversight"); while her agency is laudable, she is absent for the back half of the first season, and her showcased capabilities also mark her as different, incidentally normalizing the more gendered behaviors of almost every other woman in the series.

Each of *Jericho*'s major genre paradigms thus promotes a form of gender division: the nuclear survivalist narrative that relies on the domesticity of "Grandma's Pantry," the post-9/11 media that called for the return of "manly men" (Faludi 76–8) and the "new traditional woman" (137–38), and the wild west stories that have culturally served as a "patriarchal power fantasy" (Hassler-Forest 345). *Jericho* especially demonstrates the manner in which wild west archetypes may be incorporated into post-apocalyptic settings, and also continues the long-established American tradition of envisioning the wild west as a male playground. This means preserving stereotypical gender roles while consistently and deliberately excluding women from any possible assertion of masculine agency. When Emily and Allison Hawkins (Jazz Raycole) take up guns for season 1's final battle with New Bern (1.21, "Coalition of the Willing"), it is meant as a sign of truly desperate straits: arming the women is what the town has come to.

Jericho and Race

Jericho's frameworks have also, most particularly, prioritized the interests of white men. In American nuclear history, the racial divide was obvious in post–World War II civil defense plans and government policies that positioned "the white suburban family as the hero of the nuclear frontier" (Sharp *Savage Perils* 188) and did not provide equally for Black citizens (196). In post-9/11 popular media, Tasker and Negra have noted that the "fantasies of patriarchal protection" heralded a resurgence of straight white male heroes (13), and racial conflict (i.e., "cowboys vs. Indians") is a foundational element of the frontier discourse that not only glorifies white cowboy heroes (Slotkin

13; Limerick 73; Wright 159–60) but also erases both the cultural diversity of the historic frontier (Deutsch 5) and the genocidal history of European colonial expansion:

> American popular stories have generally portrayed white male superiority for more than two centuries. Non-white characters—blacks, Hispanics, Asians, Indians—have either not been portrayed at all, or they have usually been portrayed as inferior, primarily suitable for servitude, removal, or pity. Many of our stories have simply left them out, essentially asserting by dramatic default that only white people are important and interesting [Wright 159–160].

It is no coincidence that the resurgence of small-town rural America is a key image in U.S. white supremacist rhetoric (Schlatter 40).

Again, these genre elements combine to create an ultimately conservative narrative: the racial segregation in *Jericho* is unacknowledged but pronounced. *Jericho* features a predominately white cast; except for occasional extras, new doctor Kenchy Dhuwalia (Aasif Mandvi, eight episodes), and second-season addition Major Edward Beck (seven episodes), Hawkins, his wife Darcy, and their two children Allison and Sam (Sterling Ardrey) are apparently the only people of color in Jericho, having arrived one day before the explosions. Yet Jericho is presented as post-racial; in the only incident where the Hawkins family is acknowledged as racially different, Allison tries to distract the two white men searching her home: "Are you harassing everyone in town or just the Black people?" (1.08, "Rogue River"). This accusation, within the context of the episode, is presented as false—the men *are* "harassing" all newcomers—and moreover, Allison is only making the accusation to try and buy time for her father. The series implies that questioning the new arrivals just for being Black would never even have occurred to the local police—that all citizens are accepted and treated as equals. Such post-racial positioning, popular in contemporary liberal texts, implicitly assumes that progressive strides have already eliminated racism in any systemic sense, leaving any remaining acts or inequalities as echoes of a now-vanquished past (Valluvan 2241).

However, despite this egalitarian pretense, *Jericho*'s few characters of color are noticeably absent from the town's social and political life. Over the course of the first season, Hawkins must guard a nuclear bomb, investigate the conspiracy, fend off his murderous FBI ex-lover, interrogate the mysterious John Smith, and reconcile with his estranged family, but despite his importance to *Jericho*'s plot, most of his plot lines are kept separate from the town's politics, and he seldom interacts in depth with anyone outside his family except Jake. This segregation means that Hawkins may have influence in the town, but he is not a contender for mayor or sheriff, and he is not often present in the groups of men who decide the town's future.

The gender and race concerns here are intersectional. The other members of the Hawkins family are kept even more separate; it is eight episodes into season 1 before Darcy interacts with anyone onscreen apart from her immediate family (1.08, "Rogue River"), while Allison and Sam barely leave the house. They are victims of Hawkins' kidnapping and forbidden to go outside; here, too, gender inflects Darcy's helplessness, equating her with her children as all are held captive under Hawkins' masculine authority.

Sarah Mason (Siena Goines), Hawkins' former FBI partner (and ex-lover) now turned traitor, is another character noticeably affected by both gender and race stereotypes, as she is both a combat veteran and a woman of color. Her brief (five-episode) role as a series *femme fatale* is problematic; on the one hand, within *Jericho*, power is obtained and held through physical force, and Sarah is capable of snapping a man's neck with her bare hands. On the other, her role as FBI agent is compromised by her positioning as Hawkins' former lover; she is sexually aggressive and one of the few women to be openly sexualized by the camera, as we gratuitously see her in her bra (1.13, "Black Jack"). Not only is her body objectified, her narrative is also intertwined with the Hawkins family and thus separate from the main plot line; this removes her from direct engagement with the white masculine forces that struggle for power within the town. Sarah is more violent, more knowledgeable, and subsequently more powerful than the other women of the series, but she also dies early. Her professional capabilities are undercut by her gender in terms of her position as jilted lover, and by her race—both with regard to the positioning of her non-white body as both dangerous and objectified, and also in terms of her overall segregation from a narrative centered on the travails of white Americans in the post-apocalypse.

Summary

The mythical western frontier is "a realm noted for the limited breadth of its characterizations" (Coleman 34), and *Jericho*'s stereotypes are consistent. Its use of western tropes and focus on militarized resistance coincides with its persistent sidelining of the female characters who serve as lovers, mothers, and sisters for the men who are the inarguable focus of the series. *Jericho* harks back to notions of apple-pie Midwestern American life in positing a future that preserves truth, justice, and the American way—symptomatic of "the long-standing sense of American post-apocalyptic perfection" (Berger 136). This future is white and heteronormative by default. What little gender hybridity the series allows is a movement toward women becoming "tougher" (e.g., Allison shooting Sarah Mason [1.15 "Semper Fidelis"]) rather than men becoming nurturers or assuming domestic social roles. Further, the series assumes a post-racial society while segregating the narratives of non-white characters. Other marginalized groups, such as LGBTQ characters, are simply never represented, and while the series is notable for including a Deaf character (Bonnie), it also kills her off in a shootout (2.04, "Oversight") in order to showcase her brother's subsequent drive for vengeance. In the town of Jericho, masculine leadership prevails; in making each successive decision about the town's actions, the men in charge merely decide what *variation* on this masculinity they will adhere to. Each time a group of heterosexual white men gathers in a police station, office, or warehouse to hold intense discussions about an imminent attack, pressing resource issue, or other emergency decision, it only reinforces the notion that such men are natural leaders. Their prominence in *Jericho*'s narratives is canonically normalized.

Situated both chronologically and thematically at the beginning of the twenty-first century, *Jericho* recycles a variety of known tropes, incorporating nuclear fears, American frontier imagery, and post–9/11 anxieties. There is overlap between each of these paradigms; the atomic bomb is inextricably associated with both American military warfare (particularly World War II) and frontier survivalist imagery (Sharp *Savage Perils* 188). Both twentieth-century Cold War fears and twenty-first-century post–9/11 anxieties have been linked to the western and a post–9/11 media era which resurrected the cowboy as a reassuring figure to a traumatized baby boom generation (Faludi 4), and both produce narratives that glorify the military and military men, emphasizing combat and warfare as the masculinist keys to survival in a patriarchal world. Each of *Jericho*'s primary frameworks calls for restrictive gender performances and heteronormative white stories. As an early example of post-apocalyptic television in this millennium, *Jericho* sets the tone for many more recent twenty-first-century series; its themes wend through multiple other programs studied in this volume.

Revolution

In more recent post-apocalyptic television, NBC's *Revolution* (2012–14) has elicited a number of comparisons with *Jericho*.[4] Truthfully, however, *Revolution* owed debts to multiple series: "Fans at Comic-Con who watched NBC's big new drama pilot—about a blackout that takes out all electronic devices—only agreed on one thing: It reminded them of another apocalyptic TV show" (Hibberd). *Revolution* incorporates a fear of technology—specifically, a suspicion of computers, biotech and artificial intelligence. This fear of the "out-of-control computer ... yet another treasured nightmare in speculative fiction" (Urbanski 47) harks to a number of other popular culture texts such as *2001: A Space Odyssey* (1968), *I, Robot* (2004), the ongoing *Terminator* franchise, or the more recent *Person of Interest* (CBS, 2011–16). Unlike *Jericho*, *Revolution* shifts away from Cold War nuclear paranoia; as in other contemporary post-apocalyptic series (such as *The 100* or *Z Nation*), *Revo-*

lution's nuclear attack (a nuclear missile strike launched in the season 1 finale) is relegated to a secondary plot detail, much as nuclear fears have settled into a persistent background static in our daily lives—a "psychic numbing" (Caputi 101), or a "dread" that persists "even when not spoken aloud" (Weart 422). Instead of dwelling on the nuclear attack, *Revolution* moves further into territories marked by post–9/11 anxieties while maintaining narrative and thematic congruences with *Jericho*: both series deal with the advent of a new American Civil War, their protagonists fighting against unelected Presidents and invasive new U.S. governments, and both openly appeal to the myths of American colonial history and the frontier west.

Revolution's blackout is the result of government conspiracy and weaponized technologies gone wrong. In this world, where electrical systems and internal combustion engines have suddenly stopped working, small town enclaves dot the former continental United States, which has become a war zone divided by territorial militias. Soldiers armed with swords and guns range across a landscape littered with useless cars. *Revolution* begins approximately 11 years after the blackout, when scientist Ben Matheson (Tim Guinee) is killed by members of the Monroe Militia, who have sought him out because he is thought to hold the key to turning the power back on. Militia captain Tom Neville (Giancarlo Esposito) takes Ben's son Danny (Graham Rogers) prisoner instead, whereupon Danny's sister Charlie (Tracy Spiridakos) flees in search of her estranged uncle Miles (Billy Burke), a former militia general now in hiding. As Miles helps Charlie rescue Danny and find her long-lost mother Rachel (Elizabeth Mitchell), they become entangled with civil rebellion, scientific conspiracy, and the rising threat of war. Major characters in the ensemble cast include former dot-com billionaire Aaron Pittman (Zak Orth), rebel agent Nora Clayton (Daniella Alonso), and militia general and dictator Sebastian Monroe (David Lyons), as well as Neville's wife Julia (Kim Raver) and their son Jason (J.D. Pardo).

At first glance, *Revolution* provides more diverse gender roles and a better reflection of twenty-first-century feminism; however, closer examination reveals that what *could* be a stage for speculative new forms of government, socio-cultural relations, or gender performance ultimately fails to live up to any such potential. Burcar has noted the gendered differences coded within "hard" (aggressive, violent; masculine) and "soft" (attractive, coercive; feminine) types of power in Western societies (100); *Revolution* seems to offer more gender hybridity than *Jericho*, but the series narrative still rewards the masculine—those who can demonstrate "hard" power including military skills, tactics, independence, violence, and other traits culturally considered to be "male." While *Jericho* incorporates the same gender roles that hark back to mid–twentieth-century anti-nuclear propaganda, *Revolution* seems particularly emblematic of post–9/11 American discourse that feared men had become "weak." This is not to reinforce or subscribe to gender binaries, but only to suggest that within the series, behaviors culturally defined as "masculine" are depicted as essential to survival; prominent female characters are shown adopting masculine behaviors, but the male leads fail to develop any meaningfully "feminine" or "soft" traits. Indeed, the most peaceful and sensitive male characters must adapt, toughening in order to survive. As a post–9/11 western, *Revolution* continues to privilege masculine behaviors while placing strict limits on women's roles and focusing on white, heteronormative narratives.

"Soft" Women

Revolution rewards hard power above all; there is little place for femininity in its rough-and-tumble new frontier. Women who fill stereotypically feminine roles are featured mainly as minor or recurring characters; they tend to be either gentle victims or sexualized manipulators. Cynthia Pittman (Jessica Collins) and Sophie Hudson (Crystal Martinez) might be seen as examples of the former; both are innocents who serve as adjuncts to their husbands' stories. Cynthia dies at the hands of a man who is trying to interrogate her husband Aaron for information (2.09, "Everyone Says I Love You"); she is "fridged," a term first coined by Gail Simone, describing a woman who is tortured or killed as a plot point in a male character's story. Sophie disowns her own rebel husband Jim (Malik Yoba) when she learns of his violent past; she is later captured and held offscreen as leverage against his behavior, her ultimate fate unknown (1.18, "Clue").

Some soft women still have influence, if predominantly ineffectively: Julia Neville fulfills the stereotype of a feminine woman who survives via her sex appeal in a masculine society. Julia is the Lady Macbeth of the series, plotting her husband Tom's advancement and using her femininity as a manipulative tool against both Tom and, in the second season, her new husband Victor (Christopher Cousins). She is the vamp who moves from one male protector to the next, cultivating political ambitions that never come to fruition. Though she has more agency than Cynthia or Sophie, she is repeatedly held hostage in order to motivate Tom (i.e., 1.10, "Nobody's Fault but Mine"); at series' end (due to cancellation), she is a captive offscreen.

The president of the Georgia Federation, Kelly Foster (Leslie Hope), occupies a liminal role here: she presents as a cutthroat political leader, but exhibits no combat abilities of her own, instead acting through exclusively male soldiers. She enlists Miles Matheson as her general after holding a knife to his testicles and alluding to a previous sexual relationship (1.14, "The Night the Lights Went Out in Georgia"). Like Julia, in *Revolution*'s violent world, she is a woman who achieves power only by proxy.

In general, feminized women are seen in the background, but not accorded significant roles in the narrative; the story is not about them. Rather, families and communities—the more feminized elements of society—may be read as "victims waiting for rescue" (Oldring 13), there to motivate the men; a male scientist, for example, is forced to develop anthrax for the militia in order to save his wife and daughter (1.16, "The Love Boat"), while a mad cult leader attacks a town to seek a cure for his terminally ill wife (2.03, "Love Story"). Even Cynthia and Julia, while they have more lines than Sophie or Kelly Foster, are never fully developed as individuals. *Revolution* fleshes out its character histories through frequent flashbacks to times before the blackout, but these women are seen in flashback only as part of their husbands' pasts, never in scenes that present their own histories or points of view. They are the damsels and the victims, waiting (sometimes futilely) for men to save them.

Soft Men

Whereas *Jericho* predominantly featured manly men and feminine women, taking the masculinity of its male characters for granted, *Revolution* offers more than one version of manhood; however, it tends to reward the actions of aggressive, military masculine heroes, demonstrating part of "the ways in which different models of masculinity have been said to form a hierarchy of acceptable, unacceptable and marginalized models for the male" (Feasey 2). Men who display feminine traits are weak, and suffer accordingly. The most prominent example is Aaron Pittman, the former software billionaire now left broke and nearly useless in a world without computers. Aaron lacks the athleticism and trim body of other characters in the series; he is referred to as "Chubs" (1.19, "Children of Men"), "your portly friend" (1.20, "The Dark Tower") or "the fat guy" (1.06, "Sex and Drugs"). He is the only character to wear glasses. He is the weakest member of Miles's de facto group of survivalists; he can't use a sword or throw a punch. He is employed as a teacher of young children (1.01, "Pilot") and generally occupies a traditionally feminine role—empathetic and nurturing, and subsequently a hapless victim in need of protection. Notably, he is the only man to be included in a rape threat (1.01, "Pilot"). He is the "girly-man" of contemporary discourse in which "the controlling male stereotype is that of the muscular action-hero male as manly and of other men (non-weight lifters, nonmacho straight men, gays) as lack" (Battistella 103).

This onscreen disempowerment is symptomatic of the same post-9/11 politics that called for a return to traditional gender roles, with masculine male heroes needed to protect America against invaders. Before the blackout, Aaron was a twenty-first-century success—a brilliant, nerdy tech leader with seemingly endless funds—but in a time of crisis, his softer traits are presented as a failure of masculine responsibility. If "post-apocalyptic fiction, as a genre, is didactic: *this* is what we need to be careful of; *this* is how we survive such an event" (Curtis 17; see also Manjikian 125), then Aaron's folly was embracing his role as a twenty-first-century "new man," made vulnerable by his dependence on technology and his abandonment of physical pursuits. Neville sneers to him, "I bet you were high and mighty when the lights came on … now, you need Miles saving your fat, pock-marked ass" (1.10, "Nobody's Fault but Mine").

Aaron must toughen up in order to be redeemed. Much of his narrative evolution between seasons 1 and 2 involves him trying to become stronger and able to occupy a position in which he might protect a wife—a task at which he repeatedly fails. In episode 1.6 ("Sex and Drugs"), we see flashbacks to Aaron's past just before and after the blackout; he and his first wife Priscilla (Maureen Sebastian) are toasting their anniversary in a limousine, about to take off for a weekend on the corporate jet, when the power goes out and traffic rolls to a standstill. Soon after, Aaron and Priscilla are struggling to survive; when Priscilla contracts what seems to be food poisoning, Aaron cannot help her. Instead, tall blond stranger Sean (Michael Roark) swoops in, later saving both Aaron and Priscilla from attack. Aaron, frustrated at his inability to do so much as light a fire in the wilderness, abandons Priscilla in the middle of the night, leaving her with Sean's group. His wedding ring sits atop a folded note: "I can't protect you. You're better off with them. I'm sorry."

Years later, when Aaron re-encounters Priscilla, he has grown enough to help save her from the bounty hunter holding her captive (1.15, "Home"). It seems no coincidence that we see him, in his character development between the two Priscilla episodes, successfully lighting a campfire (1.10, "Nobody's Fault but Mine"). He is too late, though; Priscilla has a new family. She relinquishes Aaron of his responsibilities: "I want you to know I love you, Aaron. I always will. Don't worry about me anymore, okay?" (1.15, "Home").

By the beginning of season 2, Aaron has married fellow teacher Cynthia.[5] Though both are coded as "soft," Aaron's science background lends him superior knowledge; when he begins to exhibit control over the nanotech that caused the blackout, Cynthia is convinced that his abilities are a religious miracle. Ultimately, her misguided faith places her in a position where Aaron—still a "weak" male character—must seek to protect her. He fails when she is killed, an event that sends him cross-country as he seeks an end to the nanotech's increasingly intrusive artificial intelligence. Though he fails to eliminate the nanites, his efforts temporarily earn back the love of Priscilla—an event later complicated by the revelation that Priscilla is being controlled by the nanotech. While Aaron has managed to throw off the nanotech's attempted control of his brain, Priscilla has not been so strong (2.18, "Austin

City Limits"). Again, Aaron must save Priscilla as he failed to save her (and Cynthia) before[6]; while he remains the least aggressive of the series leads, his masculine positioning grows increasingly pronounced.

There are also limits to Aaron's shaming; while different types of masculinity may access different types and levels of power, masculinity itself remains privileged in popular culture (Feasey 3). Aaron's progress as a man may be measured against his relationships with women: his abandonment of Priscilla, his failed attempt to protect Cynthia, and his second chance at saving his first wife. He also gains his own special position in the narrative when he discovers that his graduate work at MIT was instrumental in creating the blackout nanotech (1.16, "The Love Boat"). Rachel compares the technical guide to "a spellbook" (1.16, "The Love Boat"), and it's difficult not to associate Aaron with wizardry or messiah-like power, particularly considering his rise from the dead in season 2 and his related ability to set enemies on fire with his mind (2.08, "Come Blow Your Horn"). Even as the "weak" male member of the party, Aaron remains privileged; other characters deride his digital-age dependencies, but his journey toward self-sufficiency also sees him elevated to a key position outside the militarized power structures of the rest of *Revolution*'s frontier society. At the end of the first season, he pleads for the technology that gave him power: "It means I don't have to be afraid of someone coming for me, or my wife" (1.19, "Children of Men"). In season 2, as he becomes a tougher man, the power comes to him unbidden, offering the narrative promise that he may yet be elevated to greater levels of influence.

Danny Matheson provides a second example of a "soft" male character, one who is killed before he can complete his journey to manhood. Danny is asthmatic and, in a world without contemporary medicine, he has been protected all his life by his older sister Charlie. He is young, physically impaired, and—it is implied—has been over-coddled, rendering him helpless when he is kidnapped by militia soldiers. As Charlie seeks out her uncle Miles to save Danny, Danny himself must learn to survive on his own—plotting escape attempts, dealing with abusive soldiers, and reaching a détente with his chief captor, Tom Neville. Though he occupies a "damsel in distress" position for much of his time on the series, like Aaron, he must learn confidence and independence, though he is too young for a wife. His progress is ultimately cut short midway through the first season, when he dies after taking up a gun in a firefight; nevertheless, he dies a man.

Hard Women

The series' lead women include crossbow-wielding Charlie Matheson, nanoscientist Rachel Matheson, and bounty-hunter-turned-rebel Nora

Clayton. If one tradition of the western is an implicit understanding that "the West is no place for a lady" (Schlatter 4), then *Revolution* skirts this by divorcing its women from "ladyship"; its female protagonists are independent and self-sufficient, having adapted to the masculine codes essential for survival in *Revolution*'s society. However, all of them are also confined by their sex. In her overview of the "tough girl" archetypes that arose in both film and television toward the end of the twentieth century (think *Terminator 2*'s Sarah Connor, *Alien*'s Ripley, or *Xena*'s titular warrior princess), Inness has noted that pop culture tends to put limitations on its female action heroes: they are tough up to a point. Their toughness may be limited in a variety of ways: female action heroes are maternally motivated, or sexualized, or just not as strong as the men (179). All of *Revolution*'s primary female characters—and most secondary characters—fall victim to these tropes, which ensure they are never quite as powerful as Miles or Monroe.

Almost every woman with a speaking role in season 1 is defined by a motherhood role. Most prominently, Rachel is driven by the need to protect her children Charlie and Danny—and, subsequently, her need to avenge Danny's death: "I want power so Monroe's enemies can wipe him off the map. I want to kill the man who killed my son. And that's it" (1.17, "The Longest Day"). Rachel is a cold and calculating killer; we see her impale a friend with a screwdriver (1.09, "Kashmir"), strangle a guard with a belt (1.18, "Clue"), and stage an assassination attempt using a live grenade (1.19, "Children of Men"). All of this, however, is in service to her children; when we see her kill for the first time, in flashback, she is a young mother with a gun trying to ensure that her family will have food in the midst of catastrophe (1.02, "Chained Heat"). Other women are also motivated by motherhood: Nora was driven to join the rebellion after having a miscarriage (1.03, "No Quarter"). Charlie, a teenager, serves as a proxy mother to Danny; she raises him and cares for him after a departing young Rachel charges, "never let go of Danny's hand" (1.02, "Chained Heat"). These themes remain consistent with regard to secondary female characters: Maggie (Anna Lise Phillips) acts as Charlie's stepmother and is also motivated by her desire to see the children in England who were lost to her during the blackout (1.04, "Plague Dogs"). Julia Neville schemes in part to keep her son Jason safe; Priscilla Pittman is arrested for killing a soldier who attacked her daughter (1.15, "Home"); and Grace Beaumont (Maria Howell) is a scientist—a former coworker of Rachel's—who also lost a child (1.20, "The Dark Tower"). The constant association of motherhood with prominent or powerful women suggests their maternal experience as a specifically gendered source of agency; the instinct of the protective mother contains their behavior within a paradigm of fierce but hegemonically acceptable femininity. While there are fathers as well—Miles Matheson's proxy fatherhood to his niece Charlie, Sebastian Monroe's discovery of a long-lost son, or Tom Neville's complex rivalry with son Jason—these relationships do not define male characters to the same extent, or serve so all-encompassingly as character traits for nearly every man in the series.

The women of *Revolution* are also sexualized, a familiar archetype Holmlund has dubbed the "deadly doll" (127). All women are thin; most are conventionally attractive. Nora appears in her bra as early as episode 1.05 ("Soul Train"); though the series' nudity is limited by its network television home, we also see Charlie's bra (1.12, "Ghosts"), and both women's naked backs (1.06, "Sex and Drugs"; 1.17, "The Longest Day"). By midway through the first season, both Nora and Charlie have posed as prostitutes (1.06, "Sex and Drugs"; 1.10, "Nobody's Fault but Mine"). When Nora has sex with Miles, we see him fully clothed and her nearly naked (1.16, "The Love Boat"). As for Charlie, considering her background as a hunter in likely-mosquito-infested forests, she has a marked predilection for wearing shirts that expose her belly or lower back. And though her body is usually less openly displayed, Rachel serves as Miles's *other* love interest, while Miles's friend Jim refers to her as "MILF-y" (1.18, "Clue").[7] She is also tied into a disturbing mix of sex and violence in the series, one that eroticizes the abuse of women; her romantic and sexual relationship with Miles comes after he betrays and physically tortures her (1.17, "The Longest Day").[8] The series' recurring women are all, at various points, threatened with rape (e.g., 1.10, "Pilot"; 1.10, "Nobody's Fault but Mine"; 1.14, "The Night the Lights Went Out in Georgia"; 1.18, "Clue"), and Nora is forced to wear a gauzy white dress when she is chained and brutally interrogated by men (1.18, "Clue").

Finally, while Charlie, Rachel, and Nora may be good in a fight, they are never as good as male leads Miles (whose single-handed battle against a squad of soldiers is a centerpiece in the pilot) or Monroe (whose hand-to-hand combat skills make him a fighting ring champion in season 2). Charlie begins the series as an innocent who must be trained by Miles (1.13, "The Song Remains the Same"), and who gradually learns to kill as she realizes her idealistic ways have no place in an uncivilized frontier. In contrast, flashbacks to a young Miles and Monroe show them to have been combat veterans well before the blackout, as they were military officers who had done multiple tours in Afghanistan. Even when they are shown as childhood friends, perhaps ten years old, they are still playing at military combat (1.10, "Nobody's Fault but Mine"). This establishes them as "natural" warriors, as opposed to Charlie, Nora and Rachel, all of whom begin as non-combatants; men's aggression is depicted as innate, while women's is learned (see Inness 124). Though Charlie learns to fire a crossbow and use a sword and a gun, she is repeatedly placed in danger—generally as a motivation for Miles, who must learn the true meaning of family in order to save her. Rachel begins the series as a damsel trapped in a tower; she has been held prisoner by Monroe for more than a decade and isn't set free until Miles comes to rescue Charlie (1.10, "Nobody's Fault but Mine"). The first time she tries to attack Monroe, with a pen, she fails (1.02, "Chained Heat"); the second time, when she has both the element of surprise and a live grenade, she fails again, tackled by his soldiers (1.19, "Children of Men"). An episode later, she must spare Monroe and give him a gun so that he can go save Charlie some more (1.20, "The Dark Tower"). On one level, the series seems to subvert notions of female helplessness: Charlie fakes a fall and pretends to hurt her leg, luring in an unsuspecting Jason so that she can handcuff him to a post (1.02, "Chained Heat"). But half a season later, Rachel is running through forest, falls for no apparent reason, and fractures her leg so badly the bone breaks through the skin (1.16, "The Love Boat"). The Matheson women are only tough to a point—generally, the point at which they need to be saved by a man.

Nora, conversely, is *not* saved by a man; in the first season finale, she nobly sacrifices herself in battle. Like Cynthia, she is "fridged" (Simone); her death primarily serves to motivate Miles. As Miles cradles her body, the camera lingers on his expression of tearful anguish, which swiftly changes to one of fierce resolve before he starts shooting his way through his enemies. Still, while Nora dies for Miles's character development, she at least has an established character outside of her romance storyline; as she is one of the tough female leads, the audience sees flashbacks establishing her back story (a teenager during the blackout, she had to learn toughness in order to protect her little sister—another proxy mother theme). She is also a rebel dedicated to fighting Monroe's forces and re-establishing the United States of America. She is a multidimensional character; the same cannot be true of less masculinized women within the series.

Overall, the women most prominent in *Revolution*'s narratives are those who at least partially master stereotypically masculine behaviors; they are violent, aggressive and ruthless in pursuit of their goals. *Revolution*'s new western frontier is one in which only men can successfully survive—even if those "men" happen to be female. But such hard-powered women must be contained. Cyndy Hendershot has detailed an uneasiness with masculine women that traces back to Victorian times:

> The threat of the New Woman was largely perceived as one in which sexual difference was breaking down; by claiming the masculine role, despite her female body, the New Woman of the popular imagination placed sexual difference in peril, creating a vision of a new society not of men and women, but of men only [378].

More recently, Inness has cited "our society's continued uneasiness about tough women who challenge our widely held beliefs about how women (and men) should behave" (136). *Revolution* mitigates this same cultural discomfort by privileging masculine behaviors but maintaining clear sex distinctions.

Charlie, Rachel, and Nora are mothers or sex objects or simply less capable than the men. Nora, arguably the strongest and most combat experienced, breaks after being captured and tortured: "I thought I could handle this. But I was wrong" (1.18, "Clue"). Rachel's scientific expertise—her assertion that she was "project lead" on the nanotech initiative (1.17, "The Longest Day")— is compromised by her lack of knowledge about the clues left by her dead husband, Ben. The women's aggressive potential is also limited: in season 2, Rachel becomes more and more emotional and morally concerned, advocating against the execution of child soldiers (i.e., 2.16, "Exposition Boulevard"; 2.18, "Austin City Limits"). Charlie, on the other hand, grows progressively more callous—killing remorselessly, engaging in casual sex—but her increased masculinity is framed as problematic, foreshadowing a future character crisis as her mother and Miles look worriedly on (i.e., 2.16, "Exposition Boulevard").

Hard Men

As in *Jericho*, *Revolution*'s technologically deficient frontier allows a return to a faux-western, Civil War–era American dream that never really was, a sort of mythological cowboy imagery that posits "Caucasian male dominance as fundamental to humanity" (Oldring 13). Originally, promotional materials for the series appeared to focus on teenaged Charlie holding a bow—quite possibly to capitalize on the popularity of the then-current *Hunger Games* (2012) movie franchise. Billy Burke had first billing in the credits, however, and by the fall finale of the first season, his character Miles had also assumed prominence in most advertising images.[9] Miles is a former soldier who, after the great blackout, joined forces with childhood friend Sebastian Monroe to form and lead the Monroe Militia, an army that conquered and now controls a large portion of the Midwest. The broken brotherhood between Miles and Monroe[10] is one of the primary relationships in the series; once Monroe's most trusted general, Miles staged a failed assassination attempt and then fled. In season 1, Miles leads a ragtag group of outcasts while Monroe is the increasingly unstable military dictator hunting them down; in season 2, Monroe is an ousted leader who must join with Miles's team in order to stay alive and possibly rebuild his dominion. Miles and Monroe are the official series warriors; either is capable of taking on multiple opponents simultaneously. Again, characters with military experience (specifically, men) take the lead in a post-apocalyptic world; *Revolution* lacks *Jericho*'s specific references to World War II, but channels Civil War imagery as uniformed soldiers roam the countryside on horses, carrying swords.

Also again, *Revolution* both privileges military themes and implies that warfare is for men. While Charlie is briefly kidnapped and conscripted to a

Monroe Militia training camp (1.07, "The Children's Crusade"), it is not clear why, since in any other episode, all of Monroe's many onscreen soldiers and officers—whether speaking characters or background extras—are male. They are coded as aggressively masculine: "brutal and smart and vicious" (1.03, "No Quarter"). "I killed fathers and sons and husbands," says Miles of his checkered past (1.03, "No Quarter"); if he fought mothers, daughters or wives, it goes unspoken. *Revolution's* clearest links to *Jericho* are here, in a technological wasteland where white male war veterans navigate the looming threat of civil war in a retrograde America. The military is where conflict and power are decided, and the military is for men only.

The masculine stereotype further extends to a certain degree of emotional stuntedness; outside of their intimate and fraught friendship, Miles and Monroe demonstrate persistently masculine performances of militarized aggression that allow for little deviation from the tough-guy role. However, the series also suggests that truly heroic men must learn to protect and care for their families; we see Miles comforting a crying Charlie (1.04, "Plague Dogs") and Rachel (1.13, "The Song Remains the Same"), while Monroe grows increasingly unstable, driven by a surfeit of ambition that leaves him "paranoid and brutal and unhinged" (1.17, "The Longest Day"). Miles is therefore the clear protagonist, advancing the idea that men must be masculine to succeed, but they must also learn to control their impulses to avoid going "too far"; it is their job to protect those (i.e., women and children) weaker than themselves. "You can't be what you were," Rachel tells Miles. "You need to take better care of [Charlie] than you ever took of me" (1.13, "The Song Remains the Same").

Bromance and the Heteronormative Future

Notably, *Revolution's* focus on the relationship between its two primary male warriors had significant queer potential:

> Over the course of the series, there's always been something going on with these two. They've been best friends, they've shared women, they've wrestled. But in "The Dark Tower," the brotherly love—which had already become a little steamier than that of a normal friendship—evolved into a possible homoerotic wonderland. Once their common threat was vanquished, they somehow rode the Tower's sewer line/waterslide out to a beach, where Miles lay there unconscious and awoke to Monroe *watching him sleep.* And then as soon as Miles opened his eyes, the pair started pounding on each other like hormonal preteens—but never to the point of real life-threatening danger. Just enough to work up a sweat and and [*sic*] tussle Monroe's hair [Surette, original emphasis].

Much of the series' plot, particularly in the first season, centers on Monroe's obsession with Miles—finding Miles, capturing Miles, killing Miles, winning back Miles. Fan fiction authors were also quick to pick up on the potential romantic tension between the two; 373 of 2160 fan-written stories on the Archive of Our Own site are tagged with a Miles/Monroe relationship.[11] By the season finale, *Revolution*'s writers had actively joined in, as Tom Neville was grousing to Monroe onscreen, "You have a borderline erotic fixation on Miles Matheson" (1.22, "The Dark Tower").

However, it was canonically not to be, as the series narrative continued to focus on Miles and Monroe as heterosexual men. Moreover, their battles are fought over and through women's bodies as the series goes to painstaking lengths to assert their mutual heterosexuality: when Miles rescues Rachel from Monroe (1.10, "Nobody's Fault but Mine"); when their conflict causes the death of Miles's ex-fiancée (and Monroe's old flame) Emma (1.15, "Home"); when Monroe captures and tortures Miles's lover Nora (1.18, "Clue"). *Revolution* both acknowledges and vehemently resists its own queer implications.

The series' only canonically queer characters are Jane Warren (Kate Burton) and Beth (Avis-Marie Barnes), reclusive lesbians who appear in only one episode (1.14, "The Night the Lights Went Out in Georgia"); they are older women who have removed themselves from society entirely. The camera does not fetishize them; they are not mothers, nor are they threatened with sexual violence. In absence of a heterosexual male presence, however, they have adopted binary masculine/feminine roles: Jane, the tough scientist who kills without remorse, and Beth, the femme girlfriend whose life Jane fights to preserve (and who passively sacrifices herself in service to the greater good). While the inclusion of lesbian characters, however brief, might seem a progressive break in *Revolution*'s otherwise straight roster, the queer relationship also reinscribes heteronormative behavior patterns.

Revolution and Race

The series also fails to challenge racial stereotypes. Miles and Monroe, both white, join a pantheon of other straight white men who are in charge in the post-apocalypse: Randall Flynn (Colm Feore), DOD representative turned weapons dealer and spy; Dan Jenkins (Glenn Morshower), leader of a group of exiled scientists (1.19, "Children of Men"); Jack Davis (Cotter Smith), exiled President of the United States (2.13, "Happy Endings"); Wayne Ramsey (Patrick St. Esprit), the rebel leader in season 1; Calvin Horn (Zeljko Ivanek), whose forces chase down Aaron in season 2; Edward Truman (Steven Culp), United States soldier in charge of occupying the town of Willoughby; Jeremy Baker (Mark Pellegrino), Monroe's trusted captain; or Will Strausser (David Meunier), chief torturer in the Monroe Republic. Tom Neville is the most obvious exception; the most prominent Black character in the cast, he serves as Monroe's head of intelligence. He is not ex-military, but rather "naturally" aggressive, calling to mind wild west (and Western) stereotypes in which non-white people are "naturally" savage (Wright 160; see also hooks 102); his flashbacks show him as a mild-mannered insurance adjuster, fired by his white male boss and disdained by his white male neighbor. But flashback–Neville has a punching bag in his basement; it's only a few days after the blackout when he beats his neighbor to death after the other man invades his home. Like *Jericho*'s Hawkins, Neville exists in a supposedly post-racial setting where he is eclipsed by a majority white cast. Though Neville does not experience open discrimination in *Revolution*, he still does the bidding of white superiors (Monroe, Kelly Foster, the President) and he is part of a pattern of untrustworthy, traitorous Black men that also includes rebel fighter Jim, and season 2's Ken Dawson (Richard T. Jones). Neville's dialogue is also the most sexist ("That pert little bitch has you soft as a kitten"—1.11, "The Stand"), racist ("Mamacita"—1.18, "Clue"), and homophobic ("your boyfriend Matheson"—1.17, "The Longest Day"). It might be possible to read Neville as a victim of discrimination who himself lashes out at the less privileged in order to gain power and security; however, his dialogue seems designed primarily to establish his character as a villain. This calls to fear-infused popular culture images of Black men (i.e., hooks 102), while also dovetailing with post–9/11 television trends in which "politically incorrect" stereotypes have become "covert" (Alsultany 90). The narrative resists charges of white political intolerance by giving the most oppressive dialogue to a Black character; it positions Neville in a post-racial world where he, his white wife and biracial son can apparently succeed based on intelligence, ambition, and combat prowess, and in which he can also placidly look on as his wife dismisses the Latina housekeeper: "All right, you can go back to the kitchen now" (1.08, "Ties That Bind").

Women of color generally receive short shrift in *Revolution*; almost all of the major female characters are also white. Nora, who is Latina, is the most experienced fighter and the least motherly—of all the women in the first season, the "hardest"—and she is also the most sexualized and the most thoroughly undermined by her own violence. Ultimately, she is "strong," but not strong enough to survive, and her characterization and early death call to mind stereotypes about hot Latina women and the disposability of non-white characters.[12] Like Sarah in *Jericho*, Nora is combat-ready, childless, sexualized, and doomed—signifying the continued marginalization of non-white women within these series.

Summary

It might have been possible for *Revolution* to serve as an extended social commentary pitting diversity and inclusiveness against the unjust forces of white male patriarchy; certainly Monroe's first-season enemies, the rebel "patriot" forces, are shown to include women and men of multiple ethnicities. But extensive re-tooling between seasons 1 and 2 derails these possibilities, as the Monroe Republic is decimated, Nora dies, and the United States—formerly a rallying cry for a plucky group of ragtag fighters—instead becomes an invading (predominantly white male) force against which the (majority white male) heroes must square off. *Revolution*'s white male privilege is perhaps best demonstrated when one considers it as television where violent dictator Monroe can order a woman to be drugged and waterboarded (1.18, "Clue"), joke about giving "smallpox blankets" to his Indigenous opposition (1.18, "Clue"), and then shift allegiance to become a series protagonist half a season later. Monroe is part of the potential that *Revolution* never quite lives up to.

Instead, the series is regressive regarding gender, race, and sexuality. It allows for a modicum of gender fluidity while still preserving binaries—characters behave as "masculine" or "feminine." Unlike in *Jericho*, some women may be masculine and some men feminine; however, feminine characters, those displaying "soft" power, are repeatedly disenfranchised, endangered, and—in the case of Aaron—mocked and shamed. Moreover, women who display masculine traits—leadership, ruthlessness, combat ability—embody the action heroine role that is "an emblematic and problematic icon of female empowerment within postfeminist culture" (Tasker and Negra 20). The series' positioning of masculinity as the key to power, and the limitations it imposes on women who would claim such power, are equally questionable. The "hard" female leads are sexualized, and their aggressions are justified by "motherhood." Their independence is learned rather than innate, and they are never as powerful or as skilled as the male protagonists. Miles and Monroe, the masculine male soldiers, are naturally dominant; their potential queerness is disavowed and they take precedence over all others, including non-white characters, women, and more feminine men. Further, the series' casting of other, smaller roles—white male military officers, political leaders, and background extras—implicitly reinforces these trends. *Revolution* does not, in fact, offer any rebellion against the hegemonic status quo.

Conclusion

There are strong parallels between *Jericho* and *Revolution*, both of which rely on a single catastrophic event that destroys electrical grids, telecommunications systems, and mass transportation networks. Each series presents a masculine world where feminine performance is marginalized or punished, white privilege goes unremarked, power is negotiated through political and physical conflicts between men, and the continuing cultural survival of the American people rests on the preservation of patriarchal order. *Jericho* pulls from multiple inspirations: twentieth-century nuclear anxiety, the twenty-first-century war on terror, and the wild west cowboy myth foundational to American concepts of national identity. *Revolution* replaces nuclear anxiety with the specter of technological rebellion but utilizes the same post–9/11 military and conspiracy themes, while replacing strict gender binaries with a more insistent glorification of the masculine and still maintaining a consistent frontier aesthetic. Both follow rebellious protagonists who must protect their communities not only against encroaching outlaw violence, but also against the fascist authoritarianism of big government.

As Hoffstadt and Schrez have noted, "so often, the end of the world *as we know it* is at the same time the beginning of a new world *as we desire it*" (33, original emphasis); if so, the identity politics in *Jericho* and *Revolution* reflect particularly conservative forms of such desire. The worlds these series present us with are, in fact, slightly different versions of the status quo—post-apocalypses that reinscribe straight white male dominance, presenting political and national infrastructure breakdowns that in fact serve as hegemonic wish fulfillment (Nilges; Oldring; Manjikian; Sharp 6–7). If unexpected attack devastates the United States, these series reassure us, Americans can survive by getting "back to basics"—namely, by re-creating the mythical wild west frontier, the perceived glories of the Civil War, and the iconic roles so foundational to American cultural identity. These regressive, heteronormative gender and racial politics are bolstered by the influx of military imagery and lead characters with combat backgrounds, ready to protect and/or dominate. In *Jericho*, men's dominance is implicit, while in *Revolution*, weak men must find their inner aggression, and women only achieve agency through violence, thus promoting ideas of masculine power and privileging masculine behaviors over more feminine traits. *Jericho* assumes that men are masculine and women are feminine; *Revolution* partially divorces sex and gender while still maintaining a masculine/feminine binary, creating a frontier where feminine traits are equated with weakness. Within this framework, both men and women can be powerful only if they act in masculine ways, but women must forever compensate for their innate femininity. The resulting highly conservative narratives exemplify a resurgence in post-apocalyptic, post–9/11 American television that repeatedly associates male agency with survival, independence, leadership, and the American way of life.

Granted, the post-apocalypse on American television is only typical of other narratives—in sitcoms, medical series, crime procedurals, news broadcasts, or any variety of other stories flooding our media. *Jericho* and *Revolution* demonstrate a devotion to white patriarchy that is neither new nor exclusive to the genre; however, if post-apocalyptic scenarios enable Americans (and others) to envision a future after the current society (along with its limitations and inequalities) ends, then these series offer a typical and highly specific set of scenarios in which the return of the west marks the return of the cowboy hero, and the global apocalypse creates an environment in which only the soldier, and those who aspire to his (inevitably "his") particular skill set, can survive. Both *Jericho* and *Revolution* fundamentally privilege military and militia characters and posit dusty, technologically stunted worlds in which warring men will decide the fate of post-apocalyptic America. Each helps establish major themes that will reappear throughout this analysis: the return to a mythological American wild west frontier, the glorification of American soldiers (both contemporary and historical), and the subsequent focus on white American masculinity that permeates both of these paradigms. Examining these series identifies the post–9/11 cultural anxieties each may represent, and most importantly, exposes the ways their frameworks function in creating decidedly conservative post-apocalyptic television trends.

— 2 —

Pandemics, Plagues and Contagion

THE FEAR OF VIRAL PANDEMICS has been situated as a cultural successor to Cold War nuclear fears (Thomas 144; Keränen 455); classical plague fictions trace back much further, including the Bible and literary works such as *The Iliad* or *Oedipus Rex* (Wald 11), while contemporary concerns may also be linked to the late 1800s, the scientific discovery of germs, and associated worries about tuberculosis and communicable disease (Tomes 628). In the 1980s and onward, the AIDS epidemic—and rumors that it had been first spread by an airline steward—highlighted new concerns about plague in an era of globalization, when the speed of air travel (and, in some pathogen cases, the onboard sharing of recirculated air) creates the potential for global disease propagation before first symptoms even appear. Within such a context, "the routes traveled by communicable disease light up the social interactions—the spaces and encounters, the practices and beliefs—of a changing world" (Wald 9).

In addition to serving as metaphors for other issues, pandemic narratives also directly reflect news about global viral outbreaks such as SARS, influenza, Ebola, or one of the most recent new outbreaks, Zika, which made headlines in 2016 for the growing number of cases reported in (and spreading from) South America, and probable links to birth defects such as microcephaly (CDC). The anti-vaccine movement in the United States has further created resurgences of measles and other preventable diseases (Sifferlin). News articles and scientific warnings predicting an inevitable global pandemic have flourished, including feature pieces such as *The Guardian*'s "Ebola isn't the big one. So what is? And are we ready for it?" (Woolf, 2014), or the U.S. Agency for International Developments' program for Emerging Pandemic Threats (USAID, 2016). U.S. research facilities are publicly known; Keränen cites "Homeland Security's sprawling collection of laboratories, open air testing sites, and knowledge centers such as the Plum Island Animal Disease Control Center, the Biodefense Knowledge Center, the U.S. National Laboratories, the Dugway Proving Grounds in Utah, and the university-based Department of Homeland Security Centers of Excellence," and further public concerns not just about the possibility of research gone awry (Keränen 452; Urbanski 66), but about anthrax mailings, terrorist attack, and the potential for infection by outside enemies (Keränen 452).

In short, it's no wonder that disease narratives have flourished in our popular culture. *The Andromeda Strain* (1971) is a classic film in the genre, remade as a miniseries of the same name in 2008 (A&E); other films include *The Last Man on Earth* (1964), *Outbreak* (1995), *12 Monkeys* (1995), or *Pandemic* (2016). While some virus narratives are intrinsically reassuring—ending with a cure and re-establishing scientific credibility (Wald 268)—the postapocalyptic pandemic narrative carries no such guarantees, and "viral apocalypse" imagery "signifies concerns that a combination of explosive population growth, ecological pressure, and biological-research-gone-awry will extinguish life as we know it" (Keränen 461). Viral outbreak narratives overlap with vampires, zombies, and other supernatural creatures in *28 Days Later* (2002), *I Am Legend* (2007), the *Resident Evil* film series (2002, 2004, 2007, 2010, 2012), *The Strain* (FX, 2014–), *The Walking Dead* (AMC, 2010–), and *Z Nation* (Syfy, 2014–); the latter two series are evaluated separately in chapter 4 of this book, but it's worth noting that many of our fears regarding communicable disease can also be applied to the infectious bites of the undead, or even the secret infiltrations of alien body snatchers (Keränen 462; Wald).

The most recent pandemic television narratives include *Jeremiah* (Showtime, 2002–04), *Helix* (Syfy, 2014–15), *Containment* (The CW, 2016), and *The Last Ship* (FX, 2014–). Of these, *Jeremiah* and *The Last Ship* are the most post-apocalyptic, taking place after most of the world's population has already been decimated. *Jeremiah* and *The Last Ship* adopt oppositional approaches to the pandemic narrative: *Jeremiah* explores the new world after the disaster, treating old institutions as malevolent relics, while *The Last Ship* situates humanity's last best hope as the preservation of the contemporary United States Navy. Both ultimately construct reassuring narratives that preserve the patriarchy and familiar social structures. Heterosexual white male leadership is maintained—in *Jeremiah*, as the promise of a seemingly diverse future, and in *The Last Ship*, as the reconstruction of American military institutions.

Jeremiah

Loosely based on the Belgian comic (1979–) by Hermann Huppen, *Jeremiah* focuses on its titular character Jeremiah (Luke Perry), one of a generation of children who survived a global plague (the "Big Death") that killed their parents, leaving a fragmented society built by orphans now in their mid-to-late twenties. *Jeremiah*'s first season aired in 2002 and its second season was split between 2003 and 2004. The focus and themes of this Showtime series fluctuate noticeably between its two seasons, likely for two reasons: first, reportedly dramatic tensions between production executives and showrunner J. Michael Straczynski,[1] and second, the September 11 attacks and the encroaching politics of a newly post–9/11 United States.

Season 1: The Road Warriors

In the first season, Jeremiah joins his partner Kurdy (Malcolm-Jamal Warner) as they act as rogue wanderers, road tripping across the former American countryside to right wrongs and recruit members for the secret, quasi-utopian community of Thunder Mountain. They operate as cowboy heroes—riding into town in a car rather than on a horse, solving a commu-nity's problems (quite often through violence), and then riding off into the sunset. This framework is similar to previous "updates" on the cowboy myth in series such as *Knight Rider* (NBC, 1982–86) or *The A-Team* (NBC, 1983–87); it harks directly to classical notions of the gunslinger hero. The series pokes fun at this notion—"Who's Jesse James?" "I don't know. Something my dad used to say" (1.01, "The Long Road Part 1")—and draws attention to the archetype in the process.

Other themes are more subdued. The series does not dwell overly on the pandemic itself; rather, it is part of a postmodern trend in series like *The Walking Dead* that "are not merely about the threat of the world as we know it ending, but which even take this impending apocalypse for granted, and therefore show little interest in offering explanations for such events" (Hassler-Forest 342), or earlier cyberpunk science fiction in which a foundational catastrophic event sets the dystopian narrative stage but has little "moral or epistemological impact" on the ensuing drama (Sponsler 253). The disease that devastated the world's adult population looms as a background threat, as embodied by Meaghan (Suzy Joachim), a sole surviving carrier trapped in biohazard containment within Thunder Mountain. Meaghan's presence in the first season serves as Chekov's virus—the narrative promise that a pan-demic carrier revealed in the first act will be used in the third. Meaghan appears in 4 of 20 first-season episodes, acting as a foreboding reminder rather than a persistent focus of the narrative; *Jeremiah* concentrates on its new post-apocalyptic society rather than fixating on the virus.

Jeremiah also flirts with religious imagery[2] and, by extension, the concept of Biblical plagues; Jeremiah's name is a Biblical reference, and throughout the first season, he is visited by Ezekiel (Alex Zahara), a wild-haired man who claims to be a prophet and seeks to keep Jeremiah from harm. An early episode deals with a man with delusions of godhood and his "angel" girlfriend (1.04, "...And the Ground, Sown with Salt"). Despite this, early *Jeremiah* episodes do not particularly embrace or explore religious themes; the events they incorporate appear to take the form of coincidence ("angel wings" as a pattern on doors) or science (the Big Death as a result of human biochemical engineering), while Ezekiel is revealed as Jeremiah's step-brother. The first season clearly singles out Jeremiah as special and plays with Christian religious symbolism without committing to any particular religious framework.

Finally, military imagery is subtle but pervasive in the early series, including settings from McLaren Air Force Base to Thunder Mountain (a former NORAD station), and costuming details like the rank insignia on the sleeve of Kurdy's coat. However, no character has formal military training. Jeremiah and Kurdy are capable brawlers, both exemplifying combat-capable masculinity, but they are defensive rather than aggressive; their mission, as emissaries of Thunder Mountain, is predominantly scouting and communications. They lack post-apocalyptic heroes' more typically direct links to the military or law enforcement. Still, throughout the road tripping and inter-community negotiations, a militarized threat (the soldiers of "Valhalla Sector") looms; the season ends on a cliffhanger when Valhalla Sector attacks and Jeremiah is kidnapped.

Season 2: War Games

At this point, *Jeremiah* undergoes a noticeable shift in which the series' western frontier theme—the notion of the wandering heroes—is abandoned, and the pandemic itself is dismissed as the series re-focuses on increasingly militarized conflicts. Religious themes are foregrounded, though ambiguously. It's difficult—and, perhaps, useless—to speculate which of these changes came about in response to network pressure and/or conflicts with Straczynski, and which were the result of shifting cultural paradigms, or where the overlap lies between these concepts. But the end result is clear: a series that formerly exhibited a variance on wild-west gunslinger masculinity while promoting notions of cooperation and peaceful unity becomes a narrative of warring armies.

The conflict between Thunder Mountain and Valhalla Sector, built up throughout the first season, lasts only two episodes into the second, during which Thunder Mountain (via Meaghan) infects Valhalla Sector with the plague, executing all adults except Jeremiah's father Devon (Robert Wisden), who then largely fades from the plot as Jeremiah becomes mayor of the town of Milhaven. This reconfigures the series, ending much of the "road trip cowboy" episode plotting as Jeremiah heads a community, Kurdy becomes a military general, and conflicts with invading pseudo–Nazi forces govern the narrative arc of the season. While both seasons feature overwhelmingly masculine protagonists and patriarchal struggles, the second is more closely focused on hard masculine power and the preservation of "American" ideals.

The brief glimpse of Valhalla Sector provided in the first two episodes of the second season suggests a *Jeremiah* that might have been. In this hidden base, a group of adults survived the plague, and now—under the auspices of the President of the United States—seeks to re-assert dominance. This aborted series, in which the scions of an obsolete American regime rebel against their predecessors, would have both echoed and pre-dated similar narratives in series like *Jericho* and *Revolution*, where the "return" of a now-illicit government to a new post-apocalyptic society allows series protagonists the opportunity to reject the corruption and constraints of pre-apocalyptic America while establishing a new masculinity (or, arguably, returning to the purer, more mythological masculinity of the American colonial imagination). This two-episode arc examines the pandemic as an engineered bioweapon, details its continued weaponization, and incorporates the accompanying implications of irresponsible/amoral scientists and the dangers of government secrecy. However, the nigh-immediate destruction of Valhalla Sector abandons any pretense that *Jeremiah* is concerned with such narratives, or with the pandemic itself: as the adults of Valhalla Sector die, so does Meaghan, the last known carrier of the disease. The prospect of a cure is raised—a vial of blood given to Devon (2.02, "Letters from the Other Side Part 2")—and then never mentioned again. Multiple threads are left dangling.

Jeremiah does nominally continue the fight against the remnants of the old United States, here reconfigured as a Nazi rebirth rather than an unelected President. In the second season, Thunder Mountain prepares to defend itself against the forces of "Daniel," an army massing along the eastern coast. These forces are associated with Nazi imagery in the form of tall banners and propaganda films (2.07, "Voices in the Dark"). Daniel's armies are aggressive and brutal, enslaving the poor and mass-murdering those who become inconvenient (2.06, "The Mysterious Mister Smith"). Their neo-fascist assimilation directly contrasts with Thunder Mountain–like attempts to establish a new cooperative union between disparate communities. "Daniel" does not exist as a person but is rather a composite graphic of a red-haired, blue-eyed white man whose features are an amalgamation of previous American presidents. He represents both fascist white male supremacy[3] and the last remnants of the world pre–Big Death. The secret adult coalition behind the Daniel image previously escaped Valhalla Sector and now manipulates the youth of "Daniel's" armies to their own advantage. This maintains the tension of old vs. new while shifting the imagery of the "enemy" from the last vestiges of the United States to the shadow of Americanized Nazism. *Jeremiah*'s new generation, as embodied by Jeremiah, Kurdy, and Thunder Mountain's leader Markus (Peter Stebbings), becomes the site of hope and a progressive future vs. a past that is not just stagnant and corrupt, but actively murderous.

Other shifts also take place at this time. Thunder Mountain becomes more visibly and actively militarized, starting with the gun-filled assault Kurdy and his forces mount against Valhalla Sector and ending with a newly unfurled American flag and the formation of a formal, uniformed army serving beneath Kurdy's command (2.15, "Interregnum Part 1"). This shifts *Jeremiah*'s male leads, particularly Jeremiah and Kurdy, from a loose affiliation with the cowboy mythos to a direct occupation of traditional soldier roles. In this sense, season 2 (airing in 2003 and 2004) sees a shift concurrent with post–9/11 cultural concerns; masculinity here is more clearly defined as military, and the United States flag changes from a symbol of outdated and suspect institutions (in Valhalla Sector) to a sign of nobility and hope (flying above Thunder Mountain's camp).

Religious and/or supernatural questions also become more overt, as the Jeremiah/Kurdy road team is broken up and Kurdy partners with new character Mr. Smith (Sean Astin), who claims to hear the voice of God. Interestingly, while first-season religious references were explicitly Christian, Mr. Smith's position is monotheistic but non-denominational—according to him, God's voice is neither male nor female and speaks without any particular language or accent. Mr. Smith's predictions and miracles are presented as the equally possible products of either divine intervention or delusion. Smith suggests, however, that having abandoned the world, God is now prepared to return and take a more direct hand in human affairs—lending Thunder Mountain's forces the promise of a divine mandate.

The break between *Jeremiah*'s first and second seasons was thus both chronological and thematic; the pandemic that served as the original basis for an episodic, road warrior series was quickly abandoned in favor of militarized conflicts and an increased focus on masculinized American patriotism. While there are also some fluctuations in terms of the series' treatment of gender and race issues, *Jeremiah*'s representations are more conservatively consistent throughout.

Gender and *Jeremiah*

Masculinity and adulthood are common themes in the series; the initial season is framed by Jeremiah's letters to his presumed-dead father, read in voice-over: "Dear Dad, I think about you every day. The end of your world. The beginning of mine" (1.02, "The Long Road Part 2"). *Jeremiah*, which preceded *Jericho* by three years, also foregrounds the narrative of a son trying to process his identity in the shadow of his father. Jeremiah's journey is presented as particularly masculine—he is a man obsessed with his own patriarchal lineage.[4] He is traumatized by the losses of his father and little brother but fails to mention the death of his mother (1.01, "The Long Road Part 1"). This initial indication that *Jeremiah* may not be especially preoccupied with women's roles holds true through the series; there are women present, particularly as victims or love interests, but the focus on Jeremiah and Kurdy's partnership means the most consistent gender presentations are stereotypes associated with cowboy adventures, followed by soldier tactics and the type of hard power that settles disputes through fisticuffs and firefights.

The series offers only limited explorations of alternatives. The first season also presents Thunder Mountain's leader Markus as a successful, admired example of non-militarized masculinity; Markus, initially a cerebral pacifist, is respected despite his lack of combat skills and even his inability to drive (1.19, "Things Left Unsaid Part 1"). Markus represents white male leadership but also a softer form of male political power, implicitly contrasted with Jeremiah and Kurdy's rough-and-tumble heroics as he openly values diplomacy and seeks community alliances. His first-season position as a visionary leader differs from other post-apocalyptic series where the strongest forces are led by resolved men with military experience and guns; more typically, men who are unable to defend themselves must learn better and are initially treated with disdain, like *Revolution*'s Aaron. The allowance *Jeremiah* makes for multiple, equally effective masculinities is initially atypical. This, too, shifts in the second season when Markus begins wearing guns strapped to his thighs and actively participating in shootouts (2.10, "Running on Empty"; 2.16, "Interregnum Part 2").

Season 2 additionally adds Mr. Smith, who is often portrayed as gentle, bumbling, and possibly deranged; Smith is consequently separate from power hierarchies, lacking any political or military position. He is also de-sexualized; though he has a young daughter, he lacks the multiple heterosexual encounters or partnerships granted to the other male leads. He arguably might be read as queer; if so, the series fails to make any such positioning explicit, instead situating Smith as both soft and isolated.

Jeremiah also fails to offer richly varied depictions of women; perhaps due to Showtime's status as a subscription cable network, the series offers frequent shots of women's bared breasts, and Jeremiah and Kurdy's burgeoning friendship is partly cemented when Jeremiah helps Kurdy arrange a liaison with a female prostitute (1.01, "The Long Road Part 1"). It is clear from the outset that in *Jeremiah*'s future, women offer themselves as sexual objects in order to survive; strip clubs and prostitution are featured repeatedly (1.01, "The Long Road Part 1"; 1.15, "Ring of Truth"; 2.07, "Voices in the Dark"). Women's biology inherently endangers them, both via rape threats (1.07, "City of Roses") and by way of the pregnancies that repeatedly threaten to kill them (1.04, "...And the Ground, Sown with Salt"; 1.05, "To Sail Beyond the Stars"; 1.06, "The Bag"); they occupy inferior social positions, limited by men's urges and by the tyranny of their own bodies. Female roles are primarily passive; women receive less screen time[5] and possess less agency than the men who are the focus of the series.

Erin (Ingrid Kavelaars), the most frequently appearing female character of the series, is cast in a nurturing role and ends her onscreen time as the instigator of a failed romantic subplot. As second-in-command to Markus, she seldom leaves the mountain. Her primary role is as a voice of support for Markus: "Even if I think you're wrong, I'll always back you up" (1.03, "Man of Iron, Woman Under Glass") or "You'll figure it out ... you're you" (2.14, "State of the Union"). She supports him when his confidence falters or his leadership is questioned.[6] She also makes sure he eats and sleeps (2.14, "State of the Union"). Further, though Erin is the only female character to recur throughout the entire run of the series, any authority she might have in Thunder Mountain is severely compromised in the final three episodes. When Thunder Mountain is under siege and being sabotaged from within, Erin cedes a briefly-held head of security position (2.14, "State of the Union"), confesses her apparently longstanding love for Markus, and invites Markus to a formal dinner for two, during which he rejects her (2.16, "Interregnum Part 2").

Nowhere is the series' preoccupation with male stories more evident than when examining *Jeremiah*'s litany of dead girlfriends. Kurdy, Markus, and Jeremiah, the three most frequently appearing male characters in the series, all lose their female partners—events which serve to motivate them in launching their final assault against the forces of "Daniel" in the latter half of season 2. The first to die is Elizabeth (Kandyse McClure), a young woman who generally stays in Thunder Mountain, gratefully accepting the gifts of glass animals that Kurdy brings to her. She is depicted as fragile, needing a man's protection, and she is killed in order to drive a wedge between Kurdy and Jeremiah. As she dies, her last words are about the two men: "Don't blame Jeremiah for this. It wasn't his fault" (1.20, "Things Left Unsaid Part 1"). She exists less as a character than as a motivation for her male suitor; her death is the reason that Kurdy breaks away from his partnership with Jeremiah in season 2.

Meaghan the plague carrier, Markus's love,[7] is the second partner to die. Hers is the most passive role in the series; since the surviving generation has now reached adult age and is vulnerable to the Big Death, Meaghan cannot leave the single room in which she lives. She is locked in a chamber below Thunder Mountain for fifteen years, able to talk to no one but Markus. She has no agency and is reliant on Markus for all her needs. Not only do her helpless entrapment and romantic entanglement with her captor mark Meaghan as the most feminized character in the series, this also calls to mind pandemic narratives that associate disease with femininity—"an insidious and mysterious force that must be dominated in order to preserve life as we know it" (Thomas 144). When Meaghan finally does leave her cell, it's to save an endangered Markus, who is held prisoner in Valhalla Sector; after Meaghan infects everyone in the base, she succumbs to guilt and despair, affirming her love for Markus before leaping to her death from a cliff (2.02, "Letters from the Other Side Part 2").

Finally, Liberty "Libby" Kaufman (Joanne Kelly), first introduced as the lab assistant to Jeremiah's father Devon, leaves Valhalla Sector for Thunder Mountain and eventually joins Jeremiah in running the town of Milhaven. It is not clear exactly what her role is: outside of Valhalla Sector, she is never shown in a lab, nor does she occupy a position of authority or responsibility within the Thunder Mountain or Milhaven hierarchies. Jeremiah is mayor of Milhaven; Libby serves tea to the men (2.07, "Voices in the Dark"; 2.08, "Crossing Jordan"), greets Jeremiah when he returns from missions (2.07, "Voices in the Dark"), does the dishes (2.08, "Crossing Jordan"), cares for Jeremiah when he is wounded (2.01, "Letters from the Other Side Part 1"; 2.07, "Voices in the Dark") and wears clothing that bares her midriff (2.07, "Voices in the Dark") or upper thigh (2.08, "Crossing Jordan"). The episode after she first has sex with Jeremiah, she is revealed as a spy and fatally shot (2.08, "Crossing Jordan").

All of *Jeremiah*'s female romantic leads are killed in service to male narratives. This is made explicit in episode 2.10 ("Running on Empty") as Jeremiah, Kurdy, and Markus discuss their emotional turmoil and subsequent actions—Kurdy reminding Jeremiah that he understands the loss of a lover, Jeremiah vowing vengeance against "Daniel"'s lieutenant Sims (John Pyper-Ferguson) for Libby's death, and Markus explaining that he will help because he suspects it's what Meaghan would have wanted. This quest for Sims, ending in a manly, one-on-one knock-down fight between Sims and Jeremiah, dovetails with the conflict between armies that marks the season—and series—climax. After Libby's death, the season 2 opening credits include only Luke Perry, Malcolm-Jamal Warner, and Sean Astin; no women merit status as series regulars.

Race and the Post-Racial

On the surface, *Jeremiah* is notable for the inclusion of characters of diverse ethnic backgrounds; however, the series is limited by its focus on white men in leadership positions, and by its supposedly post-racial setting. Its most prominent Black character is Kurdy, and Jeremiah and Kurdy come from racially stereotyped backgrounds: Jeremiah, the elder son of a middle-class scientist, living in the suburbs with his father, mother and brother, and Kurdy, a childhood victim of violence whose parents died after his father shot his mother in a euthanasia/suicide (1.07, "City of Roses"), and who has since been involved with gangs (2.12, "The Past Is Prologue"). *Jeremiah* presents Jeremiah and Kurdy as equal partners, though this presumed balance is undermined by Jeremiah's position as the title character. Jeremiah is important as the focus of Ezekiel's prophecies and as Devon's son (a familial link that ties him to the mystery of the Big Death). Kurdy receives significant amounts of screen time but at the beginning of the series, he does not occupy the center of *Jeremiah*'s story; rather, his partnership with Jeremiah echoes earlier biracial buddy cop pairings of 1980s action movies like *Lethal Weapon* (1987), or—arguably—the later relationship between Jake and Hawkins in *Jericho*. Such buddy pairings privilege male characters and masculine performance while reinscribing white supremacist systems (Wiegman, cited in Kakoudaki 127). The initial scenes of the pilot episode establish Jeremiah's dominance when he punches and ties up Kurdy; it isn't until the second season, when Kurdy and Jeremiah are no longer mission partners, that Kurdy can come into his own as a military leader. Admittedly, this second season does much to equalize Kurdy's position in the narrative, as Mr. Smith, the messenger of God, fixates on Kurdy as a figure of importance: "There are two kinds of people in this world: those who survive history, and those who make it. You, Kurdy, are one of the latter" (2.06, "The Mysterious Mister Smith"). However, despite *Jeremiah*'s increasing inclusion of a Black character as co-lead, the series is less successful in acknowledging larger contexts.

Jeremiah twice attempts to acknowledge and address race issues; each time, Kurdy is positioned as a representative of post-racial politics. The series pilot very briefly highlights a white supremacist group (1.01, "The Long Road"), complete with a skinhead who literally spits on "racial inferiors" locked in a cage. While Kurdy would retreat without rescuing the captives, Jeremiah is the one who protests, stepping in as hero. This incident reads on multiple levels: establishing Jeremiah as more conscientious than Kurdy; establishing Jeremiah as non-racist; and separating Kurdy from any engagement with racial concerns. The series then skirts mention of race for fifteen episodes, until Thunder Mountain sends Kurdy and Jeremiah to negotiate with the "Shadow of the Crescent," a Black segregationist community. Here, the Black leaders are unfairly prejudiced against Elizabeth, a biracial member of Thunder Mountain: she is "a symbol of what nearly brought our people to ruin—racial mixing" (1.16, "Moon in Gemini"). Kurdy must step in to defend Elizabeth and to decry the segregationists for their ignorant ways: "Life is not Black or white.... The real work comes in taking the time to judge people by what's in their hearts." In doing so, he cites James Baldwin, Malcolm X, and Martin Luther King, Jr., showing himself to be educated in American race history and further causing his opponents to situate themselves in the political "wrong" when they dismiss King out of hand: "King had a time and a place." Kurdy, in rejecting the segregationist Black community, serves as a mouthpiece for post-racial politics. The Big Death, he argues, has created a world where the need to survive has transcended race: "I saw unity. I saw children reaching out to other children, and it didn't matter who you were." In the color-blind philosophy that Kurdy espouses, Black civil rights rhetoric is unfair and counterproductive to social progress; this suggests that rather than promoting inclusiveness, *Jeremiah* has incorporated the type of white liberal "blindcasting" that places non-white actors in roles that echo white perspectives (Warner 13). It is surely significant that *Jeremiah* spends much more time criticizing "Moon in Gemini"'s Black leaders than dwelling on the skinheads who keep their prisoners of color literally caged. As well, since Kurdy and Elizabeth are both accepted and loyal members of Thunder Mountain, their community by extension must also exemplify equality—exonerating not only Jeremiah, but also Markus and all other Mountain characters.

Theo (Kim Hawthorne) is one of the few Black women of the series; she is the leader of the town of Clairfield and one of the first characters Jeremiah encounters in the pilot. Theo is presented as a worthy foe who later becomes a reluctant ally; she is powerful and ruthless. Her morals are suspect—a Thunder Mountain emissary dies as her prisoner—and stereotypes of race and gender intersect as Theo is depicted as savage and unpredictable, a clear opposite to Markus's calm, "reasonable" aesthetic. Theo embodies overconfident, emotional swagger while switching in and out of femme costuming such as dresses and sparkles, alternating with more masculine guerrilla clothing. In the pilot, she is promptly sexualized, as Jeremiah saves her life and she responds, "Usually I prefer to be on top" (1.01, "The Long Road Part 1"). Keeping with the series' implicit assertion of a post-racial society, Theo's dialogue highlights her gender rather than her race: "These first few years, the things I had to do to survive ... girls had it worse than anybody, you know" (1.01, "The Long Road Part 1"). According to Theo, being female has made her survival more difficult; being Black is not mentioned as a factor. This further advances *Jeremiah*'s supposedly post-racial and post-feminist future while obfuscating the prevalence of white male power and racial stereotyping, as well as implicitly ascribing Theo's emotional unpredictability—and her eventual loss of power—to her gender. Indeed, shortly after declaring her pregnancy, Theo vanishes from the screen entirely; her maternal body has no place in the coming conflicts (2.05, "Rites of Passage").

While civil rights politics are thus oversimplified, inverted, or glossed over for *Jeremiah*'s dramatizations, the series steadily advances white narratives, from its titular fixation on Jeremiah-the-character to Thunder Mountain's white leadership (as embodied by Markus and a governing council in which only one of six members is played by a non-white actor). Outside of the Mountain, white men are most often seen in charge of outside organizations—Jason Priestley's militant dictator "Michael" and his force of all-white-male soldiers are an early highlight. Other examples include the President and of course Daniel and his many representatives; Kurdy may espouse post-racial equality, but *Jeremiah*'s social structures indicate otherwise, as positions of military or political power are most frequently occupied by white men. Further, the series incorporates ethnic stereotypes—as with two Asian characters, Lee Chen (Byron Lawson) and Rachel (Françoise Yip), who are both somehow skilled martial artists despite having come of age in post-apocalyptic America without adult guidance. *Jeremiah*'s casting for small roles is arguably diverse, featuring multiple recurring characters, bit-part actors and extras of color; in this way, it avoids the pitfalls of representation in which one or two non-white characters exist against an overwhelmingly white social backdrop, but its relative lack of non-white leads also reduces this casting to "landscaping," in which extras of color are used as props—"a roster of cardboard cutouts with whom empathy is unnecessary" (Warner 20). The series implicitly claims Thunder Mountain and its would-be alliance as an inclusive post-racial utopia, while positioning Daniel as a nearly uniform white male force; this suggests Thunder Mountain to be progressive while obscuring the degree to which white men take prominence in the series.

Summary

Jeremiah's pandemic ultimately reads more as a narrative tool than a warning; the Big Death may have been bioengineered by ruthless scientists, and it may be embodied by a woman, but any attendant implications about the military-industrial complex, the trustworthiness of scientific and political institutions, or even the deadly mystery of the female body fade into the background as concerns about the plague are swept aside in favor of other conflicts. Considering the timing of the series' production, it is difficult not to read the second season as a reaction to post–9/11 American tensions and a renewed focus on the military, associated masculinity, and the patriotism accompanying notions of American exceptionalism in the face of challenge.

Jeremiah's pandemic is positioned as a cleanse that allows for the rise of new heroes who can build a new society unburdened by the constraints of the past. However, such a reading cannot be sustained. In the series finale, the warring armies of Thunder Mountain and Daniel are not set to end their conflict with a final battle; instead, Jeremiah having defeated Sims and the truth of "Daniel" having been revealed, the enemy forces are now uncertain and the final shot is of Jeremiah, Kurdy, and Mr. Smith walking to parley on Thunder Mountain's behalf. Though Thunder Mountain has mustered an army beneath a proudly flying American flag, *Jeremiah* suggests via Mr. Smith's voiceover that its new generation of children, divorced from old ways by the Big Death, may achieve a better path than war:

> Today, this day, the world would change forever. Not because of the clash of armies, not in the currency of bomb blasts or body counts, but through the proper application of the only force that matters—the only power that even God respects: the truth [2.16, "Interregnum Part 2"].

At the same time, however, it is difficult to avoid noting that the new world looks much like the old: that three men are walking to talk peace with an army of other men, and that another man's community vision is the guiding force for change. Further, while one side may claim more women and non-white members within its ranks, both are predominantly led by white men. The children once left alone, now grown, have seemingly recreated their parents' heteronormative white patriarchy—inflected with post-racial politics and paying lip service to gender equality while marginalizing women and people of color, and wholly excluding queer figures.

The Last Ship

Based on William Brinkley's 1988 novel of the same name, *The Last Ship* shifts the original book's tale of nuclear disaster to a more twenty-first-century story of bioweaponry gone wrong. While *Jeremiah* focuses on former child survivors left alone to rebuild their world, *The Last Ship* features the U.S.S. *Nathan James*, an American military naval vessel, sailing a planet recently decimated by a mysterious virus. Unlike *Jeremiah*'s bioweapon disaster Big Death, *The Last Ship*'s disease is distinctly reflective of twenty-first-century fears regarding "bird flu" or "avian influenza": it was carried by birds, transmitted to humans, and affected 80 percent of the world's population. Since the *Nathan James* was in the Arctic, retrieving scientist Rachel Scott (Rhona Mitra), its crew was unharmed in the initial viral spread. Under the leadership of Captain Tom Chandler (Eric Dane), the crew must ensure Dr. Scott has the time and resources she needs to develop a cure in her onboard lab. *The Last Ship* offers a Hollywood version of military spectacle that promises American survival via its troops; it serves as a vehicle for the same increasingly conservative values that called for a stronger American military post–9/11 (Nail and McGregor), and it implicitly calls to "support our troops" rhetoric that fetishizes the notion of white American military manhood.

Where *Jeremiah* began to explore such notions, and *Jericho* and *Revolution* incorporate them more completely, *The Last Ship* goes a step further in actively working as a public relations tool for the U.S. Navy.

Join the Navy

The Last Ship is filmed in cooperation with the U.S. Navy, and TNT released a promotional video, "Working on a Real Ship | The Last Ship | TNT,"[8] in which executive producer and writer Steven Kane states, "These are among the most noble people you could ever imagine. I mean, I think everyone watching at home should feel good about the U.S. Navy after they watch the show, because we feel that way." According to a 2014 article in the *Los Angeles Times*, the series' reliance on Navy set pieces—such as the destroyers U.S.S. *Halsey* and *Dewey*, which alternately serve as the *Nathan James*—means that producers require the continued support of Navy officials:

> The series still had to be approved by senior leaders, including Navy Secretary Ray Mabus, before the destroyers would be lent out for filming. "We have a vested interest in not having the Navy look bad," said U.S. Navy Capt. Brian Quin, a decorated officer and a former destroyer commander who served as technical advisor for the production. "This is great because we get to show sailors in an awesome light" [Braxton].

Given this context, it's unsurprising that *The Last Ship* persistently and explicitly references the American military through frequent exterior shots of the ship, neat uniforms and salutes, and dialogue laden with acronyms and jargon (i.e., "Deploy SCAT. CWIS to AAW Auto. Hold fire on," 1.01, "Phase Six"). Further, the series consistently presents flattering tales of military heroism within a simplified moral system in which the villains are always evil and the ship's fearless soldiers are noble and brave.

Chandler, the series protagonist, is clean-cut, mid–40s, and white; his square-jawed leadership is established in the pilot, when he risks his life by jamming his hand in a fuse to save the ship and crew. "I said rip it!" he yells, after which Commander Master Chief Jeter (Charles Parnell) can say admiringly, "Badass, captain. Badass" (1.01, "Phase Six"). The series is littered with comments regarding Chandler's competence and character: "Captain always has a plan" (1.07, "SOS"); "He's amazing" (1.13, "No Place Like Home"); "Do you not realize they can't do it without you? … Whether you like it or not, you're Noah, and that ship is your Ark" (2.03, "It's Not a Rumor"). One exchange stands out:

> JETER: I am here for a reason. As are you, as is everyone aboard this ship. You are
> here to lead us. And we are here to follow, to execute your vision.
>
> CHANDLER: I don't have a vision.
>
> JETER: You do… There's a voice inside you. Maybe it's your highest self. Maybe it's
> the voice of God. I don't know. But it's a voice of hope [1.04, "We'll Get There"].

As Chandler, with background music swelling beneath his speech, convinces his crew that "a 3-billion-dollar piece of machinery protected by 216 sailors in the U.S. Navy" is the last and best hope for the human race, everyone on deck salutes him (1.01, "Phase Six").

Science fiction has been used as military recruitment propaganda elsewhere, as when *X-Men: First Class* (2011) or *Independence Day: Insurgence* (2016) linked their marketing to U.S. Army recruiting material; the Navy has also previously collaborated with Hollywood on films like *Battleship* (2012), allowing site and personnel access but in turn demanding final script approval (McIntosh). *The Last Ship* is not officially connected to a recruiting campaign, but as it is reliant on Navy approval for continued filming, it ultimately serves this purpose—a type of military-friendly popular culture that also includes video games like *America's Army* (U.S. Army, 2002) and has been referred to as "militainment" (McIntosh; Singer), or "the fascinating, but also worrisome, blurring of the line between entertainment and war" (Singer). As McIntosh has noted, "science fiction can provide a simple good vs. evil narrative, one that appeals to patriotism and a desire to save the world" while whitewashing the more dangerous, uncomfortable, and complex realities of military service. On *The Last Ship*, the only future for America—and the entire planet—in deadly times rests with the training and perseverance of the American military. Chandler is the face of this message.

Women and Children First

If Chandler is the square-jawed male hero in a time of crisis, the crew of his ship is also predominantly male—including his fellow authority figures Jeter and First Officer Mike Slattery (Adam Baldwin). Repeated episodes of *The Last Ship* demonstrate a pattern of violent men, the women and children they endanger, and the (almost always) male sailors who must step in to protect the innocent. These incidents cast the crew of the *Nathan James*—and particularly Chandler—as chivalrous and further the post–9/11 fantasy of the masculine American soldier defending the hapless women and children who depend on his return to a classically gendered wartime function (Faludi). The promotional art for the first season features a young blonde girl in a frilly pink dress, holding a gas mask and standing on a pile of burning rubble, looking out at the *Nathan James* as it approaches. The accompanying text reads, "Save us."[9] *The Last Ship* sets up a conflict between male forces; its gender divisions are clear.

This is not to say that the *Nathan James's* crew lacks women completely; it includes Lt. Alisha Granderson (Christina Elmore), Lt. Kara Foster (Marissa Neitling), and chief engineer Andrea Garnett (Fay Masterson). These three women are obvious exceptions in an overwhelmingly male crew of 200-plus.

However, all of these women are in support roles; they are often seen on the bridge or using tactical equipment, but they seldom participate in off-ship missions (and accompanying action/firefights).

Kara Foster's role is most particularly gendered. When Kara is sent off ship in season 1, Chandler explicitly calls out her gender as a qualification: "We need a female for this mission." This provides a specific rationale for Kara being part of the team and apparently justifies the all-male teams that are much more common when female participation is not specifically "needed." But Lt. Danny Green (Travis Van Winkle) objects: "I don't feel comfortable having Lt. Foster on this mission. She's never seen action like this before." Danny and Kara are secretly having an affair; the mission almost fails when Danny tries to protect Kara instead of following orders. Afterward, he blames her for distracting him:

> DANNY: I lost my focus because of you.
>
> KARA: Because of me? I didn't do anything. You throttled down and wanted me to bail.
>
> DANNY: No.
>
> KARA: Danny—
>
> DANNY: This is ... this is why we're not supposed to ... I love you. Stay away from me [1.03, "Dead Reckoning"].

This speaks to conservative objections regarding women in the military—that they are less effective in combat (in *The Last Ship*, consistently sidelined) and that their presence will be a threat to male discipline.[10] When Chandler discovers the affair, he, too, admonishes Kara: "You took an oath, and you have a duty to your shipmates." Though he punishes Danny as well, his lecture is different: "You're a leader. Lead." Danny is being groomed for authority while Kara is not being a team player. Her effectiveness as a soldier is further compromised at the end of season 1, when it is revealed that she is pregnant with Danny's child (1.09, "Trials"). When her unborn fetus is a potential tool for developing a cure, Kara is kidnapped and tied screaming to a table while masked figures unfasten her clothing (2.01, "Unreal City"); after this incident, with its clear overtones of sexual assault, Kara is promoted to Tactical Action Officer and spends much of the rest of season 2 seated in front of a weapons terminal, again acting as support to the men on the ground. In season 3, after the baby is born, she leaves the ship entirely.

Women who are not sailors fare no better. Rachel Scott, the female lead in seasons 1 and 2, is a scientist rather than a crew member; she has medical expertise which is imperative to developing a vaccine.[11] Of course, she could not work without the support of the *Nathan James* and the protection of Chandler, and her position outside the chain of command further positions her as a romantic interest for Chandler without the risk of violating regulations (like the less disciplined Kara and Danny). When Rachel is eventually killed, her death is explicitly framed as being important for Chandler's continuing narrative. Just after the airing of the season 3 premiere, in which Rachel is revealed as dead (victim of a bullet fired in the season 2 finale), Steven Kane stated in an interview that in the new season, "her death sort of permeates every decision Chandler makes, and also leaves him alone as the sort of 'godfather of the new world'" (Mitovich). Rachel's execution serves as motivational fuel for Chandler's more important journey (and his apparently nearly literally paternalistic role).

One exception to the series' gender patterns proves literally short-lived. Lt. Ravit Bivas (Inbar Lavi) briefly appears as a new crew member in season 2; an Israeli soldier, she is skilled in combat and actively participates on away missions for the *Nathan James*. Her gender still limits her role; Ravit is immediately sexualized, as crewmates comment on her attractiveness and Lt. Burk (Jocko Sims) pursues a persistent flirtation—which Ravit returns, kissing him (2.07, "Alone and Unafraid") and teasing him with an invitation of forbidden shower sex (2.10, "Friendly Fire") just before she is killed, dying from wounds sustained during combat (2.11, "Valkyrie"). Her tenure on the ship is limited to six episodes, and her combat competence is continuously contained by her sexual attractiveness and her role as seductive tease.

No incident divides the men and women of the *Nathan James* so clearly as season 2's assault on Baltimore, where Kara and Rachel are escorted to safety ("Can your men get them out of here? Take them"), a bleeding Alisha Granderson is rescued and carried out of the fighting zone, and Garnett is left "in command" of a captured hostage group awaiting rescue by men with night vision goggles and guns (2.02, "Fight the Ship"). The gender distinctions on the ship, made clear here, are reinforced throughout the series by dialogue that refers to the crew as men ("our men," "your men," 1.02, "Welcome to Gitmo"; "all my best men," 1.05, "El Toro"), as well as recurring images of all-male enemy forces (1.02, "Welcome to Gitmo"; 1.05, "El Toro"; 1.08, "Two Sailors Walk into a Bar...") and armed male crew members rescuing helpless women and children (1.05, "El Toro"; 1.08, "Two Sailors Walk into a Bar..."). Former prison security guard Tex (John Pyper-Ferguson), who joins the crew, often makes casually sexist comments indicating his "appreciation" of the women around him: "She's real soulful, that one. Never mind them good looks, that brassy exterior" (re: Rachel, 1.02, "Welcome to Gitmo"), or "She is tasty now, is she not?" (re: Kara, 1.04, "We'll Get There"). He refers to Rachel as the "lady doc" (1.06, "Lockdown"). His remarks are treated as a character quirk, and since he is outside the ship's command structure, his attitudes reinforce sexist gender norms without reflecting poorly on the ship's presumably more enlightened crew—who do not correct him. He even gets a kiss from Rachel (1.13, "No Place Like Home").

These gender differences are never openly acknowledged within the series, nor is race or sexuality; *The Last Ship* presents the Navy as a pure meritocracy. Regular and recurring non-white characters include Jeter, Alisha, Burk, and Chung, but Chandler never addresses either the gender or race of his subordinates. Jeter, a Black character, is a prominent authority figure in the crew but is the senior enlisted sailor (rather than a commissioned officer)—a position that carries working-class connotations rather than elite officer status, which requires specialized education and training. Alisha, a lesbian, provides *The Last Ship*'s queer content, but this queerness is token at best, its brief acknowledgment in the pilot primarily serving to establish Chandler as accepting of LGBTQ relationships; Alisha does not have any onscreen romantic entanglements and her sexuality is a minor character detail. And while other characters are subordinate or otherwise outside the chain of command, Chandler and his first officer Mike Slattery have primary authority on the ship. They are both white and heterosexual. They frequently confer with Jeter, forming a triumvirate of male authority; later, Chandler answers to the white male President. This chain of command makes the white male supremacy on the ship official, sanctioned by rank: all members of the crew obey Chandler and Slattery before any others. Further, while there are four lieutenants— Danny, Kara, Alisha, and Burk—season 1 dialogue states that Danny, the only white male, is the one being groomed for future promotion; even as Chandler is in the process of punishing Kara for the affair, they can find common ground in agreeing that Danny is a natural leader with innate potential for greatness. The chain of succession is clear: Chandler is the leader now, and Slattery his trusted second, but the future of the *Nathan James* rests on the continuation of the patriarchy as Danny learns to be the next Tom Chandler.

The Enemy/the Other

The crew of the *Nathan James* is thus primarily composed of—or subject to the authority of—white heterosexual men wearing crisp military uniforms; they exhibit a surface-level diversity that pays homage to the U.S. Navy's supposedly post-feminist, post-racial meritocracy, while still reflecting stereotypical assumptions about heterosexual male heroism and the importance of a militarized masculinity. In turn, *The Last Ship*'s depiction of various enemies parallels both post–9/11 Islamophobia and, most particularly, Cold War–like hostility toward the Russians. If "the virus is the ultimate Other in this era of globalization; it has no voice and cannot represent itself, making it a convenient enemy" (Thomas 144), it seems significant that both *Jeremiah* and *The Last Ship* deal with the virus fairly summarily, more concerned with rebuilding the pandemic-ravaged world. In *The Last Ship*, no viral metaphors are necessary; the enemy is human, and forces that are non–American, non–English, non-white and non–Christian are consistently Othered as threats.

The Last Ship's relationship to American identity in the post–9/11 war on terror is made explicit in the second episode, when the *Nathan James* docks at Guantanamo Bay. The former prisoners of Guantanamo have over-run the facility and killed most of the guards—except for Tex, who needs the crew's help. It is implicitly assumed that the prisoners, all Middle Eastern characters, are all hardened, violent men guilty of terrorist crimes. It is 33 minutes into the 42-minute episode before one of them speaks; they are primarily nameless and faceless opponents, also referred to as "ass bags" and "animals." Tex, held at gunpoint, introduces his captor: "This here is Amir. He's a big fan of IEDs and mutilating American soldiers." When Amir and his people demand food, Chandler refuses: "There's one thing from the old world that still applies today. Something that will never change. We don't negotiate with terrorists." The *Nathan James* then attacks; in the explosion and ensuing chaos, the other prisoners are all shot by Chandler's men, as commentary from sailors watching from the ship includes "Nice," "Yes," and "Good work" (1.02, "Welcome to Gitmo"). Order restored and the generic Middle Eastern foes vanquished, Tex then joins the crew. *The Last Ship* neglects complex issues regarding Guantanamo Bay—e.g., questions about torture of prisoners, imprisonment without charge or trial (Apuzzo, Fink, and Risen), or force-feeding (Olsen and Gallagher)—as vicious Arab prisoners execute noble guards and are then justly gunned down by white American military forces. The prisoners are barely characters, short-lived and, except for Amir, unnamed. The series clearly advances a narrative of Good vs. Evil in the form of American vs. Other (with all the white male English-speaking Christian elements that "American" here represents).

Strikingly, while this episode—the series' second—appears to situate *The Last Ship* in a conflict vs. Islamic terrorists, they are not prevalent villains; rather, the *Nathan James*'s primary foes in the first season are the Russians, as represented by a rogue Russian nuclear submarine and its captain, Ruskov (Ravil Isyanov). This may be a holdover from the novel's Cold War roots; in the original work, the ship eludes nuclear war rather than disease, and pandemic may be an evolution of this fear—Keränen has also associated bioterrorism fears with 1990s "post–Cold War security concerns" (459). Certainly the Russians are also thinly sketched opponents. Much like the Guantanamo prisoners, the Russian characters lack moral nuance; in addition to firing a nuclear missile at France (with the millions of deaths that would accompany such an impact; 1.01, "Phase Six"), Ruskov is also evil on a smaller scale. He has kidnapped scientist Quincy Tophet (Sam Spruell)'s wife and child, holding them hostage on his ship and sexually abusing Kelly Tophet (Alice Coulthard) as he forces Quincy to spy for him. Unlike Chandler, he has abandoned his post: "Look around you. The world is ours for the taking." He claims, "The uniform we wear matters no more," but Chandler responds, "Well, it matters to me" (1.03, "Dead Reckoning"). This not only juxtaposes Ruskov's corruption and hubris against Chandler's disciplined self-sacrifice, it also situates *The Last Ship* and the *Nathan James* within decades of ongoing conflicts and dangers that have marked American (and world) history; in *The Last Ship*, American militarism is the solution in all cases, not just to conflicts of the present or future but also to international clashes of the past.

When the Guantanamo prisoners execute a guard and leave his body strung up, or when Ruskov destroys France and rapes the woman he holds prisoner (1.07, "SOS"), it leaves no room for moral nuance; the Navy is always in the right. Similar foes are also Othered—for example, "El Toro" (José Zúñiga), a Nicaraguan dictator who faces off against Chandler and his crew, mocks American masculinity ("John Wayne. Clint Eastwood. American macho, no?"), and subsequently pays the price. The crew of the *Nathan James* need never doubt that they are acting in the service of good, when the villains they face off against are guilty of human trafficking, slaving, and the rape of teenage girls (1.06, "Lockdown").[12]

America Under Threat

Nowhere is the essential character of the *Nathan James* crew more apparent than in the second season. The series' season 2 credits opens with images of objects sinking in the ocean, representational of *The Last Ship*'s American society in peril: a gas mask, a chemical vial, bullets, a Bible, and a U.S. flag. The makeup of the crew reflects stereotypes of a white, English, Christian America: though a few named female and/or non-white characters are featured, the majority of extras seen on ship—many of whom are apparently actual sailors ("Working on a Real Ship")—are white men. All shipboard characters appear to be native English speakers (most are American; Scott is British), and the crew is generically Christian, seen holding prayer services for lost comrades (1.04, "We'll Get There"; 2.11, "Valkyrie"). They represent stereotypes about what it means to be both "American" (white, Christian, English-speaking) and "soldiers" (predominantly male). Even when one of the fallen soldiers is Ravit, a Jewish woman, this goes unacknowledged by the line of grieving sailors touching their fingers to the Bible (2.11, "Valkyrie").

The second-season enemies are the Immunes, implicitly positioned as the antithesis to the crew of the *Nathan James*: they are former soldiers who have abandoned their mission and embraced a false religion. Again, a submarine houses the foe—"opposite" to the *Nathan James*, as subs glide secretly below the ocean instead of sailing above. While the Russians presented as opportunistic deserters in contrast with the *Nathan James*'s crew's sense of military duty, the Immunes serve as an even more extended contrast to duty and discipline. Brothers Sean (Brian F. O'Byrne) and Ned Ramsey (Nick Court), former UK officers now gone rogue, have gathered a crew of other experienced sailors—all naturally immune to the virus—and fostered a cult of fellow immunes who believe they are chosen to be the next master race. In addition to the obvious Nazi links of a "master race" narrative—again, drawing comparisons between *Nathan James*'s foes and the enemies of both today and yesteryear—the crew of the *H.M.S. Achilles* present as precisely opposite to the *Nathan James*'s neatly pressed discipline. Positioned both narratively and aesthetically as failed soldiers, they wear casual clothing or haphazard uniform pieces (for example, a British Navy uniform shirt with an open collar and rolled-up sleeves). They spout military terms but also swear and argue amongst themselves, while drinking beer and smoking on duty. In contrast to the *Nathan James*'s surface-level gender inclusiveness, they are all men—here maintaining the series' unquestioned emphasis on male leadership while also positioning the *Nathan James* crew as supposedly progressive and post-feminist. While Chandler and his crew work to spread a cure among the remaining world populace, Sean Ramsey and his people destroy scientific labs and spread the plague, trying to kill the non-immune and clear the planet for the taking. The religious cult language that fuels their crusade ("I come here as your humble messenger, spreading the gospel of the Immunes," 2.06, "Long Day's Journey") places them again in direct opposition to the Christianity more subtly but consistently espoused by *The Last Ship*'s crew.

The Immunes as an undisciplined, immoral, and dishonorable enemy force highlight the crew of the *Nathan James* as dutiful, moral, and righteous. While other series may follow protagonists in ragtag survival groups after government institutions have broken down, *The Last Ship* clearly positions such groups as dangerous, undisciplined, and delusional; American survival rests with the preservation of federal institutions. A major plot element is the *Nathan James*'s rescue of the President of the United States, Jeffrey Michener (Mark Moses), from the Immune forces, and the re-establishment of the U.S. government in a time of crisis. As the *Nathan James* spreads the cure and delivers the President to the new capital of St. Louis, there is no doubt that Navy tradition and Christian morals have prevailed; the last shot of Ramsey in his destroyed submarine is a close-up of his screaming face as he dies in agonized terror (2.12, "Cry Havoc").

Summary

The Last Ship embraces a variety of American fears and foes, from Islamic terrorists to South American drug lords to Russian nuclear vessels; the third season sends the ship to China and Vietnam. The pandemic, while it plays to contemporary concerns regarding both avian flu (such as H1N1) and bio-weaponry, is secondary to these concerns—in the post-apocalypse of the U.S. Navy and the *Nathan James*, the pandemic is less important because of the devastation it wreaks and more important as a problem for Chandler and his people to solve, giving the ship and its crew a purpose only they can fulfill. While the cast is relatively diverse, including multiple characters of color and at least one openly queer officer, the command hierarchy of the *Nathan James* continues to reflect the white patriarchy predominant in U.S. military institutions (and Western culture in general). Authority rests primarily in the hands of men—most particularly Tom Chandler, who is the frequent subject of praise from his crew and others around him, as his leadership qualities are repeatedly affirmed in order to naturalize his command position. Further, his eventual successor is assumed to be Danny Green, setting a predictive pattern of white men in command and normalizing a handoff of power from older white man to younger. This is further bolstered by first officer Mike Slattery, whose season 3 plotline as an escaping prisoner of war highlights his hypermasculinity and advances notions of the strong American soldier.

The Last Ship's dependence on the U.S. Navy for filming locations, costuming, extras, and consultant information is tangible in the series' lack of nuance. Chandler and his crew are never in the moral grey and are always resolute as they embody a fantasy of a strong American military—increasingly diverse, but securely under the command of gifted white men—fighting against one-dimensional stereotypes of American enemies. The crew of the *Nathan James* is saving not only the United States, but also the entire world. While this calls to long-time visions of the American soldier, including propaganda from both World Wars, as well as "support our troops" mantras and a long history of war stories in film, television, novels and other popular culture, it also speaks most specifically to the post–9/11 mentality that called for a stronger military and a return to traditional American masculinity. This makes *The Last Ship* one of the most conservative post-apocalyptic television series in recent memory; in its world, salvation rests not only on the gumption and initiative of a few good white men, but also on the preservation of pre-apocalyptic patriarchal institutions. Rather than rebuilding a new society in the aftermath of a catastrophic global event, *The Last Ship* clings to the last vestiges of the old to guide humanity through.

Conclusion

Jeremiah and *The Last Ship* both preserve patriarchal structures but do so in oppositional ways. *Jeremiah* envisions the destruction of previous generations in favor of new alliances built by the children who grow up alone;

its pandemic serves to cleanse America of corrupt institutions, allowing its protagonists to reject the now-illegitimate remnants of the American government while simultaneously embracing the stars and stripes as a symbol of their own new society. *The Last Ship*'s pandemic is a threat to a contemporary America whose survival is key to preserving the human race; here, the proud sailors of the U.S. Navy preserve military tradition and Christian faith in the face of overwhelming odds, not only curing American civilians but also rescuing and reinstating the President whose leadership is key to recovering a lost America. Destroying old institutions is key to *Jeremiah*; the fight to preserve them defines *The Last Ship*. In both scenarios, however, the leadership provided by straight white men is vital. Women are primarily passive, people of color are sidelined, queer characters barely exist, and it is apparent that the new world will look much like the old: a patriarchy led by heterosexual white men for whom a strong military forms the foundation of survival.

In either series, the pandemics themselves are not treated with particular depth of interest, though this is not always the case; regarding more virus-focused texts, Wald has highlighted the need for plague narratives to account for economic class vulnerabilities (265), and Tomes has noted the importance of studying how popular culture helps to shape perceptions of disease (649). Moreover, popular culture in combination with government simulations, political speeches, science journals and news may create "a widespread vision of bio(in)security ... that, in turn, licenses a proliferation of biological weapons agents in the name of biodefense" (Keränen 466). *Jeremiah*, however, briefly uses the plague as a bioweapon and then allows the entire narrative thread to drop, as the prospect of contamination is apparently no longer an issue after the destruction of Valhalla Sector and throughout the rest of season 2. *The Last Ship* removes the pandemic as a direct threat to the *Nathan James* crew (via season 1 vaccinations) and subsequently maintains the quest for a mass cure as a military mission; the plague is not a direct threat to the series protagonists. In each scenario, the pandemic reads as a timely acknowledgment of current news stories regarding health pandemics and the real threat of mass infection; however, both series ultimately present reassuring narratives in which the status quo—even in the face of annihilation—can still be safely preserved.

— 3 —

The Alien Other

ALIEN ENCOUNTERS ARE A STAUNCH science fiction tradition. H.G. Wells's *War of the Worlds* (1897) is perhaps the best-known alien invasion narrative, while films like *The Day the Earth Stood Still* (1951, 2008), *Invasion of the Body Snatchers* (1956, 1978), *Independence Day* (1996, and a sequel in 2016), *Men in Black* (1997, sequels in 2002 and 2012), and even *Mars Attacks!* (1996) have situated alien threats in our cultural consciousness. On television, invasion narratives have been featured in series like *The Invaders* (ABC, 1967–68), *Dark Skies* (NBC, 1996–97), *The X-Files* (Fox, 1993–2002, 2016–18), or 2016's *BrainDead* (CBS). Our aliens have evolved with each decade's fears regarding warfare, immigration, and the threat of foreign encroachment.

Like most popular American myths, aliens have also been associated with the wild west and the American frontier; images of the roaming cowboy have been linked with space expansion, as in James T. Kirk (William Shatner)'s famous *Star Trek* invocation, "Space: the final frontier" (Westfahl 2). As the actual "wild west" became more colonized and connected in the early twentieth century, American ambitions moved elsewhere to wartime aerial combat, air travel, and the space program: "Americans simply projected upward and outward where they had once projected westward" (Pfitzer 53). Dime novelists anticipated this trend early (52), while *Star Trek* (NBC, 1966–69) and *Star Wars* (1977) were among the blockbuster properties that helped to glorify cowboys in space (60). Not all have promoted the gunslinger hero; Bradbury's *The Martian Chronicles* (1950) have been interpreted as both using and subverting the frontier myth (60), while *The Day the Earth Stood Still*, *Cocoon* (1985), *Close Encounters of the Third Kind* (1977), and *E.T. the Extra-Terrestrial* (1982) have all speculated an Other who is here with kind intentions. Aliens in science fiction are most directly aligned with fears regarding the Other, and alien narratives have reflected both trepidation and excitement as to the strangers who might lie beyond our borders.

The 2011 film *Cowboys and Aliens* echoes the tone for television that focuses on alien invasion rather than human expansion—the type of alien invasion that leaves humans on Earth struggling to survive in a new world order. As a genre related to metaphorical fears of racial difference and hostile foreign attackers, invasion from outer space is often associated with Cold War science fiction, and easily translates to post–9/11 U.S. culture and the war on terror (Hantke). It seems no coincidence that Tom Cruise starred in a *War of the Worlds* film remake in 2005; aliens are coming again. Indeed, 2005 network television brought the triple debuts of *Surface* (NBC, 2005–06), *Threshold* (CBS, 2005–06), and *Invasion* (ABC, 2005–06), all of which have been analyzed as subversive critiques regarding the post–9/11, post–Katrina U.S. government and the suspension of American civil liberties (Hantke; Takacs). These series have ably been broken down elsewhere, in Hantke's "Bush's America and the Return of Cold War Science Fiction" and Takacs's "Monsters, Monsters Everywhere"; I turn my attention to the more recent *Falling Skies* (TNT, 2011–15), *Colony* (USA, 2016–) and *Defiance* (Syfy, 2013–15). Each analysis of these programs highlights a different type of alien invasion: *Falling Skies* as a classic, *War of the Worlds*–inspired scenario that glorifies American nationalism as resistance to globalization and immigration, *Colony* as a more critical look at post–9/11 society that both inverts and co-opts frontier stereotypes in associating white America with the positions of oppressed Indigenous peoples, and *Defiance* as most directly equating human-alien relations with racial conflict between white America and the cultural and ethnic Other.

Falling Skies

Of recent alien invasion series, *Falling Skies* is most directly inspired by Wells's *War of the Worlds*, which has served as a "prototype" for narratives wherein "Martians bent on enslaving the earth arrive en masse in cylinders and begin ravaging the world with their monstrous tripod machines and heat rays" (Lucanio 25). Here, aliens known as the Espheni invade the planet and set up giant bases over major cities, scouring the rest of the Earth with drones and scouts to either kill or enslave any remaining humans.

Lucanio has noted that in these types of invasion narratives, heroes tend to arise from science or the military; likewise, the heroes in such scenarios are assumed to be male (84), as "the alien invasion genre is profoundly patriarchal, and its appeal is especially to young boys" (86). In *Falling Skies*, only staunch, male-led American militia resistance can fight off the occupation and save the human race. *Falling Skies* appeals strongly to a white male dream of American nationalism, fostering an us-versus-them narrative that frequently incorporates verbal and visual references to the American Revolution, as well as nigh-constant images of the U.S. flag. It presents alien invaders as nameless, indistinguishable, incomprehensible, and unrelentingly hostile threats to the American family. It also presents another primarily masculine narrative, specifically focusing on white male characters and repeatedly calling back to notions of "founding fathers."

Stars and Stripes Forever

Traditional invasion stories have "stressed" nationalism as a key element of American perseverance (Sharp "Space" 153), and *Falling Skies* makes no secret of its nationalist themes; the series invokes American identity through frequent use of the national flag and through references to U.S. history, particularly the Revolutionary War and World War II. Like *Jericho*, *Falling Skies* invokes historic images of American soldiers while also incorporating the wild west mythos, positioning armed militias of determined white men as the most effective resistance force against outside dangers.

Over the course of five seasons, the changing headquarters of the human resistance provide a tour of the American dream under threat, as the militia takes shelter in an abandoned high school, an underground shopping mall, and a burned-out suburb. Against this dystopian backdrop of the beleaguered U.S.A., the most persistent reminder of the series' patriotic leanings is the stars-and-stripes flag; the red, white and blue is nearly constant. An incomplete list of appearances includes flags on billboards (3.01, "On Thin Ice"), in offices (2.09, "The Price of Greatness"), on desks (3.03, "Badlands"), on tent walls (2.04, "Young Bloods"), as tent ceilings (3.07, "The Pickett Line"), painted on the sides of buildings (3.02, "Collateral Damage"), or in a bus (2.08, "Death March"). A multi-story flag running down the wall of a military base serves as a prominent set piece in the final episodes (5.08, "Stalag 14th Virginia"). Even if a literal flag is not present, its colors may still be used to dress a scene (2.05, "Love and Other Acts of Courage"). The flag drapes *Falling Skies* and its soldiers as they defend the shattered remnants of cultural capitalist institutions.

The series also invokes the American Revolution as it follows the invasion resistance mounted by the "2nd Mass"—one of a multitude of militias fighting across the United States. The link to American history is made explicit in series dialogue: "2nd Mass? Is that some callback to the Revolutionary War? Like you're the Continental Army fighting the British again?" (5.06, "Respite") and also through protagonist Tom Mason (Noah Wyle), a history professor from Boston (itself the site of the infamous 1773 Tea Party). Tom is a living font of national memory, making overt comparisons between alien insurgency battles and American history, frequently referencing World War

II or the Revolutionary War, or extolling the virtues of Alexander DeTocqueville's *Democracy in America*. The series' use of Revolutionary War imagery ties Tom's military history stories and associated notions of white male American exceptionalism to both the marching soldiers of the 2nd Mass and the other surviving contingents that begin referring to themselves as "Mason militias." *Falling Skies'* investment in American nationalism is apparent throughout, but nowhere as blatantly as the series finale, wherein the final conflict takes place at the feet of a destroyed Lincoln Memorial, following which Tom gives a rousing speech in front of that same rebuilt monument to a cheering crowd and a background track of "America the Beautiful" (5.10, "Reborn").

Stranger Danger

Fear of the unknown Other is a predominant theme in *Falling Skies*; Revolutionary War imagery positions the soldiers of the 2nd Mass as righteously battling for their country against a colonizing empire. If alien invasions may often be taken as metaphors for concerns about immigration, the Espheni represent broad stereotypes about groups of immigrants threatening the "American" way: the Espheni forces, as represented by "Skitters," "mechs," and Overlords, lack individual names or identities and are presented as faceless hordes swarming over the American countryside. The motivations or desires of individual invading aliens are not important, as they are present only in order to be driven back by a show of American persistence, nobility, and grit. This seems congruent not only with the twenty-first-century war on terror, but with concerns about immigration policy and conflicts over incoming groups, like Syrian refugees, who are perceived as a threat to white American culture (e.g., Fausset). Certainly, the soldiers of the 2nd Mass adopt an attitude of racial superiority with regard to their invaders, cultivating a number of slurs: skitters, fish-heads, chinches, cockroaches, cooties, lobsters, elephant men. This casts the aliens within a familiar context: a vocabulary of supremacist dismissal.

Ally alien forces are also presented through metaphors of racial difference, overlaid with the western myth. If one of the traditional roles of the cowboy is to bridge the ideological distances between white "civilization" and native "savagery" (Schlatter 93; Slotkin 14; Wright 165), it seems no coincidence that when Tom is able to develop an alliance with one of the alien factions, the "friendly" alien leader is dubbed "Cochise"; indeed, Cochise admits, "We studied your pioneer and Native American wars closely" (4.09, "Till Death Do Us Part"). The congruence of alien Other and wild west native Other harks back to at least Burroughs's *A Princess of Mars* (1917) (Pfitzer 55); here, the human need to re-name Cochise (whose alien name they find difficult to remember or pronounce) is further symptomatic of white privilege. This is made explicitly apparent when Cochise's lieutenant objects to being assigned a human name:

COCHISE: Tom, Hal, Colonel Weaver. This is my second in command, Shak-Chic il Sha Shesah.

HAL: You're a tall one there, Shaq.

SHAK-CHIC: Shak-Chic.

HAL: Isn't that what I said? [4.04, "Evolve or Die"].

Despite this indication of the writers' self-awareness, however, nothing comes of Shak-Chic's objections; rather, "Shaq" is presented as being difficult to work with and unfairly prejudiced toward humans. Like the Espheni army, ally aliens are seen through the eyes of the white male military forces that represent the remnants of the American state. This reinforces the association of aliens with twenty-first-century white American concerns about "invasion" by cultural and ethnic Others.

Our Enemies, Our Selves

The threat of hybridity—of the genetic or psychological corruption of a pure human race—also looms large. The series' marketing tagline reads, "Battle them or become them,"[1] and certainly the additional threat of "becoming" the alien is as pervasive in *Falling Skies* as the aliens themselves. Against the backdrop of patriotic white American resistance, this xenophobic anxiety is expressed through fear of the changing self, and fear of unknown infiltrators. At the beginning of the series, the alien threat is clear cut: humans have been driven from their homes and they are on the run, fighting back against giant robots and multipedal aliens that shoot at them. Soon, as Tom frets over his missing son Ben (Connor Jessup), it becomes apparent that some humans—primarily teenagers—have been implanted with alien biotech and forced to become mindless slaves toiling in camps. When two teens—Ben and Rick (Daniyah Ysrayl)—are rescued, the alien symbiotes attached to their spines can't be fully removed, leaving glowing spikes that change their physiology and visibly mark them as different. Tom must defend his son against the mistrust of the regiment. This is made worse when Rick proves to be an alien infiltrator, now identifying with the Other, failing to react to his father, referring to other camp residents as "humans," and spilling all the regiment's plans to the alien forces. Rick's duplicity complicates Ben's efforts to assimilate back into his family and serve with the human military. Though Ben proves loyal, his spikes are a persistent source of tension throughout the series: they grant him superior physical endurance, power, senses, and agility, but their long-term effects on his biology are unknown and it is implied that they may lead to his premature death.[2]

Others fall victim to more pernicious forms of corruption. Tom, his son Hal (Drew Roy), and medical student Lourdes (Seychelle Gabriel) are infected with a biotech parasite that penetrates the eye. This calls back to older pop culture properties involving body snatchers or pod people—stories in which the Other not only infiltrates presumably safe spaces, but also takes the form of friends and loved ones. In such an environment, no one can be trusted; it calls to mind not only Cold War spy paranoia and McCarthyism fears about the communist threat, but also post–9/11 fears about secret terrorist cells. The fact that infected characters don't realize their own co-option makes this even more striking: in this paranoid world, those fighting the influence of the Other can't even trust themselves.

The threat of corrupting hybridity is also particularly feminized, in that it is a constant threat to the women who are loved by the Mason men. This danger is first represented in the body of Tom's daughter Lexi (Scarlett Byrne), who is modified by alien tech before she is born. Lexi could serve as a bridge between cultures, but instead she is a threat whose uncertain allegiances almost destroy her family. As a baby, she experiences accelerated growth framed as a disconcerting horror; as a sudden adult, she preaches peace and leads a cult of worshippers. Lexi's pacifism is revealed as naïve and deluded; she is the victim of a plot by the Espheni Overlords, who plan to kill her. Before she comes to this realization, she kills Lourdes and takes control of her alien-spiked brother Ben. Her only redemption comes through death, as she sacrifices herself to save her father's life (4.12, "Shoot the Moon").

Further, while the first four seasons showcase only male aliens, these aliens "speak" through Hal's former girlfriend Karen (Jessy Schram), who is captured on an early reconnaissance run and then reappears with a spine parasite; eventually it becomes clear that she is cooperating willingly. Karen displaces her alien overseer and becomes the new alien commander and the primary threat faced by Tom and his people. She is duplicitous because of her cooperation with the enemy, her assumption of hostile power, and her deception of Hal. Her power even as an alien force is inextricably linked to her sexuality as she attempts to seduce Hal away from his people; when he is infected with the alien parasite, Karen rapes him. "You saw what happened to Karen," says Hal. "They turned a sweet girl into a monster" (4.06, "Door Number Three"). It is important to note that Karen is young, white, and blonde (one of a number of such women in the series). Hal's statement thus specifically invokes historical American discourse that calls to "protect" white women from the Other—racialized as Black men, as Middle Eastern terrorists, as any number of non–white masculine threats designed "to galvanize white male readers into a virile vigilance against any invasion" (Sharp 197; see also

Cloud 289)—and simultaneously presents such women as either struggling for control or working with the enemy, their feminine alliances suspect.

Finally, Maggie (Sarah Carter), a soldier and scout, is not "corrupted" by the alien tech—her loyalty is never suspect—but she loses control of her sexual impulses when a transplant from Ben's spikes leaves her unable to control her newly carnal desires for him. More than any other character, Maggie struggles with bodily autonomy: first when the spikes are implanted without her permission, second when she fights to control her subsequent physical reactions, and third when she must fight to have the spikes removed (having been told that she is too valuable as a supersoldier to give up that advantage). Her narrative might be a fitting metaphor for women's fights to control their bodies vs. institutional interference, but such a reading is blunted by Maggie's confession that she has the spikes removed not for herself but in order to please her boyfriend Hal ("I did it for you"; 5.08, "Stalag 14th Virginia")—a purification from alien influence, as well as a sacrifice of physical power and dominance, for which she is ultimately rewarded with a marriage proposal (5.10, "Reborn"). In resisting the threat of alien corruption and maintaining her feminine role, Maggie retains her position as (another white blonde) series regular.

The season 4 finale then reveals that the Overlords serve a queen, a monstrous spider-like being whose primary dialogue consists of "smell the blood." As she penetrates Tom, he poisons her—destroying not only her body, but those of her followers and her unhatched children, ensuring that her reproductive line ends while his continues in the form of his sons and his new unborn child (5.10, "Reborn"). In this fashion, the dual threats of invasion and hybridity are vanquished, framed not only as a wartime conflict between male forces but also as a masculine victory over the monstrous female. Further, while Lexi, a hybrid child, dies, Tom and Anne's human child is yet unborn at the series finale, carrying a promise of a genetically human future (and a continuation of the Mason dynasty).

Gender and *Falling Skies*

While *Falling Skies* occasionally casts a female extra in a combat scene, or highlights gang leader Pope (Colin Cunningham)'s love of cooking, its gender divisions are generally traditional, binary, and clear. The lead female role is Dr. Anne Glass (Moon Bloodgood), who from the outset is clearly separated from the military hierarchy that grants authority within the 2nd Mass; she is instead part of the civilian group the regiment protects. She is also not a combat doctor; though she is drafted into the role, her background is as a pediatrician—a nurturing role centered on working with children. Her major storylines include her romantic relationship with Tom Mason, her subsequent pregnancy with Lexi (during which she is abducted and must be rescued), and her quest to protect or retrieve her half-alien child. This protective mother role leads her to adopt a more leadership-type position later in the series, but one which is compromised by images of female hysteria; in the absence of white men who might otherwise assume command, Anne carries a gun and commands a small squad of soldiers who consistently question both her authority and her sanity (e.g., 4.03, "Exodus"). Anne's roles are primarily wife, mother and caretaker; notably, her eventual development of more "masculine" soldier skills dovetails with young Matt Mason (Maxim Knight)'s evolution from childhood to adolescence. As the 2nd Mass is scattered, Anne commands soldiers and Matt must survive on his own in a Nazi-esque youth camp (4.01, "Ghost in the Machine"). Their increased independence and martial skill is gained separately, but each is subsequently and, subtly, almost simultaneously rewarded with participation in 2nd Mass combat activities. Season 4 sees Anne and Matt both joining command strategy sessions (4.07, "Saturday Night Massacre"). Anne goes out on patrol and so does Matt (5.01, "Find Your Warrior"). Anne loads a gun; Matt throws a knife (4.12, "Shoot the Moon"). Not only is Anne's development as a soldier congruent with a boy's journey to manhood, she is ultimately reduced to the role of Mason progenitor after she reveals a new pregnancy, is killed in the series finale, and is then resurrected when Tom demands her life as his reward for his heroic actions (5.10, "Reborn"). Anne and the future child she carries are given back to Tom because he has saved the world; they are, literally, objects of payment.

Anne and Maggie are the most prominent female characters on *Falling Skies*; they are both regulars from season 1 through to the finale. They are also both love interests for the male leads—Anne as Tom's eventual wife, and Maggie caught in a love triangle with brothers Hal and Ben. As opposed to Anne's distinctly nurturing role, Maggie is combat-capable from the outset and serves as a scout for the 2nd Mass. However, as is common for such "strong" female characters, Maggie is also the victim of trauma. Originally a prisoner of Pope's gang (who repeatedly raped her), Maggie was also a cancer survivor prior to the alien attacks; like Rachel or Charlie from *Revolution*, Maggie is not "naturally" aggressive or emotionally detached but, rather, has evolved through physical and emotional suffering. This back story serves to "explain" her abnormal behavior in a way that is seldom necessary for male characters, who do not need reasons to justify their independence or combat competence. Maggie's combat capabilities are also rare; along with minor characters Crazy Lee (Luciano Carro) and Katie Marshall (Melora Hardin), she is one of three named female soldiers in *Falling Skies*, and the only one to survive.[3]

Other notable women include Lourdes, who works as Anne's assistant and dies at Lexi's hand, as well as Lexi herself, whose initial gentle pacifism is exposed as dangerous naiveté, and Sara (Mira Sorvino), a late-season addition who is a love interest for Pope. Sara, like Anne, is not combat skilled when she first appears; rather, she uses her "feminine wiles" to try to drug and rob Pope. Eventually, though she begins to learn soldier skills under Pope's training, she is killed as a motivational plot point in Pope's story (driving him to leave the 2nd Mass and war with Tom). The only woman to occupy a position of formal authority is Marina Peralta (Gloria Reuben), who begins her onscreen tenure as Tom's assistant when Tom is briefly elected president in season 3. She first follows Tom around while carrying a series of clipboards, then becomes president herself when Tom gives her the position (unelected), but she subsequently vanishes from both screen and dialogue, presumably dying in an alien attack after Tom and the 2nd Mass move on to new locales. In general, women are either present as love interests or their parts are (literally) short-lived; they are not natural warriors and, with the exception of Maggie, are seldom incorporated in combat scenes. As in *Jericho*, they are also seldom seen during strategy planning sessions; their voices are not necessary when the men are talking tactics.

Men are also traditionally gendered throughout the series. In terms of post–9/11 anxieties, *Falling Skies* may certainly relate to concerns regarding men gone soft, particularly those media voices calling for a strong (male) military and urging the re-establishment of traditional gender roles (Faludi). As a nominal representative of the academic humanities, Tom might initially be taken as the sort of "soft" twenty-first-century man whose weakness endangers those he loves. He is concerned about his sons, considerate of new love interest Anne, and able to cooperate with sympathetic aliens. However, any demonstrations of empathy are limited; the series begins six months post-invasion and it is clear that Tom is already comfortable with guns and accompanying warfare. He is the first to capture an alien, single-handedly dragging its body down the hall while others can only gape (1.03, "Prisoner of War"). *Falling Skies* also incorporates frontier imagery and the notion of the cowboy hero; in season 3, for example, Tom's costuming consists of a long coat over a white shirt, a vest, and a gun strapped at his hip. He even sports a pocket watch on a chain as he adopts the aesthetic—if not the official title—of the new sheriff in town (3.03, "Badlands").

As the rise of the "Mason militias" indicates, it would be difficult to overemphasize Tom's "chosen one" status in *Falling Skies*; not only does he twice return from the dead, he temporarily becomes both president and a masked vigilante hero, and is the only one able to communicate with or even perceive the last of an alien race—an ally who takes the form of his dead wife and exhorts him, "We need you, Tom. Only you; no one else. If you die, everything will be lost" (5.05, "Non-Essential Personnel"). By the final season, Tom is using his elite status to in turn encourage the soldiers of the 2nd Mass to find their "warrior":

> I'm not talking about anger; I'm talking about rage.... This is the time for overkill, to fire both weapons, to give it everything we've got! Our enemy is still out there, but they're unprotected and they're vulnerable, and they're just waiting for us to take them out if we've got the will to do it. Because when the last bullet goes into the last Skitter, this war is over [5.01, "Find Your Warrior"].

Though he is warned against overaggression, nothing comes of these warnings; there are no consequences, as Tom inevitably leads his forces to victory.

The series further focuses on Tom's three sons Hal, Ben, and Matt as they come of age in the alien apocalypse. These heterosexual white men and boys are the focus of *Falling Skies;* the Mason family dynasty—as represented by Tom and his sons—is paramount to the narrative, and subsequently humanity's survival, ultimately basing the salvation of Earth and the human race on the actions of literal white patriarchy. The men in the series display emotional sensitivity only up to a point—generally, one explained by Tom's academic background or his sons' developing youth. Their primacy in the narrative rests on their combat capability and their evolving leadership skills. Within the context of *Falling Skies*'s American flags and frequent references to American military history, this firmly establishes the Mason men within an increasingly familiar pattern: as the clean-cut, English-speaking, white heterosexual male guardians of American identity, with their mastery of military skills key to national survival. Tom and his sons evolve as soldiers within a predominantly white male militia, joining other masculine leaders like Captain/Colonel Weaver (Will Patton) and anti-hero Pope. They are also contrasted against both the alien Other and the women of the series.

(Re)building "America"

Falling Skies is also primarily focused on white characters; the only two non-white characters to survive the entire series are Anne and Anthony (Mpho Koaho)—a soldier who recurs throughout but never assumes authority. Others die early: Mike (Martin Roach), Dai (Peter Shinkoda), Lourdes, and Deni (Megan Danso) all meet premature ends, while Dingaan Botha (Treva Etienne) survives but doesn't appear until later seasons. A review of episode cast listings illustrates *Falling Skies'* reliance on white characters, particularly men. The only characters to appear in all 52 episodes are white and male: Tom Mason, Hal Mason, Matt Mason, and Weaver. Anne Glass follows at 51 episodes, then Maggie (50), Ben (49), Pope (48), Anthony (46), and Lourdes (38).[4] All of these characters are also heterosexual; there are no LGBTQ plot lines or characters in the series.

This lack of diversity is consistent with *Falling Skies'* depiction of a white heterosexual America under siege. Considering *Falling Skies'* thematic emphasis on corruption via infiltration or biocontamination, this further suggests a disturbing concern with cultural, and arguably ethnic, purity. Lexi is the clearest example of this racialized threat: as the daughter of Tom and Anne, Lexi should be of partial Korean heritage,[5] but she is played by Scarlett Byrne, a white actor. Canonically, this is never addressed; it might be read as white post-racial wish fulfillment, in which people of different ethnicities are ultimately assimilated into hegemonic whiteness. It might also be interpreted as a play to have Lexi's tragic end elicit more sympathy from audiences accustomed to reading young white women as "innocent." However, since Lexi is a hybrid spy sent by the Overlords to infiltrate and destroy the human resistance, it is difficult to avoid reading her feminine white Western aesthetic, including her dyed blonde hair, as part of the duplicitous lie deliberately obscuring her ties to the alien Other, and thus symptomatic of historic American cultural fears regarding racial "passing" (e.g., Kennedy). While blonde white women such as Karen, Maggie, and Sara are part of humanity in peril, Lexi is a plant and her appearance is a disguise. As such, she is both untrustworthy and doomed.

As well, when Tom kills the Espheni queen, destroying not only the queen herself but also every Espheni, he commits genocide—a development unaddressed within *Falling Skies* as anything other than a decisive human victory. This is aided by the lack of distinct Espheni characters: since they remain a nameless horde, when they are killed, it has the same effect as a natural disaster being averted. Victory is quick, conclusive, and without guilt or moral discussion; the war in *Falling Skies* is an entirely good vs. evil, "us" vs. "them" conflict, in which Hal and Maggie high-five over bombing starving Skitters in a barn (5.01, "Find Your Warrior"), and the eradication of an entire species can only be met with cheering.

The death of the entire Espheni race reduces the alien population of the planet to Cochise, the single cooperative alien who has been accepted as an ally and collaborator. Humanity is left on its own to embrace a post-racial future—one in which human beings, having worked together to ward off the threat of the Other, can ignore racial differences among themselves in order to embrace white leadership. As Tom gives his speech ("Once upon a time, there was a place called America"), he stands onstage with Weaver, Ben, Matt, Hal, Maggie, Anne, and Cochise—Anne is the only non-white human, here as Tom's supportive and pregnant spouse, and Cochise is the single alien presence remaining. Tom calls out the American dream of cultural assimilation:

> Despite the horror, the loss, the death, the war with the Espheni might have ultimately made us better people. Human beings. We can actually christen a new melting pot, a worldwide one [5.10, "Reborn"].

As he invokes the "melting pot," the crowd here is the most multicultural, multi-ethnic in the series, including a range of people and costuming; indeed, Anne is carrying another biracial child. But Tom is the voice of leadership (his use of "christening" invoking a further hint of white Christianity), and though he has yet to become president, it is implied that this can change:

> MATT: They might even ask you to be president again.
>
> TOM: I've already said no twice.
>
> MATT: Well, you can say no a third time. You know, like George Washington [5.10, "Reborn"].

This final comparison of Tom to one of the American "founding fathers" completes *Falling Skies* as a fantasy of white American male exceptionalism; indeed, Tom is *literally* a founding father, standing on the stage with his sons and his pregnant wife and calling for democracy and cooperation as a new world order is formed.

Summary

Falling Skies thus calls back to prior alien invasion narratives, particularly *War of the Worlds*–style science fiction, that equate "alien" with racial, cultural, and gender differences and serve as metaphors for white American anxieties about globalization and immigration. The series explicitly uses Civil War and American Revolution history—as embodied by the 2nd Mass and history professor Tom Mason—to craft a framework of white male experience and colonial imagery. *Falling Skies* incorporates cowboy mythology but emphasizes military history and the notion of scrappy, outgunned soldiers fighting off overwhelming odds while forming a tightly loyal brotherhood. The gendered term is used advisedly here; *Falling Skies* is predominantly a male show. Like *Jericho*, *Revolution*, or *The Last Ship*, its story focuses on soldiers who are primarily men. Tom and his sons are central figures but Tom's dead wife is not even present in a family photo that survived the invasion— presumably, this was a practical prop decision to allow flexibility if/when Tom's wife was eventually cast (Jennifer Ferrin later assumed the role), but in the first season it has the effect of ensuring that the former Mrs. Mason is a faceless concept. The series is concerned only with the Mason men and their journeys toward manhood in a time of war.

Elements of a wild west aesthetic are still notable, visible in Tom's costuming and clearly invoked in the naming of the alien "Cochise"—a convention that not only conflates aliens and American colonial stereotypes of Indigenous people, but also illustrates the white perspective in presuming to name and define alien armies that appear (to their human enemies, and to the cameras) primarily as uniform hordes. Men are also at the forefront of series narratives, occupying positions of power and authority. Women receive less screen time and are generally nurturers and love interests—Maggie's exceptional toughness is "explained" by her traumatic back story, while the female president appointed by Tom is subsequently written out with little ceremony. When *Falling Skies* addresses the feminine alien—through Karen, Maggie, Lexi, or the Espheni queen—it serves to illustrate fears regarding monstrous femininity, the uncontrollable woman, or the susceptibility of the "American" woman (white, blonde, heterosexual) to outside corruption. The overall result is a series that posits a U.S. history professor as the savior of the human race, thus situating the secret of post-apocalyptic success as a return to the historical status quo (as seen through the eyes of white colonialism). *Falling Skies* glorifies both the American military and its masculine associations, repeatedly incorporating images of the U.S. flag as it reminds viewers that the secret to survival against alien onslaught is to look to the colonial past.

Colony

Unlike the various alien species of *Falling Skies*, the aliens that have attacked the continental United States in *Colony* do not appear onscreen throughout the entirety of the first two seasons, save for one bipedal armored suit covered by a helmet and faceplate. The aliens here exist as generalized concepts with unknown motives. Save for the sudden alien technologies that have built impossibly huge walls between cities, created flying drones that monitor each enclave, and added a prison camp on the moon, it might be possible that the invaders are only a fiction created by a human conspiracy as an excuse for fascist rule. As such, *Colony* is less an exploration of wild frontier than a successor to the 2005 alien TV series *Threshold, Surface,* and *Invasion,* in which fear and threats to family lead to "political and social repression" and the revocation of rights, suggesting that "the siege mentality ruling US public discourse post–9/11 is inappropriate to the context of global integration and poses a threat to the nation's own democratic ideals and institutions" (Takacs 3). "Antistate paranoia" has historically been more the realm of alien invasion television than film, exemplified by series like *The X-Files* (Kakoudaki 123), and *Colony*'s primary theme fits within this context as a critique of government policies that destroy civil rights in the name of security and public safety.

Homeland Security to the Rescue

The dystopian nature of the new regime is evident from the first episode: although Los Angeles still stands, cars have been restricted, food has been rationed, and telecommunications has been cut. Armed soldiers patrol the streets. A nighttime curfew is enforced by lethal drone patrol. While an elite few have retreated to the "Green Zone," where they live in luxury, the majority of citizens scrabble in the city, where Katie Bowman (Sarah Wayne Callies) is desperate to locate black-market insulin for her diabetic nephew. Meanwhile, her husband, former FBI agent Will Bowman (Josh Holloway), is trying to smuggle himself into the next enclave so he can hunt for their son Charlie (Jacob Buster), who was separated from the family during the invasion. When Will is caught in a bombing and captured by the government, he agrees to join a task force to fight the terrorist insurgency. Unknown to Will, Katie has joined that same insurgency. The Bowmans, working different sides of the conflict, each try to save their family in the midst of a fascist crackdown.

Colony's depictions of government oppression in the name of safety and security call to mind post–9/11 America and critiques of the *United and Strengthening America by Providing Appropriate Tools Required to Intercept and Obstruct Terrorism (USA PATRIOT) Act*, with its authorizations of warrantless government wiretapping, medical and financial record searches, indefinite prisoner detention, and other erosions of civil liberty (Whitehead and Aden, cited in Huddy and Feldman 455); the citizens of post-invasion Los Angeles live under constant surveillance, regulation and rationing. Even as Will is blackmailed into working for the "Department of Homeland Security," itself a tellingly direct reference to the post–9/11 American government, he is told that the work he does is necessary—that the terrorist bombers kill innocent civilians, and that human insurgent activities in the region only invite the attention (and associated threat) of the aliens. Attempts to rationalize and humanize the regime through sympathetic characters like task force head Phyllis (Kathy Baker), computer analyst Jennifer (Kathleen Rose Perkins), or local leader ("Proxy") Snyder (Peter Jacobson) allow *Colony* to present a world in which questionably moral autocratic decisions are made with "good intentions" in the name of public safety—and the ways in which common citizens suffer when rights are given up, one by one, to protect against an alien threat whose nature is nebulous and unproven. In occupied Los Angeles, citizens are poor, starving, restricted from travel, and subject to violence, search, and seizure. *Colony*'s suspect citizens are sent to "The Factory"—the moon prison—without trial or recourse. It would be difficult *not* to read the series as an extended commentary on the role of the U.S. government, facilities like Guantanamo Bay, and homeland security initiatives in the twenty-first-century war on terror.

Colony and Racial Appropriation

The regime is definitely white. Two prominently recurring visuals separate Homeland Security from the resistance; both are racially marked. First, the logo for the Homeland Security forces—a boldly designed bird in black and red, on a white background—clearly evokes the Nazi eagle. Homeland Security is also represented by squadrons of white male soldiers in identical uniforms, their faces (except their eyes) covered by masks. Their uniformity is particularly noticeable when they are infiltrated by the insurgent Broussard (Tory Kittles); any time the masked soldiers spill onto the screen, Broussard can easily be picked out (by the camera and, presumably, the viewer) as the only Black man. It's unclear whether this distinctive casting was done for pragmatic purposes (to make Broussard easy to follow), for ideological reasons, or via the same status quo casting process that leads to seas of white male soldier extras in other series. Effectively, however, it means that apart from Broussard, the uniformed Homeland Security soldiers are all part of the same nameless, faceless, white male authority force. In this sense, positioning the alien-colluding Homeland Security as a fascist white force is striking and arguably appropriate, particularly when juxtaposed with the broader racial and gender diversity in the terrorist opposition.

However, *Colony*'s racial politics are indelibly problematic. While not otherwise particularly frontier-themed, *Colony* demonstrates a clear appropriation of western oppression imagery. The human insurgency bands together in support of the unseen leader "Geronimo," a voice on the radio who is represented by posters of an Indigenous man with a painted face. The name "Geronimo" and the accompanying image are significant; alien invasion narratives may invert standard colonial narratives of the wild west, recasting settled Americans as "natives" and the aggressive alien interlopers as unwelcome colonists:

> The invasion motif enacts a reversal that allows powerful US subjects to imagine themselves as victims of (metaphorically) those they have victimized. This reversal betrays a deeper fear that our self-identified "others" will do unto us as we have done onto [*sic*] them, and, more importantly, that we will deserve everything we get. In short, the fantasy of reverse colonization enables US culture to recognize the monstrous shape of its imperial ambitions [Takacs 16].

Colony does this explicitly, as "Geronimo's" radio broadcasts and coded posters fuel the revolution. Further, there are no actual Indigenous characters in *Colony*, as members of the insurgency or otherwise; in fact, there is no "Geronimo." The posters were created by two white advertising designers in the Green Zone. *Colony* incorporates an image of racial injustice from the history of the American west without ever allowing an Indigenous character to claim the position of the freedom fighter or the unjustly oppressed; instead, "Geronimo" serves as a figurehead to represent and inspire white heroism.[6] Similar appropriation is also indirectly present in the name of Katie's bar, The Yonk—a reference to "Yoknapatawpha" in the works of William Faulkner, but also to the Chickasaw word from which Faulkner sourced the name

(Doyle 24). The image of the oppressed native is thus appropriated and projected onto a predominantly white resistance movement (in response to an overwhelmingly white colonizing force).

Gender and *Colony*

While *Colony* at first appears to break at least incrementally from the standard glorification of the white male soldier-cowboy-hero, this distinction does not hold. The series opens on Will as an auto mechanic whose Latino boss Carlos (Jacob Vargas) is helping to smuggle him out of the enclave to look for lost Charlie. But when Will is captured, his true background as a war veteran and FBI agent is revealed—like *Jericho*'s Jake or *The Last Ship*'s Tom, he possesses hypermasculine soldier skills, specifically expert knowledge of combat tactics and investigative strategies. Here, too, *Colony* toys with expectations of the hero's role: Will first assumes that he'll be in charge of his assigned task force, but fellow agent Jennifer McMahon mocks him, as he is in fact working under the purview of senior agent Phyllis. This state of affairs only lasts for four episodes before Phyllis is killed and Will is promoted to the head role: by the fifth episode, he occupies the same positions of experience and authority typical of white male protagonists in other series (and when he loses this authority, in season 2, it is to an older white man).

This pattern also applies to other gender roles, as *Colony* flirts with subverting expectations but then returns to cultural norms. Will's ostensible counterpart and main opposition in the series is Katie; the two characters share focus as *Colony*'s main protagonists. This suggests the possibility of gender equality; however, it's soon apparent that Katie lacks Will's extensive experience. While Will is depicted as an already-accomplished agent, Katie navigates the pitfalls of an unknown world. She is motivated by her maternal role ("I will not be one of those mothers who has to look her children in the eye and tell them she did nothing"; 1.02, "A Brave New World") and her participation in shootings and heists is primarily limited to holding a watch and acting as timekeeper. Her primary role in the resistance is to relay information she gleans from spying on an unsuspecting Will. In contrast, expert Will engages in multiple firefights and is the stoic type of man who can ignore a bullet wound: "I'm fine. It's blood, not guts" (1.06, "Yoknapatawpha"). Further, Will discovers Katie's duplicity despite her best efforts; he is more skilled than she, reinforcing her comparatively unnatural position in a masculine world.

Colony, like other series, advances stereotypically masculine skill sets as key to survival, and also positions male characters as inherently better at these skills; if anything, Will's primary opponent is Broussard, the insurgency's top soldier. Broussard is an emotionless, hypermasculine war veteran with all the spy experience that Katie lacks. Katie funnels information; Broussard takes violent action. The only reason Katie survives the threat of execution from the same insurgency she is trying to help is Broussard's apparent desire to save her. A conversation between Katie and fellow rebel Rachel (Kim Rhodes) makes Katie's role clear:

> RACHEL: A cause needs all sorts of people, Katie. It needs soldiers like Broussard who can pull the trigger, and it needs people like you.
>
> KATIE: Why? What purpose do I serve, other than spying on my husband?
>
> RACHEL: Broussard needs you to remind him why he's fighting. To keep him away from the edge [1.07, "Broussard"].

Katie provides both Will and Broussard with someone to protect; as Will's task force hunts Broussard across the city, it becomes apparent that the main conflict fuelling *Colony*'s narrative is between men. Throughout the first two seasons, as Katie gradually adopts more masculine soldier skills—taught by Broussard and Will—she both reinforces the association of such skills with post-apocalyptic survival, and repeatedly takes a back seat to the more experienced male leads who drive the action forward.

Katie's sister Maddie (Amanda Righetti) further reinforces gender binaries, clearly demonstrating the type of "soft" power—manipulation, emotional and sexual appeal—associated with the feminine sphere (Burcar 100). Formerly an upper-class art dealer, Maddie is now a day laborer permitted into the Green Zone on temporary manual contracts. She uses sex to advance her social position: at first, hoping to regain status, she has a sexual liaison with an old contact, but discovers that her newly lowered social class precludes a relationship. Instead, she accepts a box of food as she leaves. When she next gains a position as assistant to art curator Charlotte Burgess (Kathryn Morris), the duties include having sex with Charlotte's husband Nolan Burgess (Adrian Pasdar) while Charlotte watches. Eventually, Maddie is able to seduce Nolan, betray Charlotte to the authorities, and gain entry into the Green Zone for herself, her son, and her niece, setting herself up to be Nolan's mistress as he rises to further political power within the new government. Like *Revolution*'s Julia Neville, Maddie exemplifies the archetype of a woman who gains power through her physical attractiveness, manipulative abilities, and sexual and emotional wiles; while she lacks the nefarious motivations of a true *femme fatale*, Maddie still demonstrates multiple aspects of the character type. This is part of a pattern symptomatic of post-apocalyptic television (and wider pop culture in general) where this type of feminized manipulation is portrayed as an exclusively female survival mechanism—male characters seldom, if ever, pursue these avenues to power. Combined with the ways in which female characters seeking "hard" (masculine) power are consistently undermined by explanatory back stories and forever more competent men, characters like Maddie serve to reinscribe gender binaries and promote stereotypes about women whose only power is sexual. Maddie is additionally depicted as both naïve and immoral, buying into alien propaganda and betraying her sister to the authorities; when Nolan eventually exiles her after using her for sex one last time (2.11, "Seppuku"), *Colony* further positions such feminized power as weak and flawed.

Will's colleague Jennifer is less sexualized but still softened. She acts as a support character for the men of the homeland security task force: she is a computer specialist who seldom participates in armed conflict. Rather, she specializes in hacking and counterintelligence, and while her skills are formidable, her expertise is also distinctly gendered: before the invasion, she managed databases for a successful online dating site. The applicable nature of this experience—her genuine skills, and her repeated defense of same— could be a convincing argument for respecting feminine experience and capability; conversely, the consistent sidelining of her character, and the perplexed reactions of male coworkers (including Will) undermine this reading. When she finds herself helpless and isolated in the new regime, Jennifer's only option is suicide (2.03, "Panopticon"); compared to the men of the series, she, too, is "weak."

Summary

Colony is less concerned with the details of aliens-as-racial-Other—and any navigation of intercultural difference or even intercultural warfare—than it is with exploring the interior of an America governed by "homeland security," in which civil rights have been stripped away in the name of safety and order. As Katie fights for the insurgency and Will plots to escape his employers—and if the incorporation of Nazi imagery were not a strong enough clue—the series' subversion of security narratives regarding government oversight becomes clear, placing it in congruence with earlier programs like *Threshold*, *Surface*, and *Invasion*, and in opposition to more conservative post-apocalyptic series like *Falling Skies* (which reiterates the need for military action in the face of danger). *Colony* also incorporates dual male and female protagonists, setting it apart from many other post-apocalyptic offerings, though the gendered nature of Will and Katie's involvements is marked; at the first season's conclusion, Will is en route to rescue his son, while Katie is left alone, weeping in the kitchen of her empty house. The focus is still predominantly on heterosexual white protagonists (there are no LGBTQ characters to be found).

While *Colony* does clearly attempt to diversify its casting and focus beyond the heterosexual white male norm, its success is limited both by the gendered differences between Will, Katie, and other characters, and by the fact that it still centers primarily on the white male protagonist. Series diversity also falters in terms of non-white casting, with only two Black men in prominent supporting roles: Will's partner Beau (Carl Weathers) is depicted as lazy and jaded, while the hyper-capable Broussard loyally answers to the authority of a white man (rebel leader Quayle [Paul Guilfoyle]). Will's mechanic boss Carlos is featured in only three episodes. Positions of political power are also held by white men: Will (after Phyllis's death), Proxy Snyder, Burgess, and, clandestinely, Quayle. One blonde white woman, Helena (Ally Walker), is Snyder's superior, but while white women like Katie, Maddie, Jennifer and (more briefly) Phyllis or Charlotte are prominent in the narrative, women of color are rarely represented. *Colony* at first seems to be setting up a conflict between a neo–Nazi white male government and a more diverse group of ragtag insurgents; however, while the series maintains themes critical of government "security" policies and the suspension of civil rights in a post-invasion world, its use of "Geronimo" as an emblem of the insurgency ultimately appropriates Indigenous American history and imagery as a symbol of predominantly white resistance. Again, there are no Indigenous characters in the series; rather, the use of Geronimo inverts the myth of the American frontier by casting white English settlers as the invaded who must defend their land and culture against the encroachment of the Other. This has been done before (Takacs); in *Colony*, it is explicit, and while the setup of the series initially seems progressive, its anti-fascist themes also incorporate white heteronormative gender stereotypes and an accompanying focus on American masculinity.

Defiance

While *Falling Skies* demonstrates the alien as a generic cultural and ethnic Other, and *Colony* explores the impact of repressive government policies justified by an unknown and unproven alien threat, *Defiance* uses its aliens as direct stand-ins for human race relations issues.[7] In *Defiance*, Earth has been colonized by a disparate group of alien species collectively known as the Votan. Fifteen years past the end of the Pale Wars (around 2046), the Votanis Collective exists in uneasy stalemate with the human Earth Republic, and the former city of St. Louis—now known as Defiance—is neutral territory in which humans and aliens live side by side. When human ex-soldier Joshua Nolan (Grant Bowler) and his adopted Irathient daughter Irisa (Stephanie Leonidas) arrive, they must learn to navigate intercultural conflicts while surviving in the post-apocalyptic remnants of the United States. Like *Jericho* or *Revolution*, *Defiance* suggests a reborn wild west where the former United

States has become a new breeding ground for adventure: Nolan immediately becomes the new "lawkeeper" (sheriff) in town and appoints Irisa as his deputy. Along with other deputy Tommy (Dewshane Williams), Nolan and Irisa must strive to keep peace within a town torn by racial factions.

Like other recent post-apocalyptic series, *Defiance* ultimately centers on the straight white male lead (Nolan). Within this limitation, however, it also shows potential as a progressively feminist science fiction series that incorporates a large number of "promising female characters" (Rosenberg). Its extras include people of diverse races and genders in a variety of occupations including soldiers, miners, or merchants; the border town of Defiance teases the possibility of serving as a home for a newly equitable society in which alien influence and wartime apocalypse has broken down the white patriarchy that has historically dominated Western cultural systems. However, closer analysis of the series shows its politics to be much more conservative than its setting would suggest. *Defiance* uses alien races to explore issues of cultural and racial conflict that ultimately support Western stereotypes, while falsely claiming a post-feminist, post-racial culture within the human population of characters.

Race and the Alien Other

Defiance's setting suggests a narrative of racial tolerance: protagonist Nolan, a war veteran and former overt anti-alien racist, has adopted an Irathient daughter. The city of Defiance itself is populated by a mix of human and Votan races, and its heroes must successfully navigate frequent cultural conflicts.

Defiance reserves any overt exploration of racist themes for interspecies conflict: the Votan species comprise multiple groups whose disenfranchisement is often highlighted—particularly the Castithans, associated with organized crime and the black market, the Indogene, a manufactured race created to serve as both weapons and medical resources, or the Irathients, depicted as thieving, mystic nomads associated with Roma stereotypes. Almost all groups hold prejudices against the Irathients, whose home world was conquered by the Castithans and who still suffer ongoing marginalization and violence. Perhaps the most explicitly sympathetic example is when Irathients are rounded up and caged during a plague scare before one of them is killed by an armed human guard whose "feared for her life" defense evokes controversial U.S. "stand your ground" laws (1.09, "If I Ever Leave This World Alive").[8] But this theme of systemic group marginalization is infrequently explored; generally, the series simplifies racism against (or between) alien characters as the actions of prejudiced individuals rather than the result of historic and institutional oppression. Racism vs. the alien Other is depicted more individually through characters like the now-reformed Nolan, who has learned to accept his Irathient daughter, or through local mine owner Rafe McCawley (Graham Greene) and Castithan leader Datak Tarr (Tony Curran), who must grow to accept their children's wedding.

Most clearly pertinent to Defiance's positioning as a post–9/11 series, Castithan culture is used as a stand-in for multiple Muslim stereotypes, most directly expressed through the character of Stahma Tarr (Jaime Murray). Ostensibly, Stahma does not represent any single human religion, society or ethnicity; her Castithan culture is an amalgamation of Western stereotypes about Other cultures. The Tarr home life incorporates what might be taken as versions of Japanese bathing rituals and its caste system uses titles taken from the Italian mafia, while Stahma and other Castithan women use indirect speech patterns reminiscent of the East (as opposed to the "straight talk" preferred by Defiance's human settlers and their American heritage) ("Defiance [Series]"). However, considering the series' post–9/11 production, it seems especially significant that Stahma wears a head scarf, and elements of Castithan culture are directly suggestive of Western perceptions concerning the inevitable oppression of women in hijabs (e.g., Cloud; Droogsma; Faludi 40–43). Stahma's scarf is a visual reminder that her Castithan heritage is consistently associated with Western narratives of Muslim women in need of rescue. In Castithan culture, women are not permitted authority or independence; Stahma frequently defers to her husband as per the religious requirements laid out in the sacred Castithan scrolls, and as the Castithan male head of household, Datak has the right to beat or even kill Stahma if he chooses. Defiance clearly situates Stahma as an oppressed woman in need of Western freedom and a feminist education. Her description on the official Defiance site reads as follows: "The wife of Datak Tarr, one of the most powerful men in Defiance, Stahma is seemingly the perfect picture of a Castithan wife. Beneath the surface, however, lies a dark side that is ready to break from the traditional roles assigned her by her race" ("Stahma Tarr").

At first, elements of this oppressed–Other narrative are complex. Stahma is seduced by Kenya Rosewater (Mia Kirshner), the owner of the local brothel, who is convinced that Stahma needs her help: "I hate that you're not free" (1.08, "I Just Wasn't Made for These Times"). But Stahma is resistant to Kenya's interference; she enjoys their illicit liaison but is adamant in defending her husband and her culture:

> KENYA: Why, Stahma? Why are you like this? Your husband is so cruel. You're capable of a lot of things. And you just let him dominate you.
>
> STAHMA: I love him. And not in the way a human female clings to an abusive lover. I love Datak because of his cruelty. It is part of his strength, his willingness to do whatever it takes to achieve his goals. We are a team. I treasure that.

KENYA: You're pathetic.

STAHMA: And you're alone [1.11, "Past is Prologue"].

Defiance, at first, seems to tentatively advance the notion that there may be more than one path to gender equality and that stereotypes of oppressed women in non–Western cultures offer an incomplete picture. Stahma spends the first season resisting and subverting Western ideas of female empowerment—not because she fails to recognize her oppression, but because she has developed her own mechanisms for claiming agency. In season 1, *Defiance* establishes Stahma as confident, intelligent and culturally *different*; though the human women of the town (with their American perspectives) may pity her, she is a master of political machination constantly working to expand her family's power. "You're the dangerous one," acknowledges Nolan, to which she responds with a demure, "You're sweet" (1.04, "A Well-Respected Man"). This is not to suggest that her character's treatment is not problematic in a number of ways: not only does her fear of Datak's violence appear quite real, she is basically a hypersexualized *femme fatale*, manipulating her brute masculine husband with her physical wiles. However, it is notable that Stahma has found her own ways of ensuring survival and life satisfaction, and she rejects Kenya's ethnocentric judgments and unsolicited advice. Stahma scorns the oppressed woman stereotype that others would project upon her: she does not want to be saved. Kenya's attempts to map Western understandings onto Castithan culture only lead to Stahma's rejection and Kenya's death: in the season finale, Stahma pretends that she has realized her mistake ("I'm not as brave as you are") and offers to run away with Kenya, only to lure Kenya into the woods and poison her as the penance Datak has demanded upon discovering her affair. She then returns to her husband.

This narrative offers the possibility of complexity but undergoes an abrupt shift. One episode later, in the season 2 premiere, Stahma has changed her attitude and cultivates a sudden desire for economic power and political liberation. With Datak having been incarcerated for the nine-month time jump between seasons, Stahma has assumed control of his illicit business and is using her son Alak (Jesse Rath) as a figurehead. When Datak is released from prison, he nearly drowns her in retaliation for her unwomanly disobedience (2.03, "The Cord and the Ax"). Stahma asks him to acknowledge her as an equal partner in his business, but instead he sneers at her and burns Alak's hand. At this point, Stahma becomes both second-wave feminist and avenging mother; she asserts open control of Datak's gang and convinces them to beat him and throw him into the street. She must then face off against both her husband and her community.

The transition in Stahma's attitude is abrupt, and the scripting reasons behind it are uncertain, but the series sees a definite shift from the satisfied yet complexly problematic alien of season 1 to the frustrated, power-hungry proto-feminist of season 2. When mapped onto Stahma's association with various forms of cultural Otherness—particularly her head scarves and her suppression by a violently patriarchal religious system—it is difficult to avoid further congruences with post–9/11 Western sensibilities regarding both the war on terror and the presumed oppression of Muslim women who must (in this metaphor) need only education regarding basic feminist ideas in order to realize what freedoms they are missing. As Cloud has noted, images of Muslim women wearing head scarves and face coverings were commonly used in America to justify the invasion of Afghanistan:

> The visual manifestations of the < clash of civilizations > during the U.S. war against Afghanistan in 2001–2002 veiled the threat of terrorism with explanations of irrational hatred between superior and inferior civilizations. Metonymic, emotionally charged, and widely circulated images of terrorists and abject women established binary oppositions between self and Other, located U.S. viewers in positions of paternalistic gazing, and offered images of a shining modernity that justified U.S. intervention there [299].

Stahma is endemic to the ways in which *Defiance* maps its racial tensions onto the alien Other. Further, she is portrayed as a victim of abuse but also as duplicitous and untrustworthy; by season 3, she and Datak have actually become terrorists, serving as Votan spies and blowing up the remains of the St. Louis arch in order to save their son. Few developments in the series draw the connection between Castithan and Muslim so clearly; Stahma serves as a clear illustration of *Defiance*'s cultural contexts, in which the diverse alien cultures are stand-ins for white Western concepts of the "foreign."

In contrast to the racialized marginalization of Castithans, Irathients, and other alien groups, humans of Defiance, dominated by white characters, hold all of the power. While Defiance may claim to be an intercultural town, its leadership positions (mayor, governor, and lawkeeper) are nearly always occupied by humans, including Amanda Rosewater (mayor, seasons 1 and 3; Julie Benz), Nicky Riordan (mayor, pre-series; Fionnula Flanagan),[9] Niles Pottinger (mayor, season 2; James Murray), Governor Mercado (governor, season 2; William Atherton), Garret Clancy (lawkeeper, 1.01 "Pilot"; Peter MacNeill), and Joshua Nolan. Apart from deputy lawkeeper Irisa, the only alien with political or legal authority is, briefly, Datak Tarr, who is mayor for approximately five minutes before shivving a human general who abuses him with a racial slur (1.12, "Everything Is Broken"). Apart from individually plotted episodes' depictions of interspecies conflict, the human dominance of Defiance's government and police remains implicit and unquestioned. At no point is the human privilege within the series more subtly prevalent than when former mayor Nicky murders alien (Liberata) bartender Jered (Jessica Nichols; voice Stan Sellers), a longtime employee of the NeedWant brothel (1.09, "If I Ever Leave This World Alive"). Two episodes later, after Nicky's exposure and death, a fond eulogy is held at the NeedWant in her honor (1.11, "Past Is Prologue"). The series primarily positions a predominantly white, middle-class America as implicitly superior to the Other that Datak and other aliens represent.

It is also notable that almost all aliens in *Defiance* are played by white actors and the Castithan race in particular presents as albino, with white skin and hair exaggerated by white clothing and even uniformly white home decor. When Castithan settlers such as Datak and Stahma are the target of racial slurs ("haint") or discrimination, the racism directed at them within the series narrative is directed at whiteness—the series' metaphorical racism is thus kept carefully distinct from Western supremacist systems, and indeed evokes twenty-first-century conservative concepts of "reverse racism" against whites (an approach both complicated by and obscuring the fact that Jesse Rath, who plays Alak Tarr, is of biracial East Indian and Austrian Jewish heritage) (Brownstein).[10] Further, the casting of predominantly white actors in alien roles dovetails with the casting of predominantly white actors in the most prominent human roles, effectively presenting the city of Defiance as a presumably multicultural, multiracial society in which humanity is prevalent and whiteness is an unacknowledged default at the same time that *overt* whiteness, as an alien racial marker, has become both stigmatized and exoticized: a club where humans can paint their skin and dress in alien costume is framed as a sexual kink.

But while ethnic differences between alien species form the backbone of *Defiance*'s narrative conflicts, ethnic differences between human characters are ignored. In Defiance's "multicultural" setting, "humans" are one more group. By deflecting discussions of racial difference onto human/alien binaries, the series simultaneously incorporates supremacist and xenophobic narratives while implying a post-racial human society where ethnic and cultural differentiations no longer exist. All humans in the series speak the same language and share the same culture; in Defiance, they are perceived as a nearly homogenous ethnic group, as this exchange between Indigenous mine owner Rafe McCawley and Castithan leader Datak Tarr demonstrates:

DATAK: The sight of your pink skin sickens me.
RAFE: Does this skin look pink to you?
DATAK: You all look the same [1.10, "The Bride Wore Black"].

Facing off against alien invaders, all of the humans of Defiance are presented as equal members of the same species. Inter-human racism is presumed to be an "old–Earth" phenomenon (3.06, "Where the Apples Fell"). But the alien-invasion metaphors of *Defiance* and their themes of racial conflict only serve to gloss over contemporary racial issues while further promoting white dominance—symptomatic of a post-racial politics in which "discursively time is called on racism, whilst structurally it continues unabated" (Valluvan 2242). In Defiance's post-racial future, when white protagonist Nolan is twice (at the beginnings of seasons 1 and 2) promoted over Black deputy Tommy, despite Tommy's protests, this is presented as the result of Nolan's expertise and experience rather than a question of race.[11] Most tellingly, when every non-white human character on the series is killed off within two episodes (Tommy in 2.13, "I Almost Prayed"; Rafe, Christie, and Quentin McCawley in 3.01, "The World We Seize"), it goes unremarked, and the series immediately introduces three new actors of color (Raymond Ablack as Samir Pandey, and Conrad Coates and Nichole Galacia as new Omec aliens T'evgin and Kindzi) in apparent compensation. Casting the Omec with Black actors further continues a long science fiction tradition of hiding Black actors under "alien" makeup (Kakoudaki 127; Buchanan), conflating the fictional "alien" Other with the Othering of real-world racial divides as "the difference that science fiction always stages now becomes literalized and thematically central in the narrative" (Kakoudaki 127). Moreover, T'evgin and Kindzi, as incestuous, carnivorous aggressors, represent the forefront of a second alien invasion—one that all residents of Defiance must band together against. This further complicates *Defiance*'s racial themes, reinscribing twenty-first-century American racial conflicts and white supremacist systems.

Post-Feminism and *Defiance*

The series takes a similar approach to gender; a simplified, individualized version of feminist issues is explored through alien cultures, while human characters supposedly enjoy a post-feminist, egalitarian existence despite the prominence of male narratives. Again, the alien perspective is exemplified by Stahma Tarr, who never uses the word "feminism"; rather, her turning point comes when she asks Datak to make her an "equal partner." Stahma's explorations are strictly limited to business opportunities and her relationship with her husband; hers is an oversimplified version of feminism as a quest for personal liberty, without concern for other sociocultural factors or any wider community forces. Her demand for equality is highly focused and highly personalized; she wants to work outside the home and receive equal opportunities and recognition for her contributions to the family business. There are elements here of second-wave socialist feminism and its concerns with "the sexual division of labor," but within this context, Stahma's demands are simple; there is no discussion of domestic abuse, educational opportunities, childcare, healthcare, beauty and body standards, gender binaries, or any other concern that acknowledges wider-sweeping social constructions (Little 28). Likewise, Stahma fails to engage with intersectional issues such as race, class, age, body type, sexuality, or other factors that contribute to tiers of societal privilege. Instead, she is a noblewoman with bonded slave "hand-maidens" who enjoys her own class privilege and shows no concern for either her servants' rights or those of women from other alien groups (such as the overtly marginalized Irathients). When other Castithan noblewomen fail to immediately support her cause, she casually poisons them and frames the chauvinist cleric who was publicly speaking against her. Her social status among humans fails to concern her, and her status among her fellow Castithans is easily maintained: either she is easily accepted (by Datak's gang) or she murders anyone who disagrees with her. Her desire for empowerment comes without any sense of sisterhood or solidarity; within Defiance and the local Castithan community, she acts alone.

Though this heavy-handed approach to "feminism" lacks nuance—much like the series' approach to intercultural and race issues—Stahma's focus on personal challenges also seems entirely appropriate in the post-feminist world that Defiance's human women theoretically enjoy. As the oppressed Other who is just now discovering Western concepts of "women's liberation," Stahma is contrasted with the more complacent human women of the series, suggesting that Western human society (both before and after Defiance's alien apocalypse) is already post-feminist; Stahma must fight to attain the status of the human women around her who already have careers, finances and independence. She has the Rosewater sisters, Kenya and Amanda, as particular role models.

Kenya Rosewater, as Stahma's doomed lover, is the first to try to "free" Stahma from the constraints of Castithan patriarchy. But Kenya is a sex worker whose supposed empowerment goes unchallenged; it is implied within the series that she freely chooses and enjoys her work, as do the employees of her brothel. This is not to suggest that such a position is not possible, but the complexities of this issue are unacknowledged. Instead, Kenya's character fills the general "prostitute" role prevalent in wild west narratives (Coleman); she fills a needed archetype for the setting, but one that is "romanticized, renamed, and refigured" to overlook the "ugly realities" of historical prostitutes combating issues such as "malnutrition, tuberculosis, botched abortions, and alcoholism" (Petersen 269). The series does not explore what motivated Kenya to become a "night porter" or what other avenues of self-support might have been (or not been) available to her. Kenya is instead presented as a woman who owns her sexuality without concern for patriarchal forces or even physical health and safety. When she first appears onscreen, she is refusing a potential client and instructing him to come back after he's showered and shaved; she slaps him, then giggles, secure in her power (1.01, "Pilot"). She is a survivor of an abusive marriage but her relationship with her late husband is presented as a past aberration, as she has now established herself as independent and in control, able to reach out to Stahma to offer what she believes to be seasoned advice.

Amanda begins the series as mayor of Defiance; her position as political leader at first offsets some of the more archetypical female roles in the series (Kenya as whorehouse madam; Stahma as the *femme fatale*; Nolan's daughter Irisa as the sexy action hero). Her newcomer status as appointed mayor is repeatedly emphasized, however, and she loses a season 1 election, after which she returns in season 2 as the new proprietor of her missing sister's brothel. Second-season Amanda is thus relegated to the same role as Kenya—one in which her financial and political power depend on her sexuality and her ability to appeal to the men who are the NeedWant's primary customers. Moreover, she has very little agency in the second season, as her primary storylines situate her as a drug addict, Nolan's romantic interest, and the lust/stalking object of the new mayor (and her former rapist) Niles Pottinger. But Amanda is secure in her sense of empowerment, and in advising Stahma:

AMANDA: It's an old world saying. It means "men are dicks. Deal with it."

STAHMA: Oh. Still, I come from a culture that worships dicks. That will never change.

AMANDA: Well, look around you, Stahma. Everything changes.

STAHMA: All the more reason for us to maintain our standards. We Castithans owe our greatness to the strength and depth of our culture.

AMANDA: Mmm. And who created this culture, hmm? Old men who scribbled it on tablets a thousand years ago to keep you on your knees. Human women felt the exact same way, so we banded together. We changed things. We burned our bras.

STAHMA: Why in three hells would you burn your undergarments?

AMANDA: I don't know. It was in a book [2.06, "This Woman's Work"].

Of course the apocryphal feminist bra-burning historically never happened (Mikkelson), but Amanda doesn't need to know that; she and Kenya are not feminists, merely women who enjoy feminism's benefits and can simply shrug off lingering gender differences as "men are dicks." Their world is inflected by a feminist movement that is assumed to be in the human past. As twenty-first-century American women, it is implied, Amanda and Kenya are already free. It is up to Stahma to join them.

Kenya and Amanda's attitudes are also intrinsically linked to our present day, as Amanda—who is apparently in her mid-thirties to early forties—remembers childhood media products like *Twilight* (2008). Her post-invasion cultural attitudes are based on her pre-invasion life in the contemporary United States and are complicit with current trends by which post-feminism "suggests, among other things 'post,' that as a progressive movement, a sexual politics and a group identity, feminism is over, its goals accomplished, leaving in its wake the assumption of gender equity and cultural heterogeneity" (Badley 69). As such, it is perhaps appropriate that the Rosewater sisters are white, slender, cisgender, able-bodied, and of comfortable economic status.[12] Theirs is the middle-class white woman's post-feminism of the late twentieth and early twenty-first centuries (Tasker and Negra 15–16), carried forward to Defiance's science fiction future.

This implicit assumption of Defiance's embedded gender equality effectively downplays the more sexist elements of the series: when two of the most prominent female characters sell sexual favors to ensure their continued financial survival; when Nolan or another man explains politics to mayor Amanda; when a woman is taken hostage, sidelined in an action scene, or held prisoner for a man (usually Nolan) to save; when Irathient warrior Irisa spends most of season 1 with her midriff or lower back exposed; when Stahma repeatedly wears nothing but beads in the bath, distracting her husband with a whisper or a well-placed hand; or when the camera (in multiple instances) focuses on a woman's side breast or naked back. Stahma's desire for empowerment—particularly as explicitly stated in season 2—serves as counterpoint. She wants what human women—white Western women—have, and thus by default, almost any woman who is not Stahma is stipulated as free.

Elyce Rae Helford has noted,

> [W]hile television fantasy can be used to challenge the boundaries of lived experience through speculative metaphors ... to display female potentialities, and/or to address patriarchal structures that oppress women, such strategies may simultaneously labor to contain the radicalness of the challenge ... leaving the actual status of women unchanged [3–4].

Both narratively and in terms of production factors like camera angles and costuming, no woman of Defiance escapes the constrictions of patriarchy or the male gaze; however, Stahma's narratively simplified desire for "partnership" with her husband glosses over the more subtle ways that sexism affects the series.

Defiance's overt focus on Stahma's quest for personal power presents a narrative that ostensibly supports feminist goals while also serving as a distraction from the many ways in which the series sexualizes and marginalizes its recurring female characters. The freedom supposedly enjoyed by Kenya, Amanda, and other non–Castithan women emphasizes Stahma as a character who is (among the series regulars) singularly oppressed, thus conjuring current regressive arguments that women in Western countries should not claim their own oppression when faced with "other" women in the world who suffer more; within such nationalist rhetoric, "women's oppression is a marker of an inferior society," and gender inequalities in America are therefore ignored (Cloud 289). In this story, moreover, not only is Western human feminism the solution for the alien Other, but every human woman is implicitly the same, and the white cisgender post-feminist serves as a figurehead for all who have presumably achieved freedom within a sexually liberated system.

Feminism itself is presented as simplistic, either defined by its "pastness" (Tasker and Negra 8–9) or as a personal series of goals unrelated to wider questions of race or sexuality (or age, or ability, or any other variety of factors) and based in relatively narrow concerns such as the ability to work outside the home; if post-feminism is "an active process by which feminist gains of the 1970s and 1980s come to be undermined" (McRobbie), then *Defiance* is complicit with these politics.

Sexuality in *Defiance*

The series' queer content is also notable but limited. *Defiance* includes at least one bisexual character (Stahma; it is unclear if Kenya is bisexual or just doing her job) and one lesbian (Doctor Yewll, played by Trenna Keating). There is also one Votan species—the Liberata—whose male and female members present equally as small, bearded figures, and the Earth Republic allows polyamorous marriages (one of its ambassadors travels with her two husbands). The town apparently also contains a society inclusive of LGBQ people, nonconforming gender presentations and a variety of legalized relationships; the T is intentionally missing from the acronym as notably, there are no transgender characters or other characters who might challenge the male/female binaries still imposed on all races. Also notably, the only gay male activity is implied (i.e., Niles Pottinger's schoolboy crush on Amanda's former fiancé Connor [Gale Harold]) or fake (an alibi-making kiss that Datak Tarr plants on a Votan spy), and both lesbian relationships end in death (Stahma kills Kenya; Yewll's wife commits suicide). The overtly queer relationships in *Defiance* are transient. Stahma's relationship with Kenya apparently has little lasting impact, as Stahma's season 2 goal is to achieve equality with her husband; there is no further suggestion that she is tempted by other women, or that her season 1 dalliance was anything other than an experiment. Doctor Yewll's lesbianism is primarily confined to the two episodes where she is haunted by chaste visions of her already-dead wife. Even the minor-character polygamous Earth Republic ambassador betrays both of her husbands for money.

The character of Niles Pottinger (recurring in season 2; one appearance in season 3) is particularly regressive, as his bisexual tendencies (his obsessions with Connor Lang and Amanda Rosewater) are suggested as the result of his own childhood rape by fellow students at his all-male boarding school. In the series' canon, when Connor and Amanda were engaged, Niles stalked Amanda and raped her, then followed her to Defiance, planted a camera in her bedroom, became her drug dealer, and resurrected a clone of her dead sister solely so he could comfort her in the aftermath. Needless to say, the manifestation of his queerness as criminal deviance brought on by childhood sexual trauma does not advance *Defiance*'s narrative in any imaginative or progressive way—nor does Amanda's storyline as a vengeful rape victim who, after having been stalked and successfully seduced by Pottinger for an entire season, then shoots him.

In short, most LGBQ relationships or images on *Defiance* are fleeting and destructive, existing on the fringes of a narrative that focuses on heterosexual protagonists. There is little to no inclusion of transgender characters, and Pottinger's story arc in particular calls back to regressive stereotypes about queerness and criminal sexual deviance. The series is primarily heteronormative, as is reflected in its foundational romantic couplings: Nolan and Amanda, Datak and Stahma, Tommy and Irisa, Alak and Christie (Nicole Muñoz), or temporary variants such as Nolan and Kenya or Tommy and Berlin (Anna Hopkins).

Summary

On its surface, *Defiance*'s premise suggests it has the potential to be a science fiction series that breaks with stereotypes and explores a multicultural, multi-gendered future where disparate groups must learn to survive together on a war-ravaged Earth. However, *Defiance* uses the alien Other to suggest, through both implicit and explicit comparison, that humanity's new post-apocalyptic society is both post-racial and post-feminist—all while marginalizing and killing characters of color, sexualizing its female leads, and further presenting a heteronormative world where queer imagery is either brief, destructive, or both. Some elements of *Defiance* may be socially progressive—its diverse background extras, its high proportion of female cast members—but overall the series is firmly situated within white American culture and supports the prominence of the straight white male. To find a post-apocalyptic television series that fully addresses contemporary social issues, we will need to look elsewhere.

Conclusion

By definition, alien invasion narratives detail humankind's encounters with the Other; such stories have been popular at various times in the twentieth and twenty-first centuries, particularly at moments of tense international conflict such as the Cold War, and most recently in post–9/11 America. Series like *Falling Skies*, *Colony*, and *Defiance* illustrate different ways in which alien invasion television has been used to address issues of racial and cultural conflict from a white American perspective. In *Falling Skies*, the myth of America-that-was is invoked through repeated references to the Revolutionary War, World War II, the founding fathers, and a consistent background of stars and stripes. The invading forces are characterized as unreasoningly hostile, a threat to the American way of life generally and American women specifically, while ally aliens are confined to a "Native American" support role within a frontier paradigm that privileges the white hero in a quest to destroy the Other and nostalgically re-establish a patriarchal American dream. In *Colony*, the thematic emphasis moves from direct explorations of the Other to criticism of government crackdown and the suspension of civil rights in the name of safety and security versus an alien threat. Here, however, Indigenous American references—specifically, to Geronimo as a resistance leader—invert a frontier framework to appropriate the position of the invaded for white liberal America. Finally, in *Defiance*, tensions between human and alien races serve as stand-ins for real-world racial and cultural conflicts; the projection of Muslim stereotypes onto Castithan aliens is particularly noticeable. *Defiance*, the only one of the three series to have Indigenous characters, also actively disavows any notion of inter-human racial conflict.

Each series presents the alien Other differently. *Falling Skies* projects the Other as a nameless, faceless horde threatening "traditional" America. *Colony* criticizes the actions of an American government in the context of an ill-defined external threat. *Defiance* allows the Other individual faces and voices while still prioritizing white, English-speaking "America" in a context of intercultural conflict. Despite these differences, all three series also construct supposedly post-racial human communities in which the alien presence has elided previous human racial differences and heroic humans must band together (beneath a banner of white heterosexual male leadership). Gender binaries also remain consistent, as the threat of the alien Other calls for male heroism and the same combat-oriented skills that have been projected upon cowboy and soldier heroes throughout American culture, reinscribing masculine dominance as well as gender stereotypes and heteronormative, patriarchal family and romantic relationships.

— 4 —

The Zombie Renaissance

ZOMBIES ARE DISTINCTLY CONTEMPORARY MONSTERS. Boluk and Lenz have identified three generations of Western zombies "responding to the specific technological and cultural anxieties of each historical era" (3); the first major appearance of the stumbling undead in North America is commonly traced to William Seabrook's descriptions of Haiti in *The Magic Island* (1929), and the subsequent film *White Zombie* (1932) (Vials 42). These zombies were individual and personal: people who had been robbed of their will and forced to obey their voodoo masters in mindless slavery. This imagery, with its clear racial overtones regarding Haiti's colonial oppression (Hassler-Forest 340; Keetley 3), was co-opted by white Western Hollywood to examine fears of the racial Other but also discontent regarding the drudgery of the post-industrial workforce (Vials). In later decades, the Western zombie was popularized by George Romero's *Night of the Living Dead* (1968) and subsequent *Living Dead* movies: here were the armies of infected, brain-eating risen corpses that have set the standard for all further pop culture reference, part of the "zombie matrix" (Proctor 10) in which every zombie cultural product is "inescapably intertextual" (Ahmad 132), intrinsically drawing material from others. These zombies have shifted from their Haitian origins, appropriated as symbols of colonial attitudes and fears (Rushton and Moreman 1). They are particularly mass-media-friendly, differing from bogeymen like vampires, ghosts, or Frankenstein's monster because they are rooted in Caribbean oral culture and recent Western film rather than English literature or the Gothic tradition (Feshami 93).

Such zombies lulled in popularity through the 1990s, then resurged again in Romero's new *Land of the Dead* (2005), *Diary of the Dead* (2007), and *Survival of the Dead* (2009), as well as films like *28 Days Later* (2002) and *World War Z* (2013), the comedies *Shaun of the Dead* (2004) and *Fido* (2006), and the romantic comedy *Warm Bodies* (2013). The twenty-first century saw a "global expansion of zombie mania" (Hubner, Leaning and Manning 3)—a rise not just in zombie films, novels, comic books and other media, but also in zombie walks, zombie survival guides, and even specialized zombie-fighting ammunition (Linneman, Wall, and Green 520); in the U.S., the CDC was using zombie disaster scenarios as tools for government emergency planning (512). On television, the dead rose again in series like *The Returned* (A&E, 2015; a remake of a 2012 French series) and *Resurrection* (ABC, 2014–15). Robert Kirkman's comic series *The Walking Dead* broke sales records, and AMC's *The Walking Dead* (2010–), which adapted Kirkman's series, has been a top-rated cable program for much of its run, shattering ratings records with 17.3 million viewers for its 2014 fifth-season premiere (Pallotta). *Fear the Walking Dead* (AMC 2015–) and *Z Nation* (Syfy, 2014–) followed, along with the more comedic *iZombie* (The CW, 2015–).

Given their flexibility, the current popularity of the zombie is not a surprise. Zombies possess a malleable quality, or "blankness" (Manning 164), that allows them to serve any number of metaphors; indeed, "the zombie's utility as a metaphor is virtually without limit" (Boluk and Lenz 9), and "no one version of zombies exhausts all the narrative or symbolic uses or implications of the monster" (Paffenroth 24). The risen dead carry the same uncanny implications as the alien body snatchers that replace our loved ones with walking simulacra of themselves, linking them to distrust about invaders among us (Bishop 14). They have been associated with viral pandemics and bioweapons (Bishop 14; Boluk and Lenz 6; Keetley 4; Rushton and Moreman 5; Pokornowski 43–43), HIV/AIDS (Ahmad 135), immigration crises (Bishop 14), interracial conflict (Canavan; Pokornowski; Vials), postindustrial labor and postmodern ennui (Manning 162–3; Linneman, Wall, and Green), Hurricane Katrina (Lauro 58; Simpson 29), evolution and scientific discourse (Moreland), and terrorism and post–9/11 anxieties (Paffenroth 19; Manning 163; Simpson 29; Ahmad 132). They are a catch-all for a morass of cultural anxieties, able to represent everything and nothing, associated most broadly with violence and fear:

> It is difficult to talk about zombies with critical and historical rigor. It's not so much that the zombie apocalypse encapsulates ideas about race, or the atom bomb, or recent financial meltdown; it's that the zombie encapsulates anxieties about race *and* the atom bomb *and* the recent financial meltdown, *and* … [Boluk and Lenz 9, original emphasis].

The zombie's flexibility as a signifier lends it emotional resonance in a time of multiple threats; as such, "the replicating zombie constitutes the perfect metaphor for the dangers of the age, from the biological to the natural, to the nuclear, to the terrorist"; it can represent any danger required, even "the concept of 'terror' itself, an amorphous enemy that has no specific identity and is ever threatening because it can never be defeated" (Simpson 38).

Zombies have also been intertwined with wild west narratives since the 1950s and films like Edward Dean's *Curse of the Undead* (1954), and in the twenty-first century with *From Dusk Till Dawn* (1996) or *Vampires* (1998) (Miller and Van Riper, xiv). But such genre mergers tend toward the subversive; the undead are fundamentally destabilizing figures, standing as they do on the borders between life and death, loved one and enemy, person and object. The zombie genre has the capacity to provide "a sustained critique of conservative ideology and the political status quo, while also creating a space within its narrative where (sometimes radical) social alternatives can be explored" (Hassler-Forest 345; see also Ahmad 132–35). A zombie apocalypse presents a society in which both foundational institutions and individual lives are destroyed by friends, lovers, and family members (Paffenroth 20); the living protagonists must fight off formerly trusted loved ones while simultaneously grieving that same loss (Kremmel). As such, while zombie narratives incorporate the same wild west archetypes and structures as other types of post-apocalyptic series, they do so despite a fundamental tension between the disruptive zombie and the reassuringly hegemonic western: "There is no fair play, no honorable death, in the West of the undead—only cannibalism, evisceration, and mutilation" (Miller and Van Riper xiv; see also Hassler-Forest 345). Thus, series like *The Walking Dead*, *Fear the Walking Dead*, and *Z Nation* are limited by familiar cultural stereotypes, but each also challenges hegemonic structures in different ways: *The Walking Dead* by presenting forms of patriarchy that are continually crumbling, *Fear the Walking Dead* by attempting to incorporate more diverse characters and settings, and *Z Nation* by partially shifting focus away from white male heroes while half-advocating for a hybrid zombie future. Each reflects varying degrees of struggle between the zombie disruptor and a stubbornly strong cultural status quo.

The Walking Dead

AMC's *The Walking Dead*, based on the comic series by Robert Kirkman, is a quintessential story of displacement and the repeated search for sanctuary, as a mismatched group of survivors roams the ravaged United States seeking shelter from the zombie apocalypse. As former Deputy Sheriff Rick Grimes (Andrew Lincoln) leads a rotating band of desperate humans across a dead American wasteland in search of safety, he establishes an authoritarian "Ricktatorship" over his people while encountering a series of alternate groups and false sanctuaries. The series has been frequently linked to post–9/11 anxieties regarding security and law enforcement in a world perceived to be under constant threat (e.g., Bishop; Pokornowski; Nurse; Keetley); unlike *Colony*, it reads as a highly conservative narrative in which civil rights cannot co-exist with the aggressive actions required to ensure community protection in a dangerous world. The series illustrates a "neo-apocalyptic" paradigm, demonstrating "a bleak shift in emphasis from the belief in an ordered universe with a cogent history to one in which the overriding sense is of a chaotic, indifferent, and possibly meaningless universe" (Rosen xiv), and further echoing zombie texts in which the monsters and their creators have come "to represent those elements of society which America's white middle class found disturbing or troublesome and over which it wished it could exert control" (Kordas 6). While *The Walking Dead*'s persistently failing communities ultimately suggest a nihilistic end, their repetitive configurations also promote violent security and survival philosophies and fail to present compelling alternatives to contemporary Western power structures. These structures are inevitably patriarchal; as each encounter degrades into conflict and death, *The Walking Dead* presents a future in which different presentations of white masculinity battle for supremacy. If zombies may be read as allegories for a number of contemporary challenges to hegemonic Western culture—including feminism, LGBTQ rights, or civil rights—then elements of *The Walking Dead* also represent the struggle to maintain white patriarchal privilege in a changing world, suggesting the frightened paranoia of a twenty-first-century patriarchy that can envision its own downfall, but only at the end of human civilization.

Pragmatism and Patriarchy in the New Wild West

The Walking Dead first suggests the breakdown of traditional social systems through the perversion of wild west influences that are established early, as the pilot episode showcases Rick in his wide-brimmed hat and police uniform, riding a horse down an abandoned highway into the ruined city of Atlanta (1.01, "Days Gone By"). Rick is clean-cut and honorable; he is "a synecdoche for the pre-zombie social order" (Canavan 436) and represents the ideals of a now-defunct American justice system. He is looking for his wife Lori (Sarah Wayne Callies) and son Carl (Chandler Riggs), and he is positioned for a mythological narrative arc wherein he might protect his family while bringing law and order back to the new frontier. However, "the brutal necessities of his new world … quickly illustrate the shortcomings of the very qualities that made him such a sympathetic character" (Simpson 29). Multiple events in the pilot signal Rick's compromised position. First, he awakens from an eight-month coma to find that the world has ended, an event during which he was passively unaware; he begins from a position of confused ignorance. Second, the episode's opening scene shows Rick in his uniform attempting to help a young blonde girl holding a stuffed toy; however, the girl is already a zombie and Rick, too late to save her, must instead shoot her in the face (Rees 80). And finally, Rick obtains a horse and a bag of guns only to immediately lose both by riding heedlessly into a zombie horde (Coleman 82–3). Rather than being the new sheriff in town, Rick is literally the old sheriff, whose services are no longer effective or required. His status as frontier hero is thus undermined; his traditional American cowboy heroics are ill-suited for *The Walking Dead*'s new world.

This ongoing theme is most notable in the series' first two seasons, which pit Rick against his best friend and former police partner Shane (Jon Bernthal) as the two men jockey for control of the group. While Rick advocates for the preservation of a moral code ("We don't kill the living"; 1.05, "Wildfire"), Shane is violent and self-serving. Their competition for leadership is framed as a confrontation of ideologies: Rick's compassionate, democratic law and order versus Shane's brutally dictatorial practicality. This is marked not just by dialogue or narrative action but also by visual cues: in early episodes, Rick's uniform retains visible links to traditional authority structures, while Shane's abandonment of police trappings reflects his embrace of paramilitary approaches (Nurse 72). Moreover, the series "verifies Shane's cynicism more often than not, so while viewers are encouraged to prefer Rick's hope, we are never allowed to confirm it" (Coleman 87). Critics have invoked comparisons to the 1953 film *Shane* (Coleman 87), in which noble cowboy Shane leaves town rather than act on his attraction to a married woman; in *The Walking Dead*, ex-officer Shane has sex with Lori and becomes a father figure to Carl when Rick is presumed dead. At first, it seems that Lori's subsequent second-season pregnancy carries a paternity question that symbolizes the ideological conflict—who will father the future? (Coleman 88)—but on both philosophical and domestic levels, the conflict between Rick and Shane is ultimately futile. Though Rick kills Shane (2.12, "Better Angels"), in the act of gunning down his friend, he is already *becoming* Shane. Season 2 sees Rick give up his badge and his increasingly blood-splattered uniform, and as Shane's corpse lies cooling in a field, Rick announces to the ragtag group, "You're staying? This isn't a democracy anymore" (2.12 "Better Angels")—thus beginning the "Ricktatorship."

It seems no coincidence that just before Rick kills Shane, the previous episode brings the death of Dale (Jeffrey DeMunn), an older man who served as the voice of humanist empathy in the group (Simpson 33). Dale, a steady and vocal conscience advocating the preservation of morality and inner goodness, supports Rick and detests Shane, but dies in a night-time field, the victim of a zombie attack—symbolizing also the death of old morals and old ways of being human (Kremmel 93; 2.11, "Judge, Jury, Executioner"). Rick's slow descent into fascist monstrosity harks back to Romero's films, wherein predominant themes included "the identity of zombies and living humans, and the greater threat posed by the living humans" (Paffenroth 19); likewise, "the obsessive object of scrutiny in *The Walking Dead* is the human propensity for violence, a propensity mirrored in the zombies, who are defined by their drive to devour, and then reflected back on the humans, who are themselves infected with the 'zombie virus'" (Keetley 8; see also Bishop 77–78, Feshami 88). The series focuses on the breakdown of both society and the moral condition, as the zombies become a secondary threat when Rick's group is forced to face much greater danger from other humans. In *The Walking Dead*'s nihilist world, the traditional cowboy hero cannot survive, and Rick can only save his extended survivor family through increasingly horrific actions—by season 6, when people stare at his blood-drenched features, all he can muster is an irritably puzzled, "What?" (6.11, "Knots Untie"). Here, there are no hopeful futures or concrete moral choices: "The presence of the undead ... complicates what, in traditional Westerns, had been a simple moral equation, highlighting degrees of savagery in all characters—heroes *and* villains—while at the same time mitigating their moral differences through their shared opposition to the undead" (C. Miller 16).

In a recurring pattern on the series, Rick's band stumbles upon a new community or shelter and thinks they have found safety, only to discover that safety was a lie and, after some violent encounter, they will have to move onward. At first, it is a CDC research center where the lone remaining scientist, Edwin Jenner (Noah Emmerich), allows the group to enter. Jenner serves as an indicator of *The Walking Dead*'s disinterest in exploring the origins of the zombie plague; he is also representative of surrender. He has failed to find a cure, he is running out of gas for his generators, and he plans to destroy the lab (as well as himself and everyone else) rather than confront the horrors outside. His explosive suicide forces the series' main characters to choose continued survival over despair.

Next, Hershel Greene (Scott Wilson)'s rural family farm (reminiscent of the setting for Romero's *Night of the Living Dead* [Bishop 23]) seems like refuge. Hershel was the farm's legal owner, pre-zombies, and he leads a group primarily composed of his teen-to-adult children, as well as former neighbors. Hershel models a "zero tolerance" defensive stance (Nurse 75), reactive and rule-keeping; he is a doctor who forbids guns on his land and keeps a barn full of captive walkers, under the assumption that the undead are sick people who may someday be cured. Rick, respecting the rule of law, dictates that the group obey Hershel's rules on Hershel's land; Shane, the ruthless rebel, advocates a takeover. Even as Rick kills Shane, Hershel's defensive stance fails his family: a wave of zombies destroys the farm, and Hershel—along with his daughters Beth (Emily Kinney) and Maggie (Lauren Cohan)—joins Rick's fleeing group under the newly established Ricktatorship.

Bishop has linked the Ricktatorship to "the post–9/11 Bush Administration's creation of the Patriot Act and its increasingly aggressive military actions overseas," as "Rick claims the old laws won't protect them, but self-defensive action and preemptive violence will" (81). The dominant survival philosophy in the series is certainly aggressive rather than reactionary, as Hershel's farm falls and Rick adopts Shane's pragmatic, us-before-them approach. But there are limits imposed on this expression of self-interested, military masculinity: the group's next foe is The Governor (David Morrissey), who leads the town of Woodbury—a seemingly idyllic recreation of small-town America, protected from zombies by both walls and a trained paramilitary militia force. The Governor embodies the fantasy of a "secure society" (Keetley 10):

> The Governor's obsession with guns and walls ... is everyone's obsession on *The Walking Dead*. No one who has watched the show can fail to be aware of either the importance of fences ... or the omnipresence of guns—the use of guns, training people in how to use guns, debates over who should have guns, giving guns to children, retrieving guns, lamenting the scarcity of guns [10].

However, The Governor is militant and fascist to the point of perversion. He kills anyone he perceives as a threat to his power: "In Woodbury, the state, while legitimately protecting itself against a tangible threat, indeed becomes illegitimate in its use of force" (Nurse 77). The Governor's excesses distinguish him from Rick, defining him as dangerously dystopian: he maintains a trophy wall full of his enemies' heads, channels his people's aggression via staged fights between soldiers and chained zombies, and keeps his own zombified daughter walled up in a secret room. The Governor's overt viciousness must be defeated, but the victory is pyrrhic as Hershel—like Dale, a vestige of an old moral system—is beheaded and Rick's group is forced onward.

From there, the scattered survivors follow signs promising "sanctuary" and regroup in the *Soylent Green*–esque town of Terminus, where pragmatic survival means that cannibal town leader Gareth (Andrew J. West) and his people lure in unsuspecting strangers, then line them up along a trough to be slaughtered. Unlike The Governor, who offers shelter to some but proactively and too brutally seeks out potential threats, Gareth and his people prey on the weak by entrapping and literally consuming all those around them; anyone who is not a member of the Terminus community is Othered to the point of being food. But the brutal, dehumanizing pragmatism of the cannibal approach is again too far; Rick's group, protecting themselves once again with violence, burns Terminus as they flee.

The suburban community of Alexandria then appears to provide a welcome respite. Here, the promise of the frontier myth is briefly renewed as Rick gets a haircut, puts on a uniform, and resumes the old sheriff role that he abandoned in season 2. Unlike the cannibalistic depravity of Terminus, Alexandria is an optimistic promise that the world can be as it was; it has electricity, water, large modern houses, white picket fences, and plans for expansion. Its citizens have preserved their pre-apocalyptic social structures. Like Rick, Alexandria's leader Deanna Monroe (Tovah Feldshuh) is a remnant of past institutions of authority: she was an elected congresswoman. She attempts to maintain democratic discourse within a peaceful community, holding the zombies at bay with large fences and avoiding the notice of more hostile human groups. But while Rick and his people first attempt to fit in, they soon discover the citizens of Alexandria to be naïve and unprepared for the brutality of the world outside. Rick's now-habitual aggression ensures that his tenure in the now ill-fitting sheriff role is short lived. When he beats the town doctor, Pete (Corey Brill), for domestic abuse, he is captured and almost exiled, only to be proven correct after Pete kills Deanna's husband. Though Rick's attack on Pete proves prescient, his actions cannot be rectified with the outdated system of justice he used to represent—nor can Alexandria continue as is. Indeed, Alexandria's survival pre–Rick is credited to luck, as zombies have been falling into a nearby quarry instead of attacking the town (6.01, "First Time Again"). When human invaders and then zombies flood Alexandria, they prove Rick's paranoia right.

Rick takes over Alexandria and subsequently goes to war against Negan (Jeffrey Dean Morgan) and the Saviors gang, in order to obtain a trade agreement with the nearby community of Hilltop (and keep Alexandria from starvation). This configures Rick as a more bloodthirsty leader than he has been previously; when he and the group break into a Savior stronghold at night, killing sleeping (and therefore defenseless) Saviors, Tara (Alanna Masterson), formerly a member of the Governor's forces, observes that she has taken similar action before (6.12, "Not Tomorrow Yet"). As Rick persists in provoking the Saviors despite the reservations of others in the group—forcing Glenn (Steven Yeun) to take his first human life, alienating the pacifist Morgan (Lennie James), traumatizing Maggie, and driving Carol (Melissa McBride) to leave—*The Walking Dead* seems to question whether its core group has gone too far; as Savior Michelle (Jeananne Goossen) states to Maggie, "You're not the good guys" (6.13, "The Same Boat"). In the conflict between Alexandria and the Saviors, it is difficult to identify with either side as "good": the Saviors, who commandeer fifty per cent of Hilltop's supplies, beat a teenage boy to death, and nearly kill Daryl (Norman Reedus), Sasha (Sonequa Martin-Green), and Abraham (Michael Cudlitz) in the road (6.11, "Knots Untie"), or Rick and the Alexandrites, who murder sleeping people in the night. As its narratives explore increasingly murky conflicts, *The Walking Dead* lends itself to "a new symbolic manifestation, one that reflects not cultural fears about what terrorists *might* do, but rather what the good guys *can* do against potential or suspected terrorists. In other words, that which we most fear is not the monstrous Other but our monstrous selves" (Bishop 78, original emphasis). In some ways, as *The Walking Dead* descends into moral anarchy, it doesn't seem to matter; all of these communities and groups are destined to fail, ending in violence and death as Rick's people either messily succumb or are forced to move on.

The series functions as a metaphor for conflicting philosophies regarding both morality and security in insecure times. Ultimately, however, *The Walking Dead*'s America is crumbling, and no attempt to rebuild can last for long against endless ravening zombies—or, more pointedly, against other humans desperate for increasingly scarce resources. Each confrontation becomes increasingly brutal, but also increasingly repetitive. Even as the series subverts classical notions of the cowboy hero and the code of the American west, it continues to support notions of patriarchy and the importance of the white male hero: almost every group is led by a heterosexual white man. The series' grim future becomes a war zone of masculinity, even when the cowboy myth is fracturing. Indeed, *The Walking Dead* arguably rejects Rick's cowboy heroism but instead echoes the more Latin American concept of the *caudillo*, in which a hero of the wild frontier provides life-saving order rather than championing individual freedoms, and in which—even if a leader is brutal or cruel—"the personal law of one man" is still "better than no law at all" (Sullivan 10). As American society collapses, patriarchy in *The Walking Dead* yet persists—even if, like any still living, it is ultimately doomed. Much as Rick and Shane's battle for supremacy goes unchallenged by other group members (Greene and Meyer 70), male leadership is taken for granted through the first five seasons.

This is also typical of the horror genre, which equates masculinity with survival:

> anger and/or displays of force belong to the male, while crying, cowering, screaming, fainting, trembling, and begging for mercy belong to the female. This is a significant distinction, because in horror films, anger and force often facilitate survival, while cowering and fear generally lead to death [Greene and Meyer 66].

The leaders of *The Walking Dead* may model slightly different moral codes or venues of aggression, but ultimately the results of each encounter are the same: two men enter, one man leaves (or, more specifically, Rick's group encounters a new enemy and eventually prevails, with most surviving, under Rick's continued dictatorship). Deanna is the only exception, and her leadership is highly gendered; the only leader who doesn't take or keep power by force, she is the remnant of a democratic system now depicted as both unworkable and ignorantly optimistic. As the previously peaceful Alexandria is finally invaded by both walkers and human raiders, Deanna willingly surrenders her authority to Rick ("They don't need me. What they need is you"; 6.05, "Now").

The Walking Dead thus presents a cowboy hero who fails to maintain a code of honor but still acts as protagonist within Western patriarchal tradition. As Rick assumes control and the group stumbles from one failed sanctuary to another, Rick's leadership is contrasted with other models of masculinity; male dominance is taken for granted.

Race in a Time of Zombies

Like so many other series, *The Walking Dead* is ostensibly post-racial; this is established early on by the character of Merle (Michael Rooker). A violent, hostile white supremacist, Merle is an original member of the survivor group. He uses racial slurs (e.g., "n***er," "taco-bender"), and is, additionally, openly sexist ("sugar tits") (1.02, "Guts"). However, Merle's initial tenure on *The Walking Dead* is brief; at the end of his initial episode appearance, he is chained to a rooftop pipe and by the time the survivors return for him, he has already sawed off his own hand and vanished (1.03, "Tell It to the Frogs"). Though he reappears in season 3, "his blatant and overt racism is dampened, and he is removed again before the end of the season.... [T]he eradication of Merle (and the excesses of his racism) evacuates the character's function as a reminder of racial strife" (Pokornowski 52). Merle primarily serves the purpose of establishing Rick, in comparison, as *not* racist, and to allow Rick to give the following speech: "There are no n***ers anymore. No dumb-as-shit, inbred white-trash fools either. There's us, and the dead" (1.02, "Guts"). In Merle's absence, the remaining group members can band together for survival, human vs. zombie in a presumed color-blind future—despite the fact that an episode after Rick gives this speech, Glenn is using his own Korean ethnicity as a reason to defer to Rick: "I don't mean to bring race into this, but it might sound better coming from a white guy" (1.03, "Tell It to the Frogs").

Merle's brother Daryl also espouses racist beliefs at the beginning of the series, but as he is a protagonist, these beliefs could not be allowed to persist—instead, Daryl's racial slurs begin as offensive, progress to being a "joke" that Glenn can laugh at (1.06, "TS-19"), and soon vanish entirely from his dialogue, save when Merle reappears in season 3 and Daryl can knowledgeably correct him that Glenn's heritage is Korean and not Chinese (3.10, "Home"). Merle, the unrepentant white supremacist, must be exiled and eventually die (3.15, "This Sorrowful Life"); Daryl, the younger brother, must learn the error of his ways and become a "better person" (Garrett 31, 74–75) to gain the approbation of his non-white co-survivors and progress as a hero. This reduces racism in the series to the behavior and dialogue of two characters, establishing everyone else as non-racist by default and obfuscating the ways in which *The Walking Dead* privileges white narratives. Daryl himself is part of this—he is presented as the woodsy survivalist character in tune with nature, a stereotypical role normally reserved for Indigenous Americans in the wild west world (Coleman 91). Even this shallow stereotype is appropriated for a white lead, however, as Daryl tracks, hunts, and embarks on spiritual vision journeys (2.05, "Chupacabra").

Further, Rick and *The Walking Dead* may claim a post-racial world, but while the series has an extended cast of non-white characters, notably Glenn, it has also been critiqued for narratively neglecting these characters in favor of white stories. In particular, the series has incorporated a rotating roster of seemingly disposable Black men, who are nominally included in the group but are given very little back story and have relatively little onscreen presence before their inevitable deaths. These men include T-Dog (Irone Singleton, seasons 1–3); Oscar (Vincent M. Ward, season 3); Tyreese (Chad L. Coleman, seasons 3–5); Bob (Lawrence Gilliard, Jr., seasons 4–5); and Noah (Tyler James Williams, season 5). The first Black people seen onscreen in the pilot are anonymous dead bodies. Morgan (Lennie James) is one exception to this trend, but though he has lived from the pilot episode through the series (so far), his story has been mostly offscreen; he appeared in only 13 episodes of the first five seasons, and his initial role was enabling Rick's journey, as he and his son Duane (Adrian Kali Turner) found a confused post-coma Rick and explained to him what the walkers were and how to survive them. While season 6 has seen the return of Morgan and the continued recurrence of Father Gabriel (Seth Gilliam), these characters are not sufficient to disrupt *The Walking Dead*'s overall concentration on white male narratives. Apart from Glenn (seasons 1–6)[1] as the only Asian lead, other non-white men have appeared even more rarely: Latino character Morales (Juan Gabriel Pareja) splits from the group and departs with his family in the fourth episode. The series makes an early and minimal effort to address both cultural stereotypes and the possibility of non-white leadership when Rick's people encounter an apparent Latino gang that turns out to be a group of nursing home employees struggling to help the elderly (1.04, "Vatos"). This single episode initially and briefly suggests "gang culture" as a socially constructed response to "perceived threats from dominant groups within society (which here includes both the walkers and Rick's mostly white group)" (Nurse 74); however, these characters are never seen again, and in a deleted scene from a later episode, the nursing home is reportedly shown to be an empty ruin (Simpson 35).

Women of color are also secondary to the series, and their presence rarer than the men's—T-Dog's wife Jacqui (Jeryl Prescott) is barely a presence onscreen before she commits suicide in Jenner's lab explosion (2.01, "What Lies Ahead"; T-Dog never mentions her again), and Rosita (Christian Serratos), who appears in season 4 onward, evokes sexy Latina stereotypes when she first dresses in a midriff top and short shorts (4.11, "Claimed"), her primary story being her sexual relationship with former soldier Abraham (Michael Cudlitz). Two Black women, Sasha and Michonne (Danai Gurira), have been presented as more intricate characters—Sasha has dealt with post-traumatic (or perhaps more accurately, ongoing traumatic) stress, and Michonne is one of the group's best fighters, given plenty of onscreen time and impressively choreographed battle scenes. Michonne in particular is a complicated read in terms of the series' politics; first, she "eerily echoes colonialism and racism. This tall, cloaked African American woman wielding a sword and leading chained zombies not-so-subtly evokes the slave trade" (Pokornowski 52). But she is also a central character who, as of season 6, is romantically linked to Rick; this may potentially impose gender restrictions on her character, but the onscreen inter-racial partnership has also been seen positively by fans who view the pairing of a white man and a dark-skinned love interest as refreshingly progressive (e.g., Sharon).

Certainly *The Walking Dead* is not post-racial, however, and Rick's claiming such only serves to obscure the zombie's long association with racial oppression and slavery, from its origins in Haitian culture (as "the nightmarish figuration of a slavery that would continue even after death" [Canavan 447]) through to Romero's films and other undead artifacts of the twentieth century. Among their many metaphoric uses, zombies are closely related to anxieties about "others" and the disruption of white middle-class social norms (Nurse 68; Pokornowski 52; Canavan 431; Kordas 16); while *The Walking Dead* ostensibly rejects the notion of post-apocalyptic racial tensions, its embrace of white leadership (Ho 63) and patriarchal security narratives says otherwise. Merle's overt racism and Daryl's reformation serve as smoke screens for the way characters of color are repeatedly marginalized and slaughtered in service to Rick's story. Of course, this obfuscation is destructive: "Recognizing that the logic of survival put forth in zombie narratives is racially-motivated, based on exclusion, and that it reflects real-world issues of race, class, and sovereignty, is a crucial step toward identifying and resisting the self-destructive politics of fear popularized by zombie narratives" (Pokornowski 42). It is not possible to separate the zombie from its racialized slave history (Lauro 201). Alexandria, a vision of a "safe" (white) gated community (Canavan 443), only supports the projection of zombie imagery on real-world marginal groups—"the literal embodiment of those dispossessed and socially dead others borne of late-capitalism" (Linneman, Wall, and Green 519), with images of the hordes outside suffused with notions of killability and disposability (520). As well, if *The Walking Dead* serves as a conservative critique of liberal law and order policies that use "deadly force only when necessary and as a last resort" (Nurse 71), and Rick's gradual shift to a more aggressive stance suggests the need for "a proactive response to lawlessness" (Nurse 77; see also Bishop 81), this stance is already racially charged when considering

American legal systems that both criminalize and violently disenfranchise marginalized groups (Linneman, Wall, and Green).[2]

Dead Girls and Gender Roles

Beyond issues of Deanna's leadership and the suppression of women of color, *The Walking Dead* also further enforces gender essentialisms. This is apparent from the opening scenes of the pilot, when Rick shoots a small zombie girl, "pink-robed and bunny-slippered, carrying a soiled teddy bear, the epitome of innocence" (Young 61). The scene with the zombie child establishes a precedent that carries throughout the first five seasons of the series: the horror of the apocalypse is represented by the maimed bodies of young girls, most particularly blonde white girls. These symbols of putrefied American innocence include the first walker girl (Addy Miller), Carol's daughter Sophia (Madison Lintz), The Governor's zombie daughter Penny (Kylie Syzmanski), Carol's briefly adopted daughters Lizzie (Brighton Sharbino) and Mika (Kyla Kenedy), as well as adolescent victims such as Andrea's younger sister Amy (Emma Bell) and Hershel's youngest daughter Beth. Girls die quickly and frequently as the story moves past; the only girls to survive (so far) are Rick's infant daughter Judith and season-five addition Enid (Katelyn Nacon). In contrast, boy deaths are rare: Morgan's son Duane dies offscreen (3.12, "Clear"), Michonne's son Andre died pre-series, and Rick's son Carl improbably survives multiple dangers, including being shot in the chest (2.01, "What Lies Ahead") and face (6.09, "No Way Out"). It isn't until season 6 that we see young boys killed, and these boys—Alexandria residents Sam (Major Dodson) and his brother Ron (Austin Abrams)—first have their own narratives. Sam, in particular, suffers a protracted multi-episode breakdown and his onscreen death is presented for maximum dramatic effect, as he is pulled screaming from his mother (6.09, "No Way Out"); after, he is remembered, as Carol puts a cookie on his grave (6.12, "Not Tomorrow Yet"). The deaths of young boys are rare and notable; the deaths of young girls are both series wallpaper and affective constant, soliciting a nigh-continuous run of viewer sympathy and emotional investment. As in zombie films and traditional tragedy formulas in which pity "usually centers on female characters and children" (Bishop 45; see also Keetley 3), the intrinsic hopelessness of *The Walking Dead*'s nihilistic apocalypse is expressed through the shambling bodies of the dead girls that the survivors (and, by extension, Rick) have failed to protect—presumably as girls, and particularly blonde girls, are seen as the *most* innocent and *most* vulnerable members of American society. As Coleman has noted,

> *The Walking Dead* produces a grotesque hybrid, a changeling Western, animated yet altered, infected with a strain of postideological nihilism that disempowers its heroes,

creates child monsters from its child victims, and turns sheriffs bound to protect children and avenge harm done to them into their grim killers [81].

Additionally, "the proliferation of female children represented in horror films can … equate adult women with children, marking them as being in need of constant male protection" (Greene and Meyer 66); and "whatever else might be said about *The Walking Dead*, or about zombie narrative in general, its uncritical relationship to a particular pre-feminist narrative about the need to 'protect' women and children cannot be glossed over" (Canavan 444). The women of *The Walking Dead* are too often seen as vulnerable, as well as intrinsically irrational and emotional. This also stems from the pilot, when a pre-apocalyptic flashback scene opens with Rick and Shane in their squad car, Shane asking, "What's the difference between men and women?" Shane describes a woman as a "pair of boobs" and laughs at her apparently irrational behavior: "I've never met a woman who knew how to turn off a light." Rick, in turn, is frustrated because his wife Lori always wants to talk about their marital problems. This initial scene "foreshadows the rest of the season"; sexist behavior is normalized, even humorous (Greene and Meyer 67), and women and men are presented as fundamentally, essentially different—a regressive position "particularly troubling for a 21st century television series" (64). After Rick is shot, Shane brings him flowers in the hospital, but quickly disavows any involvement: "Linda and Diane from dispatch, they picked these out … probably could tell, huh?" The female officers (unseen) are associated with flowers, nurturing, and dispatch duties, unlike the four men constituting Rick's onscreen police team. Further, the narrative emphasis is on the men throughout the pilot episode—it is 50 minutes in before we hear a woman (Amy) speak. Men's dialogue overall repetitively invokes sexist stereotypes about feminine weakness: "They gonna pussy out" (Shane, 2.11, "Judge, Jury, Executioner"); "Hey, while the others wash their panties, let's go hunt" (Daryl, 3.01, "Seed"); "There ain't a pair of nuts between the whole pussy lot of you" (Merle, 3.07, "When the Dead Come Knocking"). More subtly, the need for men to protect women and children is often invoked: "You don't think I can keep Lori or Carl safe?" (Rick, 2.10, "18 Miles Out"); "Thanks for looking out for her" (Hershel, 3.09, "The Suicide King"), and women are assumed to be the natural and perpetual targets of sexual violence: "They roll through here, our boys are dead, and our women—they're gonna wish they were" (Daryl, 2.11, "Judge, Jury, Executioner").

These binaries are preserved most visibly in the work divisions of the series' initial seasons, when the men patrol with guns while the women cook and do "a seemingly infinite amount of laundry" (Greene and Meyer 68). When the women, washing clothes at the riverbank, watch Shane teaching Carl how to catch frogs, Jacqui explicitly calls out this dichotomy:

JACQUI: I'm beginning to question the division of labor here. Can someone explain to me how the women ended up doing all the Hattie McDaniel work?

AMY: The world ended. Didn't you get the memo?

CAROL: That's just the way it is [1.03, "Tell It to the Frogs"].

The division of labor is thus normalized—at the fall of civilization, without the political pressures of feminist movements, the people of *The Walking Dead* return to "tradition" and "essentials," relegating women to their domestic place because this is voiced by the group members as the best and most practical way to survive.

Andrea (Laurie Holden) best exemplifies this trend. A former human rights lawyer and a childless professional—thus, a remnant of feminism and the "politically correct" past—she rebels against the male/female constrictions within the group. She demands a gun and wants to patrol with the men. First, she doesn't know how to use a gun properly; when she pulls one on Rick, he has to tell her how to turn off the safety (1.02, "Guts")—a situation in which, "while Andrea's possession of a gun could have provided her a position of power, Rick's commentary strips her of this power and repositions her as hyper-emotional and irrational" (Greene and Meyer 69). Her subsequent insistence on arming herself is a source of strife; moreover, when she does have a rifle, she accidentally shoots Daryl, mistaking him for a walker (2.05, "Chupacabra"). Her refusal to engage in cooking or laundry is also a source of conflict with Lori and the other women, who resent the extra "burden" of having to do more work: "The men can handle this on their own. They don't need your help.... You don't care about anybody but yourself. You're sitting up on that RV, working on your tan with a shotgun in your lap" (2.10, "18 Miles Out"). Finally, Andrea's poor choices are both highlighted and punished in season 3, entangled with her sexual choices when (after also having had sex with Shane) she embarks on an ill-advised affair with The Governor and dies after he locks her in a room with a dying man who turns walker (3.16, "Welcome to the Tombs"). Andrea is portrayed as irrationally headstrong, seeking to assume a position of power and agency to which her gender does not entitle her.

Lori, in comparison, plays a particularly passive role within the series. It is unclear whether she had a career before the apocalypse, as her personal back story is left blank apart from her marriage to Rick. In the series' first two seasons, she is at the center of the show's romantic drama, and a major focus of the conflict between Rick and Shane. Lori exemplifies a predominantly conservative mindset: she blames herself for any difficulties in her marriage (she is a "shitty wife"; 3.02, "Sick"; also 2.02, "Bloodletting"), stays in that marriage despite her own discontent, accepts her role as domestic support, and cannot emotionally or morally opt for an abortion even under the worst of circumstances (Simpson 36–7). Her decision to have a child in the middle of an apocalyptic wasteland—without any kind of supplies or consistent shelter, and when the sound of a crying baby will attract the undead and endanger the entire group—is questionable on pragmatic grounds but reasserts a conservative sense of morality and positions Lori in need of further protection. She needs a man for survival (Greene and Meyer 71). Her authority in the survivor group comes via her marriage to Rick (she is "unofficial First Lady" [2.05, "Chupacabra"]). After Shane's death, when Lori is no longer the symbol of a battle between two masculine forces, she dies during childbirth (3.04, "Killer Within") and subsequently haunts Rick—first as a voice on the phone, but then as a silent ghost, without power or agency. She is a symbol of his faltering masculinity and a tool to further his character development, further advancing wild west tropes wherein "if a man wins the fight but not the woman, his strength and dominance must be questioned and he cannot be a true hero" (Wright 150).

In contrast to Andrea's problematic desire for masculinity and Lori's passive domesticity, Carol represents *The Walking Dead*'s main foray into gender hybridity—again, as in other series like *Revolution*, as a woman who adopts independence, aggression, and power rather than a man who embraces nurturing and empathy. Carol is the survivor of an abusive marriage—a notable change from the source material comics, in which her never-seen husband is already dead and comic–Carol is sexually promiscuous, needy, and emotionally unstable. This change to Carol's back story—and, subsequently, her character—suggests a line of logic similar to that of *Falling Skies*, in which, if a woman is "strong," it is because she has survived some (usually sexual) trauma—women are not "naturally" strong (like men, who do not need such back stories), but can evolve to be so. Further, they are granted more cultural latitude with regard to gender hybridity, as there is less pressure for them to "prove" themselves (Kimmel 185). Carol, at first, fails to stand up to her abusive husband Ed (Adam Minarovich) when he threatens her on a riverbank, and the attempts of straw-feminist Andrea and the other women to verbally intervene lead nowhere—it isn't until Shane punches Ed that the incident ends. Carol's evolution is slow: we see the first signs of her resentment after Ed is killed by a walker and she must stab her husband in the head to prevent his undead rising—she violently and repeatedly drives a pickaxe into his skull (1.05, "Wildfire"). In season 2, she is the nurturing soul who brings loner Daryl into the group, and she is still primarily defined as a distraught mother as the group searches for her lost (and doomed) daughter Sophia. It isn't until season 4 that the changes in Carol are most noticeable: she adopts two young girls while lecturing them about the importance of strength (4.02, "Infected"), then subsequently has to kill the older girl, Lizzie, after Lizzie turns out to be a sociopath who murders her sister Mika (4.14, "The Grove"). Carol is a repeated failure as a mother: first, when she is too gentle to protect Sophia, and then when she is unable to save Lizzie or Mika despite her newfound survival skills. Her aggression also strains her relationship with the group after she kills two plague victims to keep them from infecting the colony (4.04, "Indifference"), and is subsequently exiled for much of season 4.

Still, Carol's growing gender hybridity is presented as a strength, though one in which masculinity is still privileged: her demure attitude and domestic skills are used as a cloak that allows her to appear unthreatening, masking a cutthroat nature still seen as the key to post-apocalyptic survival. Notably, however, despite the repeated suggestion that Carol is maternally flawed, her predilection for motherhood is also professed as the reason for her toughness:

> TOBIN: You can do things that just terrify me.
> CAROL: How? How do you think I do those things?
> TOBIN: You're a mom.
> CAROL: I was.
> TOBIN: You are. It's not the cookies or the smiles, it's the hard stuff. The scary stuff. It's how you can do it. It's strength. You're a mom to most of the people here [6.12, "Not Tomorrow Yet"].

Unlike Andrea, Carol is defined as a "mom" and her aggression is contained within an acceptable paradigm that allows for female protectiveness, particularly as long as feminine skills are maintained; in this fashion, she can be reincorporated as an accepted member of the group. This is typical of contemporary zombie films, in which

> many female main characters ... embody physical strength and emotional toughness in the heat of a zombie attack, while happily coupling in domestic tranquility after the threat has passed. This performance of both power and traditional femininity represents an ethos quite acceptable to contemporary ways of viewing women as capable and strong although still always essentially embodying feminine difference [Cady and Oates 322–23].

Further, Carol's murderous tendencies are a source of increasing angst for her: she keeps a journal guiltily detailing her victims (6.12, "Not Tomorrow Yet"), panics over her desire to avoid killing (6.13, "The Same Boat"), takes up smoking for her stress (6.12, "Not Tomorrow Yet"), and leaves the group voluntarily to avoid having to commit further violence to protect her friends (6.14, "Twice as Far").

Carol's breakdown in season 6 might be compared to Rick's in season 3, when after Lori's death, Rick turns over the governance of the group's then-sanctuary (an abandoned prison) to a voting council and instead tries to build a garden inside the prison walls. While season-six Carol stress-bakes cookies and casseroles, adopting a post-apocalyptic facsimile of a traditional housewife role, season-three Rick becomes a farmer—a role, like the cowboy, associated with American masculinity and endurance (Schlatter 85). Each adopts the gendered colonial role associated with survival in the American west. Both characters attempt pacifism, but Carol is haunted by the violence she has had to commit to save those she loves; Rick is tormented by visual and auditory hallucinations of people he has *failed* to save. Further, while Carol's breakdown comes after seasons of series-typical but escalating violent acts, Rick's occurs post-*hyper*violence, when he single-handedly clears the prison of zombies in his grief at Lori's death. Carol flees Alexandria, causing Rick and Morgan to go after her—Morgan must rescue her after she is injured. In contrast, Rick must voluntarily reclaim his leadership of the group in order to fight off The Governor, thus undermining his own attempts at establishing democracy and reinforcing the narrative link between survival and the white male Ricktatorship. The causes and expressions of Carol and Rick's breakdowns are both clearly gendered.

Morgan also adopts pacifism through much of season 6. Like Rick's crisis, Morgan's psychotic break is triggered by his failure to protect his son and wife; he is haunted by those he failed to save, as well as the unnecessary atrocities he committed in his grief after. However, his newly adopted pacifist philosophy comes with a mastery of martial arts and the bo staff; he becomes an accomplished fighter who remains calmly effective in battle despite his aversion to killing. In other words, he can choose not to kill because his martial skills have already assured his victory; only from a position of superior combat prowess is he free to make nonlethal choices. Like Rick, he maintains a masculine role, while Carol reverts to baking. Morgan also spends much of season 6 telling Carol how she feels and ignoring her requests to be left alone. While Rick must reclaim his gun and control of the group, Morgan must commit homicide once again in order to protect the wounded Carol. At this point, Carol's narrative arc has not concluded—she may or may not become resolved to violence again—but it seems clear that her struggles are particularly gendered and reflect a conflict between her feminine and masculine binary traits, while Rick and Morgan's temporary pacifist streaks are presented as manly.

The Walking Dead "has consistently raised the possibility of female empowerment only to decisively shut it down" (Simpson 35): plucky farm girl Maggie is humiliated and threatened with rape; Andrea is "symbolically exiled" and slaughtered (36); Carol's early steps toward independence are punished through the loss of Sophia (36); and Michonne's "phallic katana" is "often being seized from her by men" (37). Certainly, bad things happen to every character in the series, but particularly and immediately to those who contradict or defy Rick, and most particularly to female characters: "any boundary-crossing by women, the slightest move toward claiming male prerogatives, is typically punished by subsequent plot twists" (37). Greene and Meyer have proposed five categories for *The Walking Dead*'s regressive depictions of gender issues: "sexist rhetoric, division of labor, the role of protector, white male leadership, and the role of the dutiful wife" (67). A close examination of six seasons only upholds this analysis. While some gender divisions begin to break down post-season 3, this mainly reflects the idea that any women who survive so long (saving the residents of Alexandria) do so by becoming more masculine; the series echoes *White Zombie* and its derision for the soft, white-collar American male, as well as its attempts to contain women (Kordas 26–7).

Like most other post-apocalyptic series, then, *The Walking Dead* presents masculine traits as key to survival, while focusing on male characters as leaders and allowing gender hybridity only to a female character who evolves as a victim of trauma. The series primarily follows the narratives of white characters and is almost entirely heteronormative. It does add LGBTQ relationships in season 4 onward with secondary characters Tara and Aaron (Ross Marquand) and their respective same-sex love interests. These relationships are present but not central to the plot: both Tara and Aaron are recurring (rather than regular) characters. Tara's girlfriends tend to be (literally) short-lived and receive the occasional chaste kiss, while Aaron and his husband seldom share screen time; this comes in comparison to steamier scenes shared by Lori and Shane, Rick and Lori, Rick and Michonne, or Glenn and Maggie. Further, all characters are cisgender. *The Walking Dead*'s inclusion of queer figures is present, but minimal.

Summary

The Walking Dead exhibits a dying world where the apparent last of humanity struggles for basic food and shelter, the threat of death (via zombie or human monster) is imminent and constant, and aggressively masculine systems of leadership and governance are implicitly acknowledged as flawed but are still the only systems presented as options. There are many ways in which to interpret both zombies and *The Walking Dead*, but popular analysis of the series as a panicked, post–9/11 pro-police conservative security narrative proves valid (Pokornowski 52), as a series of false refuges and community structures demonstrate, one after another, the pitfalls of surrender, defensiveness, hyperfascist over-aggression, and the supposedly naïve democratic status quo. Additionally, Hassler-Forest has described *The Walking Dead* as enacting the death of the patriarchy: "its perpetual cycle of narrative play ... seems to stage the same fundamental dynamic over and over again, offering no alternatives, but also quite convinced that this kind of centre simply will not hold" (354). *The Walking Dead* both espouses proactive violence and portrays the breakdown of white masculine patriarchy through one failed refuge after another, as each community inevitably falls apart and Rick's struggling group of survivors becomes a mostly revolving cast of soon-to-be-corpses.

The Walking Dead also incorporates wild west imagery while corrupting the wild west narrative: so far, no one has ridden off into the sunset, and the good guys are increasingly indistinguishable from the bad. This challenges the western frontier myth and its associated stereotypes of white American male exceptionalism: Rick, no matter how much of a cowboy he may be, cannot prosper and cannot save those he loves. He only becomes more violent and more morally corrupt as he quixotically attempts to achieve safety and community as resolution in a story that, according to its creator Kirkman, is intended as a horror movie that never ends (Canavan 435). In light of Hassler-Forest's reading, though—in terms of *The Walking Dead* as a study of the last days of patriarchy, and multiple examples of failed communities and crumbling patriarchal structures—it seems telling that the series can envision the death of patriarchy but not the birth of any new, more successful social structures:

> What clearer metaphor could there be for the nagging American anxiety than that there is no better future waiting and that we ourselves are monsters or potential monsters? Against that kind of backdrop, Rick's journey to find his family and bring them to a safe harbor in a world gone mad represents an achingly poignant American desire to do the same: to retreat from the never-ending geopolitical perils of the post–9/11 world, to create a post-apocalyptic domestic utopia where one can feel secure once again [Simpson 38].

If post–9/11 apocalyptic stories may be seen as both metaphoric of the war on terror and as a straight white male reaction to twentieth-century cultural forces like feminism or the civil or LGBTQ rights movements (Nilges), then *The Walking Dead* is not the comforting "reset" button offered by more optimistic series like *Jericho* or *Falling Skies*, in which white men take the lead in rebuilding new frontier worlds that hark back to colonial notions of the American Dream. Rather, the series suggests, the only way to survive a dangerous world is for such bold white men to stop playing nice—and, even then, there are no guarantees.

Fear the Walking Dead

Even at first glance, *Fear the Walking Dead's* aesthetic appearance marks its intended difference: it is filmed using warmer color filters, with more yellow and orange than *The Walking Dead's* washed out grays and blues. *Fear the Walking Dead*, created by AMC as a spinoff for its most successful series, begins during the eight months when Rick Grimes was in a coma; it traces the downfall of American civilization that had already occurred when *The Walking Dead* began, and follows its protagonists through the beginnings of the zombie apocalypse and beyond. Its characters often still retain hope that authority will be restored and the world they know will return; this series traces the slow dissolution of that hope. *Fear the Walking Dead* reads on many levels as a response to criticisms of its parent property: it incorporates more non-white characters, contains more queer content and alternate family structures, and dispenses with the strictly segregated gender roles that particularly infused *The Walking Dead*'s first two seasons. The series had the potential to explore an alternate style of post-apocalyptic survival based on community and cooperation. However, it has instead morphed into a version of *The Walking Dead*, exploring a narrative in which its central characters grow to embrace masculine power, suspicion and violence.

Some of *Fear the Walking Dead*'s attributes are distinct. Though it ultimately treats with many of the same themes as the mother series—a descent into nihilism, the embrace of violence in order to survive, the protection of self and family above all other considerations—there are differences in *Fear the Walking Dead* that highlight the possibility of diversity in the post-apocalypse. While zombie narratives typically "reinforce the idea that the heteronormative nuclear family unit is the only safe solution when faced with a threat" (Cady and Oates 323)—and both series advance this theme—*Fear the Walking Dead*'s extended family connections, including interracial couples, a biracial child, divorce, and remarriage, situate the spinoff series as embracing more contemporary family structures than *The Walking Dead*'s endangered nuclear family unit. Unlike *The Walking Dead*'s primary focus on Rick Grimes, a white police officer, *Fear the Walking Dead* follows Travis Manawa (Cliff Curtis), an English literature professor who is non-violent. He is also non-white (played by an actor of Maori heritage) and not associated with the legal system or the military-industrial complex. Travis is married to Madison ("Maddie"; Kim Dickens) and is stepfather to her two teenage children, Nick (Frank Dillane) and Alicia (Alycia Debnam-Carey); he also has an ex-wife, Liza (Elizabeth Rodriguez), with whom he shares a son, Chris (Lorenzo Henrie). In *The Walking Dead*, the division in the Grimes family is both external (the strain of living in an undead hellscape) and domestic (as per Lori's affair with Shane), representing on multiple levels the threat posed to the white heterosexual family unit, particularly via the emasculation/cuckolding of the father. In *Fear the Walking Dead*, the divisions in Travis's extended family are more variant: Nick's battle with drug addiction, Chris's feelings of abandonment, and Alicia's resentment of her mother's unintentional neglect. Travis's relationship with Maddie is strong. This allows for more complex focus on family tensions.

Additionally, while the shadow of the *caudillo* looms over *The Walking*

Dead's broken cowboy mythology, *Fear the Walking Dead* evokes *la frontera*—a more historically inclusive version of the frontier that acknowledges Mexican and Black settlers, among others, as well as the complexities of culture and class differences (Limerick). The series frequently incorporates Spanish, including significant exchanges of Spanish dialogue (with English subtitles). This is particularly notable in the second season, when the survivor group flees the United States for Mexico. *The Walking Dead* is situated exclusively in the continental U.S. (particularly the environs surrounding Atlanta); *Fear the Walking Dead* ranges more widely. This both acknowledges the world outside the United States (which is, it turns out, just as ravaged by zombies as Georgia) and includes bilingualism as a post-apocalyptic skill. In *Fear the Walking Dead*, not all characters speak English, and in Mexico, monolingualism is a disadvantage; Nick, for example, must learn Spanish (2.11, "Pablo and Jessica"). *Fear the Walking Dead* relies much less on specific wild west imagery but also explores a wider post-apocalyptic landscape, crossing international borders and acknowledging settings and characters outside the continental U.S.

Initially, *Fear the Walking Dead*'s approach to race also appears far more inclusive. In addition to Travis, a Maori man, in the lead role, the series also includes Liza, a Latina woman; Daniel (Rubén Blades) and Ofelia (Mercedes Mason) Salazar, a Latinx father and daughter; and Victor Strand (Colman Domingo), a Black man who is half con artist, half multi-millionaire businessman. Strand, in particular, is a mentor to Nick and an early leader of the group; his is the yacht on which the family escapes a ravaged Los Angeles, and his former economic and social status pushes back against stereotypes—prominent in early seasons of *The Walking Dead*—that mark Black men as violent or working class. However, this is where the differences between *The Walking Dead* and *Fear the Walking Dead* begin to break down. The success of *Fear the Walking Dead*'s apparent attempts at inclusiveness is ambiguous from the outset: three Black men are the first major (named, speaking role) walker victims in the pilot episode, which seems a particularly tone-deaf development in light of *The Walking Dead*'s previously (and publicly) critiqued brutality toward a rotating roster of Black male characters. Liza fails to survive season 1. The series also consistently neglects Ofelia, who has few lines and leaves the group in Tijuana part way through season 2, only to have the narrative occasionally flash to her solitary trip toward the United States border. A scene where Ofelia crosses through the abandoned border fence seemingly highlights the futility of such nationalized dividing lines, as the desert stretches identically (and dangerously) on either side; the fact that she is soon captured by a militant white American man with a gun belies this imagery, as does the general neglect of her character throughout the series' run to date.

The series aspires to the same post-racial politics as *The Walking Dead*, and, like its predecessor, focuses on white narratives in the process. While Travis may be the lead character in season 1, the second season's focus begins to shift away as the family is separated; Travis and Chris split from the group and Nick strikes out on his own. This provides more leadership opportunity for Maddie but also allows for extensive narrative focus on Nick, shifting him to prominence as a white male lead.[3] Nick joins a Mexican *colonia* of survivors, where he begins as a captive but soon rises to prominence as a community leader. As Maddie supplants Mexican survivors to assume control of a Tijuana hotel, and Nick devises a plan to save his new community, their leadership roles inscribe white authority in an otherwise Latinx setting. Again, an overtly racist role is played by tertiary characters: Brandon (Kelly Blatz) and Derek (Kenny Wormald), Americans vacationing in Mexico when the zombie plague began. Brandon and Derek are quite comfortable cracking jokes about "Mexcrement" or "border bandits" (2.14, "Wrath"), and Maddie's disgust with this both establishes her own character as "not racist" and obscures the narrative trend that once again sees white people rise "naturally" to positions of power. Most tellingly in terms of the series' shifting attentions, Travis only lives for two seasons, meeting his undead fate in the season 3 premiere; while Rick Grimes has survived at least seven seasons on *The Walking Dead* and remained at the center of the series narrative, Travis's death clears the way for *Fear the Walking Dead* to most closely follow Maddie and Nick—returning white stories to prominence.

The series also repeats one of *The Walking Dead*'s major themes, as surviving humans become the true monsters of the zombie world, and violent aggression becomes the only route to survival. Travis is a pacifist who thinks the best of humankind and hopes for the return of the United States. He initially presents as a clear contrast to *The Walking Dead*'s Rick: he is a gentle, idealistic man whose primary motivation is fulfilling his role as a father—not just in terms of protecting Chris, or teaching him to fight, but in attempting to pass on a sense of empathy and a strong moral code. However, Travis's narratives in the first two seasons are repetitive: he begins horrified by the changes he sees in the world around him, but must become ruthless in order to survive. His morals are seemingly contrasted with Chris's more psychopathic tendencies, but like the contrast between Rick and Shane in *The Walking Dead*, the initial differences between Travis and Chris are challenged by Travis's evolution into a more violent man: he mercy-kills Liza at the end of season 1, then snaps and beats Chris's killers to death in an extended sequence in the penultimate episode of season 2 (2.14, "Wrath"). His love for his family motivates him, but he is narratively punished for his pacifism when he is repeatedly too late to save both Liza and Chris. By the end of season 2, he has declared the loss of his previous self, warning Maddie that he is no longer the man she knew. But she accepts this, as well as her own violent acts and their acceptability in this new world: "I know the world changed and made you this. Me, I've been like this a long time. I understand what you did. Why you did it. And I'll understand when you do it again, because you'll have to. We will have to" (2.15, "North"). In each season, Travis's arc finds him more violent; however, his initial reluctance means that he fails to protect both his ex-wife and his son, and subsequently dies a failed provider.

Maddie suggests a challenge to more standard gender binaries, but she primarily achieves power through masculine behavior and her success is inflected by whiteness. She is less empathetic than Travis and more pragmatic. She attempts to maintain a sense of morality—a frequent source of discussion between her and Travis—but is quicker to abandon previous principles. Her related propensity for leadership challenges some of the patriarchal structures of *The Walking Dead*, but though she assumes control of the Tijuana hotel, she does when there are no white men to compete with; Maddie leads a group that consists of Alicia, Strand, former hotel manager Elena (Karen Bethzabe), Elena's nephew Hector (Ramses Jimenez), former hotel guest and wedding groom Oscar (Andres Londono) and his family, and a crowd of Mexican refugees who swarm the hotel gates. Maddie then gives up her authority in order to stay with a returned Travis and look for Nick—abandoning power in favor of domestic responsibility and resuming her position as a wife and mother.

Other women also occupy positions of leadership and/or authority: former housekeeper Celia (Marlene Forté) leads the community at Strand's partner's compound, and Luciana (Danay Garcia) heads the scouting for another nearby colony. One gang of villainous pirates even includes a heavily pregnant woman (Veronica Diaz-Carranza) who fully participates in ship hijackings. Remaining characters are varied in their gender performance; in general, the men are masculine and the women are permitted more hybridity. Daniel, a former torturer, is pragmatic and violent. Ofelia is more feminine. Alicia is self-sufficient. Nick is self-destructive and subsequently fearless. Strand is both ruthless and charming. Chris is a budding sociopath. Again, this varies from *The Walking Dead* in that multiple women are shown occupying "masculine" roles early in *Fear the Walking Dead*'s run. However, this does not challenge the essential premise that masculine aggression is the key to survival in dangerous times. Compassion and empathy are not rewarded; when Alicia reveals the location of Strand's ship to what she thinks is a sympathetic fellow survivor, it only opens the group to pirate attack (2.04, "Blood in the Streets"). Ultimately, despite lip service characters may pay to making "good" choices, *Fear the Walking Dead* embraces the same nihilist survivalism as its parent series, and packages this in the same philosophy of necessary violence so often coded as masculine.

The series also lacks queer content, though it does feature Strand as the most prominent gay character in the *Walking Dead* television universe. Strand's masculinized, ruthless competence belies feminine stereotypes of gay men, establishing him as a powerful force in *Fear the Walking Dead*'s universe. However, his partner Thomas (Dougray Scott) almost immediately dies, leaving him without onscreen romance or sexual consummation. While the series may explore Maddie and Travis's marriage, or Nick and Luciana's budding sexual relationship, Strand remains single and chaste. This allows the series to present Strand as a powerful gay man whose gayness is seldom performed, obscuring its significance and downplaying its challenge to heteronormative structures.

Summary

Fear the Walking Dead is an ambiguous series, more inclusive than *The Walking Dead*—featuring more prominent non-white characters, a powerful gay man, women in leadership positions, extended lines of Spanish dialogue, and a setting partially outside of the United States. On the surface, *Fear the Walking Dead* tells a different story than its parent series—one in which the post-apocalyptic future has a place for more than heterosexual white men and those they lead and protect, and other types of community than those based on white patriarchal systems. However, its fatalist narratives are the same: only characters who shed conventional morality in favor of pragmatic and unflinching violence may survive, and even those characters are ultimately doomed in a world where the swarming undead (and humanity's most aggressive and amoral remnants) routinely destroy any hope of safe haven. More, the longer the series continues, the more its focus shifts to hegemonic norms and particularly the white family at its core—allowing, at least, more varied roles for white women, but increasingly reinscribing the status quo.

Z Nation

An ongoing but less commercially successful series than the *Walking Dead* programs, *Z Nation* embraces a campy B-horror aesthetic, showcasing an ever-increasing assortment of novelty zombies mutated by radiation or methamphetamines, or storming across the country in a massive "zunami" wave. Hybridity and contradiction are both key to the series: *Z Nation* simultaneously incorporates familiar reductive stereotypes and sexist, heteronormative constructions while also presenting a narrative that is fundamentally more hopeful and more radical than *The Walking Dead*'s. In *Z Nation*, the government experimentation that caused the zombie outbreak is more of a concern—emblematic of "the modern zombie ... as a critique of science" (Lauro 54)—but more importantly, the survivor group that is the focus of the series is trying to enact a cure. Unlike *The Walking Dead* and *Fear the Walking Dead*, where characters are just trying to survive as long as possible, *Z Nation* follows protagonists who are trying to save the world (or at least, as is the focus of most U.S. television, the continental United States). The series walks a fine line between radical change and conservative, predictable stereotype. While most other examples of post-apocalyptic television exhibit some hybridity (e.g., a blend of western and horror or science fiction tropes) and political or cultural ambiguity (*The Walking Dead* casts a swath of diverse characters but fails to treat them equally), *Z Nation* is consistently in conflict with itself, simultaneously radical and regressive.

Subverting Expectations

In early episodes, it appears that *Z Nation* will, predictably, concentrate on the travails of a heterosexual white man in the post-apocalypse. Charles Garnett (Tom Everett Scott), a Marine sergeant, leads a small survival community with his military partner, Roberta Warren (Kellita Smith), after zombies have risen and decimated the United States. Former federal prisoner Murphy (Keith Allan), an unwilling subject of medical experiments, is the only survivor of a zombie vaccine and now appears immune to infectious zombie bites, but the prison where he was captive was overrun and records were lost. Now Garnett and Warren must escort a still-unwilling Murphy across country from New York to a CDC lab in California. They are joined by former engineering student Addy (Anastasia Baranova), her boyfriend Mack (Michael Welch), elderly drug dealer Doc (Russell Hodgkinson), escaped sex trafficking victim Cassandra (Pisay Pao), and teenaged sniper Ten Thousand (or "10k") (Nat Zang). The group is intermittently monitored and helped by a single remaining member of the NSA, "Citizen Z" (D.J. Qualls), who broadcasts from a station in the Arctic.

At first, Garnett takes charge as the survivors embark on their road trip, and it seems as though *Z Nation* will follow a similar pattern to *The Walking Dead*: the group finds a place that appears to be safe refuge, a military base under the governance of Garnett's old comrade Major Williams (Roy Stanton). Of course, this promise of safety is false, and Williams is secretly the leader of a zombie-worshipping cult. In the process of escape, however, Garnett is killed—only six episodes into *Z Nation*'s run (1.06, "Resurrection Z"). This is moments after he has consummated a new romantic relationship with Warren. In a more standard progression of such a narrative, Warren would be the one killed as a development/plot point in Garnett's story, providing him with motivation and character growth; in *Z Nation*, the inverse is true, as Warren (a Black woman) must put the mercy bullet in Garnett's undead skull and then assume leadership of the remaining survivors. There is no *Walking Dead–like* ideological conflict between morality and pragmatism; rather, Warren retains her ideals and sense of purpose, escorting Murphy ever closer to California.

The series also embraces its share of western trappings—a bar fight in a saloon, for example, or Warren introduced with a guitar twang (1.07, "Welcome to the Fu-Bar")—and it's noticeable that while *The Walking Dead*'s most iconic cowboy imagery is focused on Rick, *Z Nation* reserves its western iconography primarily for Warren and Addy. It is influenced by a more contemporary hillbilly-style motif; the opening credits soundtrack features an electric guitar wailing over gun shots being fired through a highway sign. *Z Nation* offers a subversive take on class as well as, to limited extents, gender and race; its protagonists were not wealthy or influential before the zombie apocalypse, nor do they hold significant positions of power now. Charlie and Warren, as sergeants, were enlisted soldiers and not commissioned officers. Addy and Mack were postsecondary students, presumably privileged but with their educations and credentials incomplete. Doc was an addictions counselor. Murphy and Citizen Z were both federal prisoners (for fraud and hacking, respectively).[4] The series combines predominantly working-class heroes with a campy, back-country aesthetic that subverts common Western notions regarding traits that lead to heroism, leadership, and success in the patriarchy.

One Step Forward; Two Steps Back

But *Z Nation*'s ideologies are never well defined. The series is unique in this volume for featuring a Black woman in the leadership role; however, after Mack meets his own grisly fate at the beginning of the second season (2.02, "White Light"), the group is noticeably absent any white men of prime adult age who might otherwise assume command. Doc is elderly, 10k is young, and Murphy is established as both untrustworthy and increasingly alien (his makeup/skin color gradually changes to blue). Warren, as a soldier, assumes the prominent position, since her combat and tactical skills—her masculine skill set—give her an edge over men whose masculinity is otherwise compromised by age or medical condition. *Z Nation*'s casting also features a revolving assortment of non-white characters, including short-lived group members Cassandra (seasons 1–2), Vasquez (Matt Cedeño, season 2), and Hector (Emilio Rivera, season 3), before adding Kaya and Sun Mei (Ramona Young and Sydney Viengluang, seasons 3–).[5] Doc, Addy, 10k, and Murphy all survive to date, but by season 3, Warren is the only non-white original cast member remaining.

The series is still notable for its repeated inclusion of non-white women (Warren, Cassandra, Kaya, and Sun Mei) and women of at least marginally different body types (Warren and Addy in particular are more muscular and more sturdily built than women commonly seen as protagonists on American television). However, *Z Nation*'s ideological conflicts are also apparent when examining one of its most problematic characters: Cassandra exemplifies the ways in which *Z Nation* can be drastically more regressive than other post-apocalyptic programs. She first appears as a mysterious warrior, skilled in combat, who joins with the group in their mission to escort Murphy to California. It is later revealed that she is an escaped sex slave who was formerly used to lure unsuspecting victims to feed her cannibal captors (and presumably herself as well). In part, this reinforces the rape culture of the post-apocalypse, in which women's bodies are always under threat; in the first season, Cassandra also confronts the man who leads the twisted cannibal "family," reclaims her agency, and becomes a free woman. This development is undercut when Cassandra suffers a leg wound that goes septic, eventually killing her—but not before she is bitten by Murphy to prevent her from rising as a zombie. Murphy's bite instead turns Cassandra into a half-undead creature with limited speech ability and no free will; she essentially loses her newfound freedom, becoming Murphy's slave (1.13, "Doctor of the Dead"). He dresses her in a gold llamé bikini top and hot pants, knee-high white boots, and a white fur coat, an outfit that she wears for the remainder of her time on the series. This is apparently meant as a commentary on Murphy's lowbrow character (he describes Cassandra's new appearance as "classy lady" [2.01, "The Murphy"]) but has the effect of sexualizing Cassandra's body. Not only is her agency entirely lost, but she becomes increasingly animalistic in her behaviors, crouching on all fours and rubbing against Murphy. She obeys his every command. Her tight, revealing outfit, worn consistently across the first half of the second season, is one of *Z Nation*'s campiest examples of excess; the narrative context is all the more disturbing.

The series takes a similarly ill-defined tack in season 3 with the introduction of Kaya, an Inuit girl living in the Arctic with her aunt and uncle. Kaya rescues a hypothermic Citizen Z and he later takes her and her family back to the military station, where she assumes duty as co-host of his post-apocalyptic radio broadcast. Kaya's oft-demonstrated familiarity with pop culture and her immediate mastery of the NSA computer systems present her as worldly, knowledgeable, and hyper-competent. Conversely, in the early scenes that introduce her, she strips down to cuddle with a naked Citizen Z—presumably for "first aid" purposes. She is subsequently flirtatious, entering into a sexual relationship with Z and ending season 3 by declaring her pregnancy; moreover, she and her aunt are left behind in the station as Z and Uncle Kaskae (Cecil Cheeka) dramatically pilot a plane south to contact Warren and help save the group. What is apparently an attempt to push back against racial stereotypes is simultaneously undermined by gender tropes that place Kaya in a position as Z's ardent admirer—including making her jealous of Addy—and use her as a substitute in his previously-passive observational position, so that he can play the active hero. Further, Ramona Young, who plays Kaya, is of Chinese heritage, not Inuit ("Ramona Young"), suggesting white notions of a generic racial and ethnic Other; Kaya, too, thus serves as an example of *Z Nation*'s challenge to, and reinforcement of, hegemonic norms.

Still No Shelter

As in *The Walking Dead*, the protagonists of *Z Nation* move from one community to the next, though here they seek respite rather than permanent refuge. Other ways in which the two series' philosophies differ become apparent, though *Z Nation* remains ambiguous: it provides significantly more variance than *The Walking Dead*'s limited visions of single white male authority, while at the same time incorporating a swath of gender and racial stereotypes. A first-season all-female community, for example, serves as a straw exaggeration of second-wave feminism: male children are exiled at the age of 12, while men are used as passing sperm donors and forbidden from entering the encampment (upon pain of being fed to a zombie bear) (1.11, "Sisters of Mercy"). Likewise, a second-season episode featuring an Indigenous tribe on reservation land showcases a casino and a mistrustful, xenophobic leader—additionally sending white man Doc on a peyote-fuelled vision quest (2.10, "We Were Nowhere Near the Grand Canyon"). *Z Nation* also depicts Mexico as a green, prospering paradise now guarding its borders against unwanted American immigrants; the Mexican forces are led by a woman, La Reina de los Muertos (Gina Gershon), who is an intelligent and confident foe for Warren. But Gina Gershon is not Latina, and La Reina is a drug lord's widow who has expanded her dead husband's empire through a network of violent Hispanic drug runners; her iconography is clearly based on sugar skulls and other *dia de los muertos* imagery common to American visions of Mexican culture. These communities suffer a variety of fates: the all-female commune falls to zombie attack, the Indigenous tribe is still surviving when Warren's group leaves, and La Reina and her people are infected by Murphy. The context differs from *The Walking Dead*, where destruction is inevitable and no cure is in sight (or even in discussion); *Z Nation* offers more hope, and more communities that are not under the purview of white male leadership (or that do not, as in the case of Alexandria, exist purely through naïve luck). Each of these examples demonstrates *Z Nation*'s contradictory embrace of both alternative community types and lazy cultural stereotypes.

Hybrid Futures

The Walking Dead offers continued variations of a doomed patriarchy, but no better alternatives, and it maintains masculine/feminine binaries while consistently advancing masculinity as the key to post-apocalyptic survival. Conversely, *Z Nation* offers hints of gender hybridity that allow men to exhibit femininity as well as women to be masculine: Charlie is both an able soldier and good with small children; 10k is a lethal sniper but also a sensitive teenager; Doc is a former social counselor turned drug dealer and user. Masculine traits are necessary for survival but not necessarily privileged in the manner of other series; no one presents as a hypermasculine hero. Warren and Addy, both fierce and formidable in combat, are also still emotionally sensitive—Warren via her failed romance with Charlie and her guilt over the loss of her husband (e.g., 1.05, "Home Sweet Zombie"), Addy via her PTSD and stress over her new violent life. Addy's eventual psychological breakdown (1.09, "Die Zombie Die … Again") in another context might be seen as an example of inherent female weakness; in *Z Nation*, however, every character exhibits varying forms of compassion and/or emotional trauma. Admittedly, the series' transgressiveness on this level is limited; Burcar has noted that zombies, being "ungendered," "call for the destruction of the 'old order' by rethinking the ways post-industrial economies conceive of gender and sexuality" (98) and, further, erase heteronormativity by "reproducing" via bite instead of sexual intercourse. If so, while the subversiveness of gender performance is muted but notable, these themes do not—in this case—extend to the sexualities of human characters or to Murphy: *Z Nation* plays with the possibility of Addy's bisexuality (2.03, "Zombie Road"; 2.11, "Corporate Retreat") but is generally lacking in queer characters, and its zombies are forced (by Murphy) to perform strip teases and lesbian sexuality for Murphy's voyeuristic heterosexual pleasure (2.01, "The Murphy").

As well, *Z Nation*'s most radical narrative move is the suggestion of Murphy as the hybrid future. Like *Falling Skies*'s unsuccessful Lexi or more hopeful previous alien/human hybrids in series like *V*, *Invasion* (Takacs 10), or *Babylon 5* (PTEN, 1994–97; TNT, 1998), Murphy is neither human nor zombie. This makes him an innately subversive protagonist figure when "the conflation of difference and danger has been central to the formation and maintenance of 'American' identity" (Takacs 2). Though Murphy is human at the beginning of the series, his slow reaction to the zombie vaccine has him turning blue and craving brains. He is also able to command many of the undead, forcing them to do his bidding while also treating them more kindly than he does his human companions. Murphy's bite can also infect others, preventing them from rising as zombies but turning them (like Cassandra) into his puppets, though they retain limited abilities of thought and speech. The implicit question of the vaccine looms over the narrative: if a treatment *is* extracted from Murphy's blood, will it transform all human recipients the same way it has transformed him, creating a new race of thinking, living, autonomous zombies? Is the only way for humanity to survive to accept a vaccine that will fundamentally change the human race? So far, *Z Nation* has yet to present alternatives: either the undead win, or the world becomes populated by a new hybrid race of Murphys.

Murphy is the most prominent example of hybridity in the series, and his role is as ambiguous as his character; he is neither protagonist nor antagonist, or rather, he vacillates between the two roles depending on the episode. Murphy could be humanity's salvation or he could be its downfall—it is a frequent source of concern whether he identifies more with the group he travels with or the zombies they are fighting. *Z Nation* positions Murphy as the potential savior of the human race, but makes it clear he is no hero and he is not in charge. He begins the series powerless, strapped down on a table as scientists perform experiments on him; he is subsequently left for dead as the medical team flees and zombies chow down on his still-restrained body. He does not volunteer for the vaccine and he is not certain he wants to go to California, but he is given little choice. He continually waffles between trying to escape and helping his erstwhile allies survive. At the end of the first season, he causes a nuclear strike and flees the site, leaving the rest of the group to fend for themselves (which they do, somehow driving safely away from a radioactive missile explosion with seconds to spare—such are the series' B-movie roots). He roams the apocalyptic landscape wearing colorful tailored suits and hats, getting drunk and taking refuge in abandoned strip clubs (2.01, "The Murphy"). While he is a primary focus of the series, he is not the only focus, nor is he aggressively masculine. Rather, without any training or proclivity for physical self-defense, he must rely on the group for protection, or force zombie servants to fight for him. He is also empathetic: he is upset by zombies being abused or needlessly destroyed, and he will act or beg to protect them. *Z Nation*—and, by extension, Warren—can't decide if Murphy is friend or foe, and he often serves as comedy relief or at least camp exaggeration.

In season 3, *Z Nation* directly addresses the question of Murphy as hybrid future by having him attempt to found a community of people he has "saved." The people Murphy bites, however, are enslaved to his will; they gain safety at the cost of their personal autonomy. 10k, who is bitten by Murphy in the season premiere, spends the rest of the season arc attempting to rebel against Murphy's unwanted control, to the point of his own near death. This reasserts the primary threat of zombies: the destruction of identity (Feshami 91), and the reduction of the human condition to chemical and biological processes (Moreland). As 10k struggles to regain autonomy and Murphy begins to devolve into a brain-eating monster who abuses those he controls, it appears the hybrid future is untenable—save that Murphy's daughter Lucy (at various ages Tara Holt, Bea Corley, Madelyn Grace), half-human and half-zombie, is presented as a new potential source for a zombie cure. Lucy's unnatural development—a series of "growth spurts" that changes her from a young child to a teenager in the space of days—and blue skin highlight her non-human origins, while her curly blonde hair situates her as a classic "American" white girl, one who needs to be saved from The Man (Joseph Gatt) who is hunting her. Like her father, Lucy vacillates between potential monster, hybrid hope, and comedy relief; the series' end game remains unclear.

Summary

Of *The Walking Dead, Fear the Walking Dead,* and *Z Nation, Z Nation* comes the closest to embracing the disruptive potential of the zombie; it repeatedly plays with the notion of a hybrid zombie future. Through Murphy and Lucy, it also gives the zombies a voice; in one notable episode, scientists who were infected with the zombie virus are still conscious and able (through Murphy) to ask questions about loved ones and vocalize their desire to die (3.01, "No Mercy"). Through Murphy and his daughter, the lines between self and Other, living and dead, are blurred.

The series' more progressive elements are hampered, however. Its inclusive casting, most notably Warren in a leadership position, is undermined when non-white characters are cycled through while white characters endure. Cassandra's assertion of agency is undone by her subsequent sexualization and return to slavery. Kaya subverts racial stereotypes but assumes a typically gendered romantic role. The series flirts with alternative sexualities—specifically the suggestion of Addy as bisexual—but fails to explore them; a scripted same-sex sexual encounter for Addy was cut from episode 2.11 and limited to a kiss instead (Michaela). *Z Nation* is simultaneously subversive and regressive; its lack of ideological consistency offers a strong demonstration of the zombie's destabilizing influence.

Conclusion

We are living in a time of zombies:

Increasingly prevalent in popular culture, the zombie (at various points and places a tenet of spiritual belief, a folkloric bogeyman, a cinematic cash cow) has come to be legible as a global mythology and interpolated in society nearly as a symbol, a kind of icon of disempowerment that can be made to signify everything from distrust of the government to fears of terrorist attack and viral pandemic to suspicion of science or a critique of consumerism [Lauro 9].

Within such infested dystopias, Canavan has theorized that the most radical move a zombie series could make would be to let the zombies win and allow the human race to die out, leaving a world populated only by the shambling dead (450). If zombies are essentially destabilizing figures, then *The Walking Dead*, *Fear the Walking Dead*, and *Z Nation* show how such destabilization may work to different ends. *The Walking Dead* perpetuates regressive tropes from both horror and western genres in order to advance a narrative wherein white men are leaders and protectors even in a world that is crumbling around them; they may not live long (and, the series suggests, probably won't), but no alternative forms of community can either, and the only security and survival tactics that work are aggressive, amoral and masculine. *Fear the Walking Dead* attempts to diversify series casting but seemingly inevitably still privileges white leadership within the same crumbling universe. *Z Nation* adapts similar themes, drawing from both westerns and camp horror (as well as, likely, *The Walking Dead*), but presents a more ambiguous world in which a Black woman occupies the leadership position and a half-human, half-zombie hybrid might present the best hope for the preservation (and the annihilation) of the human race. Both franchises challenge the stereotypes of the western genre and the hero arc of the white male American cowboy; both are limited in their subversiveness, *The Walking Dead* and *Fear the Walking Dead* by regressive race and gender roles and an inability to envision non-hegemonic societal structures, and *Z Nation* by sexist imagery and an overall casting skewed toward white male characters. In each case, the resurgence of the zombie as a monstrous figure can serve as a metaphor for a variety of cultural anxieties, particularly in post–9/11 America; the question is whether we can envision a future at all.

— 5 —

Parody and
the Post-Apocalypse

IN THE BEGINNINGS OF THE TWENTY-FIRST CENTURY, the rise of apocalyptic
and post-apocalyptic comedy has been notable on screen—in film, *Shaun of
the Dead* (2004), *Fido* (2006), or *This Is the End* (2013), or on television pre-
apocalyptic series *You, Me and the Apocalypse* (Sky, 2015; NBC, 2016) and *No
Tomorrow* (The CW, 2016), alien invasion political satire *BrainDead* (CBS,
2016), the early-outbreak-set *iZombie* (The CW, 2015–), and the post-
apocalyptic *The Last Man on Earth* (Fox, 2015–). It's uncertain what this
means for the longevity of the post-apocalypse in its current forms. Cawelti
has argued,

> One can almost make out a life cycle characteristic of genres as they move from an ini-
> tial period of articulation and discovery, through a phase of conscious self-awareness
> on the part of both creators and audiences, to a time when the generic patterns have
> become so well-known that people become tired of their predictability. It is at this
> point that parodic and satiric treatments proliferate and new genres gradually arise
> [cited in Turner 219].

Parodies may mark the inevitable decay of a popular genre. Few new post-
apocalyptic television series seem to be in the works; news has petered regarding the previously-rumored CW zombie series *Awakening* (Crider), and the
pre-apocalyptic *Salvation* (CBS, 2017–) appears to have debuted its impending asteroid threat within a television landscape where new productions have
moved elsewhere for inspiration.

But parodies may also help revitalize a flagging genre (Turner 220, citing
Harries); "zomedies" (Bishop 41) like *Shaun of the Dead*, *Fido*, or *Zombieland*
(2009) were hardly harbingers of doom, either for post-apocalyptic dramas
or for zombie narratives. Later filmic entries such as *The World's End* (2013)
and *This Is the End* have likewise added to a cultural comedic library without

calling an end to more "serious" entries. Such productions may be the surest signs of the apocalypse genre's ongoing ubiquity. The 2017 television season included multiple returning apocalyptic series—again, *Z Nation* and *iZombie*, as well as *The 100*, *The Last Ship*, and final seasons of *The Leftovers*, *The Strain*, and *Zoo*. Despite the first signs of struggling ratings (Otterson), the Walking Dead franchise (including *Fear the Walking Dead*) lumbers on. It remains to be seen, therefore, whether *The Last Man on Earth* is an inevitable but productive symptom of the glut in post-apocalyptic television or a herald of the genre's imminent fall from televised grace. Regardless, the series' very existence highlights the pervasiveness of post-apocalyptic genre conventions.

The Last Man on Earth

If parodies cannot happen until people are familiar with the standard trappings of the genre (Turner 220), then not all comedies are parodies, but *The Last Man on Earth* functions as both. On a comedic level, *The Last Man on Earth* adopts an uncomfortable style that would be familiar to fans of contemporary series like *The Office* (BBC, 2001–03; NBC, 2005–13), in which the audience follows a terrifyingly inept man as he unwittingly negotiates his existence among a group of eccentric but generally more capable peers. The series' parodic elements are seldom, if ever, explicitly acknowledged; however, an evaluation illustrates multiple ways in which it skewers many of the same tropes demonstrated by other recent programs.

Enough Space for Everyone

While many post-apocalyptic plot lines involve a violent struggle for dwindling supplies, *The Last Man on Earth* immediately subverts this expectation by presenting one man alone in a world of riches. The pilot episode's opening scenes depict Phil "Tandy" Miller (Will Forte) driving across the continental United States, crossing off one state after another as he futilely hunts for other survivors. This post-apocalyptic world is empty and peaceful—unimaginably so, as the pandemic that has destroyed the world's population has apparently also left the rest of society's infrastructure untouched. There are no looted grocery stores or burned-out hospitals; indeed, there are no bodies throughout the first season. Tandy doesn't need to become vigilant, violent, or ruthless; he has more restaurants, shops, and pharmacies at his disposal than any person would ever need. He amasses a private collection of formerly priceless artwork, moves into a convenient mansion, and fills a wading pool with margarita mix he can both bathe in and drink from. Tandy's ridiculous excesses also illustrate his utter lack of danger; his main challenge is a desire for human connection. He creates a collection of sports balls with faces drawn on them (a nod to the 2000 film *Castaway*) and flirts with a window display mannequin. After two years alone, he begins attempting suicide just before discovering that his lonely "Alive in Tucson" graffiti, left on billboards across the States, has brought in Carol (Kristen Schaal), the first of a handful of other survivors. The arrival of another survivor gives Tandy a reason to keep living; as more people trickle into Tucson, forming a small community of strangers, their petty interpersonal conflicts form *The Last Man on Earth*'s comedy setups while simultaneously presenting a post-apocalypse where cooperation and empathy—rather than military experience, ruthlessness, or firepower—are paramount attributes for success.

Breaking Character Molds

Each of the characters in *The Last Man on Earth* implicitly challenges the post-apocalyptic genre—and, specifically, recent post-apocalyptic television—by failing to follow the basic tropes and narratives that would normally be assigned to them. This includes issues of gender and race. Tandy, though he is the titular protagonist, is selfish, dishonest, narcissistic, and manipulative, and most of the series' humor arises from his attempts to ingratiate and aggrandize himself to his fellow survivors. In a more typical American series, the only white male in the cast—as, in the first season, Tandy notably is— might be expected to rise to a leadership position, based perhaps on his "natural" talents but also his prior experience as a soldier, police officer, or government agent. Instead, Tandy is a former office temp whose "swimming pool toilet" alienates others in the group and whose petty attempts to denigrate other men and sleep with as many women as possible keep him consistently lowest in Tucson social standings. The supposed hero utterly fails at establishing his leadership or even helping other members of his group. The series consistently challenges notions of what it means to be a successful human being in the post-apocalypse; Tandy is routinely shown up by more considerate, thoughtful characters, as each new arrival adds new strengths and, by doing so, highlights Tandy's many weaknesses.

Carol's initial arrival subverts a genre convention in which strangers are to be mistrusted at best and attacked at worst; Tandy and Carol are not competing for resources or looking to rob or assault each other, but are only relieved to have discovered another human person. Their initial conflict is that each finds the other annoying, even though Tandy is hoping for sex and Carol also decides that they are (scientifically improbably) responsible for repopulating the human race. Though they are the series' primary couple, there is no dramatic will they/won't they tension, as Tandy and Carol are married in the third episode (1.03, "Raisin Balls and Wedding Bells"), and as they can barely tolerate each other. Carol is also positioned counter to narratives about women's helplessness; she does not look to Tandy to save or reassure her, but only expects him to be a working partner (and clean out his toilet pool). While her insistence on a wedding and her fixation on cohabitation are gendered—the woman dragging the reluctant man to the altar, nagging for a commitment he isn't prepared to make—she is also shown as more intelligent, loyal, and adaptable than Tandy. Likewise, while she is slender and white, she is presented as sexually less appealing than other women in the series, adopting a shorter hairstyle, dowdier dress, and a nasal voice, with an added proclivity for "dirty" talk using camping analogies. Carol is a terrible cook (her specialty, "raisin balls") but an accomplished knitter; she walks a fine line in terms of gender depiction but importantly challenges genre notions of the post-apocalypse harboring ideal opportunities for heterosexual romance, or the female lead requiring guidance and protection. While the two maintain a core of affection in their relationship, it is continually marred by interpersonal conflict.

Melissa (January Jones)—slender, conventionally attractive, white and blonde—is the immediate target of Tandy's lust, and early episodes focus on his machinations as he attempts to convince Melissa and Carol that repopulating the Earth requires him to have sex with them both. Melissa, however, has no romantic interest in Tandy; her rejection curtails his would-be status as a sexually desirable lead. Though her character initially serves primarily as a foil for Tandy's thwarted attempts at sexual conquest—an admittedly limited role—it is also clear that her interests and aspirations lie elsewhere; she would rather be friends with Carol.

The third arrival, Todd (Mel Rodriguez), is friendly and emotionally open; while he might perish almost immediately on a violent series like *The Walking Dead*, here his cooperative nature is a strength, as is his knowledge of dairy farming. Todd's presence is subversive because he is large (a rare trait in post-apocalyptic television characters) and gentle, and because his inherent amiability makes him a better fit for life with the Tucson group. Todd demonstrates strength in the form of friendliness, generosity, kindness and trust, consistently thinking the best of Tandy even after Tandy shames his weight (1.06, "Some Friggin' Fat Dude") and almost abandons him in the desert (1.07, "She Drives Me Crazy"). The fact that Todd is large also subverts cultural notions about fat men being lazy, unintelligent, or unattractive, as well as the implicit genre assumption that only hard bodies survive in a hard world. Todd is both capable and attractive; he becomes a love interest for Melissa. He is a successful competitor who does not realize that he *is* competing; rather, he just goes about his pleasant life while Tandy stews in frustration, illustrating Tandy's pettiest characteristics and also casting Tandy's multiple personal and practical inferiorities into sharp relief (Todd, after all, isn't even trying).

Tandy's initial relationship with Carol is a conflict between equals; his relationships to Melissa and Todd establish him as subordinate within the group dynamic as he fails to impress Melissa and is less socially and sexually successful than Todd. Though he attempts to establish his authority as President of the United States (as voted by him and Carol), Tandy fails to achieve leadership within a group that governs by campfire consensus, and his attempts to woo Melissa and/or exile Todd constitute comedic flailing.

The core group is completed with two new women, Gail (Mary Steenburgen) and Erica (Cleopatra Coleman)—both of whom, like Carol and Melissa, have survived quite nicely in the post-apocalypse without needing male protection. Again, both are sexualized by Tandy's lascivious desires, and both reject his advances after realizing he has lied to them about his "dead" wife. Gail is particularly notable as an older woman whose cooking skills, while stereotypically gendered, are credited to her background as a professional chef; moreover, she is fashionable, cantankerous, hard-drinking, and occasionally drug-seeking. She actively resists Carol's attempts to remake her into a nurturing mother surrogate. She is also sexually active, with multiple partners (including, again, Todd). Women over the age of 50[1] are already scarce in post-apocalyptic television; some of the most prominent examples are housewives and mothers (Gail Green in *Jericho* or *The Walking Dead*'s Carol). Gail additionally escapes the threat of "reversed stereotyping" (Kubey, cited in Vernon, Williams, Phillips, and Wilson 58), in which a character is the exact reverse of an expected archetype. Her behaviors are not cartoonishly exaggerated; her flinty, independent character provides an alternative model for older women at the end of the world.

Finally, Tandy's sense of self-worth is most directly threatened by the subsequent appearance of Phil (Boris Kodjoe), whose name is also Phil Miller, and who most clearly represents traditional masculinity. Phil is a former soldier (1.11, "Moved to Tampa"); he is muscular and handsome. Tandy—who has been known as "Phil" up to this point—almost immediately loses his identity to the new Phil, as the other survivors begin addressing him by his middle name, "Tandy," to avoid confusion. Phil is immediately attracted to Carol and begins a romantic relationship after she divorces Tandy—and, of course, just as Tandy decides he wants Carol back. Phil fixes Carol's broken door (which Tandy has been promising to do for almost the entire length of the season) and "runs" against Tandy for President of the United States (winning the title handily via group election).

In another series, Phil might embody the idea of the soldier whose skill with tactics, combat, and ruthless action will save survivors adrift in a hostile world. However, there is no need for combat in an empty city; instead, Phil uses his knowledge to rig up electrical power, engage in door carpentry, and drive a big truck. This combines with Todd's farming and dairy knowledge to highlight the necessity of non-combat skills in the post-apocalypse; in *The Last Man on Earth*, those who can grow food and engineer are the ones who survive. Phil's presumed tactical or fighting abilities are not required; further, though his knowledge of electrical equipment makes him a useful member of the group, his military training does not make him an ideal romantic partner, as the ruthless lack of forgiveness or empathy he shows Tandy ultimately leads to the demise of his relationship with Carol. He is also unable to defend himself against the appendicitis that causes his death in season 2; his combat abilities are of no use when his primary enemy is a basic medical ailment. Phil provides a superior model of "manhood" to Tandy, but does not represent any model of ultimate survivor.

These initial characters set the pattern for much of the series, in which Tandy—the ostensible lead—is repeatedly undermined by his own self-absorbed incompetence while others prove to be more emotionally available, more technically capable, better organized and generally better equipped to build a new community. Todd, Phil, and Gail in particular push back against stereotypes—of large men as undesirable or lazy, of military men as the key to post-apocalyptic survival, and of older women as desexualized mother figures.

The (Almost) Last Straight White Man

Tandy is generally the only white man in the group—Todd is Latino[2] while Phil is Black—and though he is occasionally joined by other white men (Will Ferrell, Jason Sudeikis, or Mark Boone, Jr.), they are not permanent additions to the cast. Non-white characters Erica and (in season 3) Lewis (Kenneth Choi) and Jasper (Keith L. Williams) also help to ensure *The Last Man on Earth*'s future is diverse. Markedly, however, it is not post-racial. An early exchange between Tandy, Gail, and Erica establishes that the world of *The Last Man on Earth* is not one in which previous racial and social differences are cast aside in the name of survival:

> TANDY: Hot older lady, Black girl. Yes, please! Don't mind if I do.
>
> GAIL: Older lady?
>
> ERICA: Glad my skin color matched up to your bucket list [1.09, "The Do-Over"].

Gail and Erica take immediate offense to Tandy's remark—and its attendant racism, ageism, and sexism—which immediately undermines the notion of a post-apocalyptic struggle in which tensions surrounding race and gender no longer exist. Instead, characters are aware of the lingering context of social inequality, and are in no way willing to subsume their previous identities in service to white leadership or the support of the only white male character. *The Last Man on Earth*'s establishment and maintenance of social tension, though subtle, might constitute its most subversive challenge to the post-apocalyptic television trope of the white male savior.

Almost every character (with the exception of Mark Boone, Jr., as Pat) is more even-minded, popular, and adept than Tandy; Tandy is not the future. It seems particularly marked that Phil, a Black man, not only claims Tandy's name but also fathers—with Erica—the first child of the apocalypse, a baby girl named Dawn. Further, the child Jasper, who joins the group in season 3, is a young Black boy who resists Tandy's attempts to adopt him, and instead also gravitates toward Erica (3.14, "Point Person Knows Best"). Carol, at this point, is also pregnant; however, Carol and Tandy's child will be the third in the group, not the first hope of a new age.

The series also includes queer characters. Lewis, as a gay man, endures Tandy's attendant social cluelessness: "I was pumped when you were just Asian. But a gay Asian? That checks off two boxes for us" (3.04, "Five Hoda Kotbs"). Tandy's shock at Lewis's sexual orientation and his subsequent assumptions that Lewis is attracted to him are contrasted with the rest of the group's matter-of-fact acceptance of Lewis, and Lewis's own calm protestations in the face of Tandy's assertions. Though Lewis's partner Mark never appears (and, presumably, died in the plague), and Lewis is not romantically or sexually active during his time onscreen, *The Last Man on Earth* also incorporates a romantic partnership between Gail and Erica, both of whom are established as bisexual at the end of season 3. As this is the same episode in which Todd and Melissa are married (3.16, "The Big Day"), *The Last Man on Earth* acts to preserve heterosexual tradition only within a wider context that acknowledges queer relationships and alternate modes of community and family.

The Last Man on Earth's comedy is situated in following Tandy, a man of great ambition and little brain, as he repeatedly strives and fails to become the great leader he perceives himself to be. Its parody, arguably, is situated in the same circumstance: a future in which the only heterosexual white man in a community is consistently its least tolerated, least respected member. His gender, race, and sexuality avail him no privilege—and, further, the other characters are well aware of, and unwilling to tolerate, his microaggressions. *The Last Man on Earth* seldom draws attention to these details, incorporating them as quick jokes or glancing references at most; however, this is how the series most directly challenges genre tropes.

Same Old Stories

There are limits to this analysis. A series that implicitly criticizes the archetype of the white male hero cannot fully realize such criticism while simultaneously following the adventures of a white male lead, flawed though he may be. In one example, the last few episodes of the first season—in which Phil appears, woos Carol, and ultimately loses her to Tandy before Carol and Tandy leave Tucson to strike off on their own—both reinforce and complicate readings of *The Last Man on Earth* as a subversive text. Phil's relationship with Carol might be taken as a tweak of long-standing cultural fears regarding Black men "stealing" white women (e.g., Sharp *Savage* 97), but Carol's final acceptance of Tandy reinstates the heterosexual white man's primacy in the narrative. Despite Tandy's multitude of personal failings and his repeated neglect of Carol, he gets the girl in the end. *The Last Man on Earth* flirts repeatedly with Tandy as a disreputable human being who serves only as a detriment to the small community of survivors gathered in Tucson, but the first season finale reassures viewers that Tandy is a good guy after all, one who will still come out ahead. This threatens to undo the subversiveness inherent in much of the series—which, though it repeatedly denigrates its white male lead, still does concentrate on the narrative of the white man in the end times. His is the point of view that drives the story. According to Forte (who is the series creator and executive producer), Tandy's character is as disposable as any other in a narrative where anyone could die (Ausiello); unless this happens, however, a shift in *The Last Man on Earth*'s focus seems highly unlikely.

Conclusion

    The Last Man on Earth challenges genre conventions by presenting an empty world in which a small group of survivors possesses an overabundance of resources, and in which the most important traits for social success are cooperation, diplomacy, generosity, and kindness. In post-apocalyptic Tucson, the greatest challenge the titular "last man on Earth" faces is crushing loneliness, and the most impressive skills include the ability to milk a cow, hook up a solar panel array, and bake a pie. While much of the series' comedy involves the *schadenfreude* of watching Tandy's many failed exploits, its narratives and setting are also notable for their rejection of standard post-apocalyptic tropes. *The Last Man on Earth* features a survivor group in which the white male lead is outnumbered not only by people of color but also by a majority of women. It features a community in which the most effective skills are not violent, aggressive, or martial, but instead associated with the production of food and electricity; when a military character appears, he is embraced for his engineering skills but rejected for his ruthlessness. While the series' corpse-free setting avoids the "gritty" aspects of the world after the virus, allowing for the use of the premise as a sitcom, it also allows for a narrative in which characters act in ways entirely opposite to the genre norm.

The Last Man on Earth reads as more a comedy set in the post-apocalypse than a consistent or deliberate takedown of post-apocalyptic convention; nevertheless, in injecting levity into a dire scenario and in repeatedly differing from the genre norm, it also lampshades a variety of familiar tropes. A wider selection of contemporary television parody might reveal more; series like *You, Me, and the Apocalypse* or *No Tomorrow*, which take place before the cataclysmic event, fall outside the purview of this analysis. Still, parody has potential for exposing the repetitive nature of the genre and, in turn, provoking a revitalization of ideas. While its continued focus on a heterosexual white male lead compromises some of its subversive potential, *The Last Man on Earth* could also help spark change—if it doesn't herald the impending demise of an overplayed premise.

— 6 —

After the Fall:
The Post-Post-Apocalypse

MOST POST-APOCALYPTIC SERIES TAKE PLACE within living memory of the catastrophic event, featuring characters who remember existence before the pandemic, the nuclear blast, the invasion, or the rise of the undead. But some are set farther in the future, with protagonists who neither know nor particularly care how the world ended; such characters are not scrabbling to form new societies from blasted rubble, but instead already living in a normalized aftermath. *Into the Badlands* (AMC, 2015–), *The 100* (The CW, 2014–), and *Wayward Pines* (Fox, 2015–16) are three examples; others might include MTV's *The Shannara Chronicles* (2016–17) or films like *After Earth* (2013). Such future settings might potentially allow series and the fictional worlds they present to further divest themselves of old myths, cultural tropes, and patriarchal structures—providing more fertile ground for diverse characters and explorations of non-masculine, non-white, queer-friendly narratives. A cursory glance at either *Into the Badlands* or *The 100* distinguishes these series from the norm; *Into the Badlands* stars Sunny (Daniel Wu), an Asian male hero, and the protagonist of *The 100* is teenaged Clarke (Eliza Taylor), a bisexual white woman. However, the constraints of twenty-first-century writing, ratings, and network decisions still apply, and each series is also limited in its inclusiveness. *Into the Badlands* repeatedly incorporates Southern Antebellum imagery that insists on post-racial politics while simultaneously evoking slavery and the conflicts of white masters; meanwhile, *The 100* is hampered by a myopic focus on white women, and season-three choices that create a focus on militarized male narratives while perpetuating stereotypes about dead queer characters. Further, an examination of *Wayward Pines* reveals a straight white male law-enforcement hero in a far-future town that entirely preserves the stereotypical American status quo. The post-post-apocalypse demonstrates variety but fails to fully break free of genre constrictions.

Into the Badlands

With the exception of occasional supporting characters, such as Glenn in *The Walking Dead*, it is rare to see an Asian actor heavily featured in a post-apocalyptic series (or, arguably, other genres of contemporary television). This immediately marks *Into the Badlands* as unusual: protagonist Sunny first appears on a motorcycle, riding alone through open fields, on a mission to retrieve stolen cargo: teenage boy M.K. (Aramis Knight). Sunny both rescues and captures M.K., taking him to a sprawling mansion at the center of vast poppy fields. Sunny is in service to Quinn (Marton Csokas), one of six local "Barons," who controls the plantation and the region. *Into the Badlands* is a narrative of escaping slaves, as Sunny gradually comes to realize the limits of his position and the corruption of his lord. However, though the series features a diverse cast, it ultimately presents a blend of martial arts "wire-fu" and Southern slave imagery that distances its narratives from any examination of racial conflicts. Instead, it uses racially charged images as fantasy trappings in an ostensibly post-racial world. Further, *Into the Badlands'* strict gender binaries reinforce a future in which hypermasculine behaviors once again dictate political, social, and physical dominance. The series offers a glimpse of a post-post-apocalyptic future that promises difference but also adheres to many aspects of a standard genre template.

Race and the Post-Racial

Into the Badlands consistently suggests a post-racial future, incorporating a diverse cast while simultaneously relying on racialized stereotypes, images and settings. This is evident through both the series' reliance on martial arts action, and through its frequent use of slave images and references to the American south.

Into the Badlands has been marketed as AMC's attempt to bring Hong Kong action cinema to North American televisions. The series includes multiple showpiece martial arts action sequences, as well as Chinese-style costuming and props; *Into the Badlands'* creation relies on Hong Kong action experts, including Wu as an executive producer, as well as martial-arts coordinator Huan-Chiu Ku (L. Miller). Wu has stated in interviews that he sees *Into the Badlands* as breaking down stereotypes regarding Asian male leads—presenting Sunny as a romantic, sexually active hero who speaks with an American accent (Yang). This leads to complex readings: while effeminacy has indeed historically been one stereotype associated with Asian men in Hollywood, assumptions of martial arts prowess and the shadow of the "kung fu master" have also limited actors' roles (Ho 64). Here, *Into the Badlands* suggests Sunny's skills as separate from his race; the series ascribes martial arts abilities to most characters. Sunny learned from Waldo (Stephen Lang), who is white, and he fights primarily against white opponents. However, Sunny's distinction as the best of the best continually reinforces kung fu master archetypes, even as his diction and his sexual virility subvert Western television constrictions. The series is simultaneously progressive and conservative in its depiction of a male Asian action lead.

Into the Badlands is more regressive in its repeated invocation of slave imagery and (particularly in the first season) the pre–Civil War American south, as it shies away from any links to racial identity or Black American history. The series is set in the remains of the United States, hinted at by scattered clues such as a decorative model of the White House, an old copy of *Wired* magazine, and battered subway signs in English. In this dystopian remnant, people known as "cogs" are a slave population in thrall to the Barons, but the series resists interrogating the racial implications of this setup. Many of the cogs are white—immediately divorcing *Into the Badlands* from any direct discussion of Black slavery. Equally notably, the trader who ships them—the "River King" (Lance E. Nichols)—is Black. This might position the series setting as a direct inversion of American slave history, except for another prominent detail: Quinn and his family are white. There might then be a case to be made for *Into the Badlands* as an escape narrative that follows non-white Sunny and his compatriots in their struggle to flee white patriarchy, as embodied by Baron Quinn and his family. Instead, *Into the Badlands* becomes, again, confusingly post-racial: a narrative about predominantly white slaves sold by a Black merchant to a white overlord, further complicated by the presence of non-white characters Sunny, M.K., and Veil (Madeleine Mantock)—all of whom are also controlled by the Baron, but whose differing ethnicities are never acknowledged. The elements of *Into the Badlands* that most directly evoke the historic American south—the sprawling fields harvested by pickers, the elegant plantation house, the neo-colonial costuming of antiquated suits and wide-skirted gowns, even the Baron's Southern drawl—thus become set dressing in a story of Sunny and M.K.'s quest for freedom that fails to address wider questions of racial oppression or include the cogs as anything more than background detail. Quinn and his family may be white, but it is never suggested that their race is related to their dominance; a rival Baron, Jacobee (Edi Gathegi), is Black, as though to deflect any such arguments.[1] Rather, authority in *Into the Badlands* is held through aggression and martial supremacy, which situates it within similar narratives of masculine conflict and limits its capacity for subversiveness. These patterns are reinforced by stereotypical gender roles.

Gender in the Badlands

Into the Badlands offers standard divisions of male and female behavior and power. Among the men, Sunny has risen to prominence as the Baron's pre-eminent enforcer, responsible for training new youth as well as acting as bodyguard, controlling plantation security, and carrying out the Baron's more violent requests. Like other masculine heroes, Sunny is skilled in combat; here, his masculinity is expressed through his martial arts mastery rather than military jargon. He is stoic and independent; his back is covered with tattoos that mark his extensive number of kills. While he has spent his adolescence and adult life serving Quinn, he is only motivated to leave when he must protect his partner and his child—and, subsequently, only motivated to return when he is separated from them.

M.K., Sunny's rescue-turned-protégé, must likewise learn to excel in combat and does so by navigating the conflicts of the Baron's trainees as he learns to survive through cunning and ferocity. His position among the Baron's soldiers reinforces the fact that the Baron's men are, in fact, all men (or boys); there is no place for women in these fighting groups. Further, M.K.'s major challenge is learning to master the hyperviolence within him, as the release of his own blood (for example, a cut on his arm) causes him to enter a murderous fugue state during which he becomes a remorseless killing machine. He is *too* masculine; while Sunny, older and wiser, exhibits self-control and nigh-perfect bodily mastery, M.K. is an adolescent killer who must control his violent tendencies in order to become a man. In the first season, his supernatural abilities act as a metaphor for male adolescence and cultural concepts of innate male violence. In the second, M.K.'s status as a "Dark One" is shared with others both male and female, and he trains under the auspices of a female Master (Chipo Chung), though this does little to challenge *Into the Badlands*'s binary separation of hard and soft spheres. M.K. professes his relief at being free of the hyperaggressive "Gift," but retains his role as Sunny's protégé and continues to act as a martial arts warrior. The series implies both that M.K.'s powers may return, and that in their absence, he has become a more mature character. In this way, it continues to privilege masculinity within limits: martial ability but not hyperaggression; controlled power, used to protect the weak.

Conversely, Quinn and his son Ryder (Oliver Stark) both exemplify the excesses of male privilege (here also coded as wealth/class); they exhibit contempt for life and particularly the lives of the cogs who serve them. Quinn struggles for dominance over both his family and his physical territory, and Ryder's bid for power is exemplified by their shared lust for Quinn's soon-to-be second wife Jade (Sarah Bolger). As Quinn's health fails him, Ryder attempts a coup; this Oedipal narrative provides the primary character motivations for father and son, an image of competing masculinities wherein Quinn must struggle to hold his political power without the physical strength (either his own, or by proxy, Sunny's) to back it up. Ryder is consistently portrayed as weaker than Quinn; he is not a skilled fighter and runs from combat (2.04, "Palm of the Iron Fox"). Though he does briefly become Baron, his reign is short-lived. His failure to follow through on killing Quinn means that he is slaughtered by his father in turn. Both Quinn and Ryder serve as studies in excess, exhibiting power that is corrupted by politics, character weakness, and selfish ambition; as Ryder fails to seize the position of strength, and Quinn fails to use his power for anything other than domination and personal gain, both must be vanquished—they demonstrate a masculinized lack of control, arguably the same murderous excesses that the more heroic M.K. manages to overcome.

Women's roles are also visibly defined by gender stereotypes. While Quinn and Ryder struggle for power both against each other, against Sunny, and within a wider conflict between other barons, Quinn's wife Lydia (Orla Brady) and fiancée Jade pursue more domestic ambitions, each fighting to be the head of the household and Quinn's favorite wife. Their struggles are not physical and they primarily compete for Quinn's attention; they are at his mercy. They dress for aesthetics rather than combat, wearing long skirts and traditionally feminine attire, and they smile a great deal—theirs is soft power, conventionally feminine, surviving via emotional and sexual manipulation. It is clear that Lydia has little agency in her marriage, as she is forced to arrange her husband's wedding to Jade despite her own dislike; likewise, while Jade is ambitious, it does not appear she has any ability to refuse Quinn's choice, and he has apparently chosen her primarily because she is physically attractive and significantly younger than either himself or Lydia. Apart from skill at manipulation, the only weapon each woman uses is poison: Lydia to murder Quinn's previous second wife, and Jade to frame Lydia for using the same tactic against Jade. As Lydia is marched into exile, her long skirts a sharp contrast to the uniform pants of the male soldiers escorting her, she passes from one man's control to another's: she must return to her father and, publicly on her knees, beg his forgiveness for having abandoned him, as only abject humiliation permits her continued survival. Jade, meanwhile, rises to prominence through deception and coy manipulation, furthering stereotypes of the *femme fatale* and women who must use their sexual wiles and physical appeal to obtain both protection and recognition in a man's world. In the Baron's family, the men fight over politics and warfare; the women fight over the men. In the second season, both women's roles are reduced, particularly Jade's as Ryder's wife, then widow, who becomes Baron for approximately twenty minutes before she is defeated and exiled. Lydia becomes Quinn's captive and abused prisoner. Without involvement in their husbands' stories, neither character is apparently necessary to the plot.

Sunny's romantic partner Veil exemplifies a similar feminine aesthetic; she also dresses in long skirts, eschewing combat or weaponry. As the hero's love interest, she is more innocent and nurturing than Lydia or Jade; she is the local healer and also occupies the role of the damsel in distress, here as the mother of Sunny's child. Her pregnancy is forbidden, as cogs are not permitted to breed without permission (another detail incorporated from American slave history and divorced from any overt division of race within the series, though notably, Veil is Black). Though she was adopted by the local doctor as an orphan, the exact details of Veil's history and relationship with Sunny are unclear; when M.K. asks her about it, she literally tells him it doesn't matter (1.03, "White Stork Spreads Wings"). Veil serves as the plot rationale for the relationship between M.K. and Sunny, who offers to train M.K. if M.K. will get Veil out of the territory: "There's a woman. You'd have to take her with you and protect her" (1.02, "Fist Like A Bullet"). After she gives birth to her and Sunny's son Henry, Veil becomes a further pawn in the struggle between Quinn and Sunny: Quinn attempts to usurp Sunny's position, forcing Veil into marriage and adopting Henry as his own. Veil's death at the end of season 2 is particularly gratuitous, when Quinn (who has already been run through the chest twice with a sword), rises to slay her in order to prevent Sunny's victory. She sacrifices herself to save her child, then gracefully expires; "Teach him to be good," she breathes to her weeping lover, as he apologizes for failing to protect her.

Veil, Lydia, and Jade are caught in machinations between men. Jade in particular is part of a series aesthetic that treats women's bodies as sexual objects: in one of her first scenes, she walks naked to Ryder's bedroom, the camera lingering on her legs and panning up her back. Naked women abound in brothels ("doll houses"), and women are offered as rewards for Quinn's forces ("Clippers get the best of everything: food, weapons, women" [1.01, "The Fort"]); while "every boy" may attempt life as a Colt (1.01, "The Fort"), the avenues for women to escape lives harvesting fields of poppies are distinctly gendered and rife with sexual violence. Lydia is subject to Quinn's sexual dominance when he captures and assaults her (2.06, "Leopard Stalks in Snow"). Even Veil, first called as a doctor to attend the ailing Quinn, is clearly at the mercy of his whims, as the threat of his potential sexual aggression charges their interaction (1.03, "White Stork Spreads Wings"), from which beginnings he eventually force-marries and nearly rapes her (2.08, "Sting of the Scorpion's Tail"). While racially-charged slave imagery is used without acknowledgment of its implications, sexually-charged assault imagery is used to bolster over-simplified "gender equality" discourse that stereotypes feminine women as vulnerable and reduces feminist concerns to blunt doctrine.

The series' unsubtle treatment of "feminism" is exemplified by The Widow (Emily Beecham). Against a backdrop in which women's bodies are used as props, particularly in the brothel scenes, The Widow is aggressively different, a woman skilled in combat who seeks recognition as a Baron in her own right, despite Quinn's derision ("Just because she murdered her husband does not make her a Baron" [1.01, "The Fort"]). The Widow and her forces are presented as opposites to *Into the Badlands'* post-apocalyptic gender stereotypes: a female Baron aided by a trained cohort of female soldiers (the "Butterflies"), presenting a challenge to patriarchal norms and, thus, overtly acknowledging these norms within the series. Focus on The Widow as a figure of power and a legitimate threat to Quinn paints her as an exception to more "typical" women—for example, when The Widow also arranges a meeting in a brothel, and engages in combat amid a room of topless female prostitutes (1.02, "Fist Like a Bullet"), this only highlights how unusually she is meant to be perceived, particularly in comparison to those same prostitutes and to more feminine, non-combat characters like Lydia, Jade, and Veil. However, The Widow herself still occupies a restrictive archetypal role in which women are allowed to be "strong" as long as they are also sexually appealing, thus reducing their threat to masculine power. The Widow's verbal assertions of equality, and her participation in the martial arts sequences that bind the series, further belie her own sexualization via exposed cleavage and impractical spike heels—or the way that she swings around a stripper pole during a fight (1.02, "Fist Like a Bullet"). Men in the series are not treated the same way—their costuming and fighting styles are not highlighted for sex appeal, nor does the camera linger on their individual body parts—but The Widow's presence is consistently contained by the male gaze. Her combat prowess is also limited as she comes second to the male leads, losing one-on-one fights against both Sunny (1.05, "Snake Creeps Down") and Quinn (1.03, "White Stork Spreads Wings").

The Widow is also vocally (and simplistically) a feminist, explicit not only in her quest for power but about her desire for "a peaceful world where all women have a voice that's heard" (1.06, "Hand of Five Poisons"). While The Widow's overt drive for power in a patriarchal world is an exception to the matter-of-fact acceptance of gender roles in many post-apocalyptic series, it is also a caricaturized acknowledgment of the most basic feminist issues that serves to obscure the series' overall treatment of female characters and feminine traits, as well as the complexities of feminist desires. The Widow and the Butterflies have rebelled not because of restrictive gender roles or concerns about work, political agency, or property rights, but because the men who previously controlled their lives violated their bodily autonomy. A single concern—here, domestic and sexual assault—becomes the foundation of The Widow's professed political stand, wherein the other Barons' chauvinistic behavior can likewise be simplified into direct physical threats and broad comments about a woman being too naturally incompetent to hold power.

The Widow's wish to assume a traditionally male position and be acknowledged within masculine power structures also supports readings of feminism as a female desire to enter male spaces—a one-sided approach which continues to privilege masculine spaces and behaviors as superior and desirable. Moreover, The Widow and her forces are all young, cisgender, white, and able-bodied, their sexuality generally unaddressed, obscuring any intersectional issues as all of the women are advanced as one. The series echoes both *Defiance*, in which Stahma Tarr's feminism is framed as personal ambition, and *Revolution*, in which power is wholly masculinized and the women who best survive all demonstrate "hard" masculine abilities while still being limited by consistent sexualization.

The Widow's position as a "feminist" rebel is further undermined in the second season, when she is no longer the only female Baron,[2] and when her stated goals are expanded to include freedom for all cogs. This idealistic stance becomes swiftly untenable as The Widow's political ambitions require her to cease offering sanctuary to escaped cogs, align with the disgraced Quinn, and betray Sunny and M.K. Most damningly, she trades an escaped Veil and baby Henry back to the abusive and violent Quinn, cementing an alliance at the cost of another woman's body; this could easily be read as a critique of white feminism's dismissal of women of color, though again, *Into the Badlands* avowedly post-racial position leaves such interpretations implicit. Most directly, The Widow is portrayed as a failed idealist whose naïve demands are soon abandoned in favor of a pragmatic quest for power for which she betrays any who believe her promises. She is a woman grasping at masculinity whose "feminist" ambitions are depicted as impractical and insincere.

Finally, Tilda (Ally Ioannides), The Widow's adopted daughter, occupies a more nuanced role but, like The Widow, is still constrained by sexual threats and her always-limited embrace of a masculine position. Like The Widow, Tilda is frequently portrayed as a warrior whose competence is startling and unexpected to the men who cartoonishly underestimate her. Tilda also shares the Widow's background of abuse; she was raped as a child by The Widow's spouse, and is further contained by rape threats and harassment that continually remind the viewer not only of her gender, but of the patriarchal culture that suggests rape against women is a natural consequence or threat of innate male aggression. As Tilda is first introduced, fighting a male opponent while The Widow wagers on her success, another man leers, "if she can't … we get to keep her" (1.02, "Fist Like a Bullet"). Though Tilda, who is underage, escapes overtly sexualized treatment by the camera, she is instead restricted by her emotional romantic entanglements: she is unable to resist her attraction to M.K. While M.K. is equally entangled in the romantic subplot, his innate violent tendencies mean that he is ultimately the stronger of the two, and must learn to control his supernatural aggression in order to protect Tilda both from other men and from himself. Tilda is also, briefly, offered by the Baron to M.K. as enticement: "She could live in the fort, and you could be with her whenever you want" (1.06, "Hand of Five Poisons")—a reminder of the limitations the setting places on women, and of the oversimplification of the feminist objections to such attitudes. It isn't until M.K. is exiled that Tilda begins to come into her own, first as The Widow's Regent and then as a bisexual woman, eventually turning on the Widow and fleeing the Badlands with her lover Odessa (Maddison Jaizani); in doing so, she escapes the patriarchal structures of the Baron-ruled lands, though it is uncertain for how long.

Summary

Into the Badlands features an ethnically diverse cast and an impressive percentage of female regular characters[3]; it adds Tilda's bisexuality in season 2, includes Waldo (an elderly and still-deadly martial artist in a wheelchair), and also incorporates season-two monk Bajie (Nick Frost), whose large body type is atypical for post-apocalyptic television. Ultimately, however, the series both teases the potential for difference and undercuts its own distinctiveness at every turn.

It first features a setting rife with images of the southern American cotton trade, complete with a slave-owning, upper-class white man who speaks in an exaggerated drawl—yet when Sunny is sold to the River Master at the conclusion of the first season, the series even then resists racial readings, as power roles within Into the Badlands are played by actors with a variety of racial backgrounds, and no ethnic group emerges as singularly dominant or oppressed. Into the Badlands continually references elements of the historic American slave trade, but simultaneously insists on post-racial casting and fails to engage with the implications of its own aesthetic. Instead, it further showcases its Asian male lead within martial arts stereotypes sanctioned and fetishized by white Western culture, while enslaved "cogs" are marginalized as a reductively stereotyped economic class from which advancement is possible via martial prowess (for boys) or sexual manipulation (girls).

Into the Badlands then incorporates a thinly sketched version of "feminism"—a female character who excels in the male-dominated public sphere and openly states her desire to make society a better place for women—but the series' internal acknowledgment of its own patriarchal structures is limited by the cameras that follow The Widow's body and the rape threats directed at Tilda. The Widow claims power via her mastery of the masculinized combat skills that are the key to advancement in the series. This supports limited readings of feminists as wanting to be "like men," appropriating male roles and male spaces wholesale, and implicitly advances masculine-associated behaviors and traits as socially superior, practical, and more desirable than the nurturing abilities or emotional sensitivities associated with women. Further, The Widow's "feminist" actions are revealed as a political cloak for a selfish fantasy of individual power. Though *Into the Badlands* avoids directly advancing white male patriarchy, portraying Quinn as corrupt and focusing more positively on those who rebel against him, this is where the series' progressiveness ends. The series is race and gender *inclusive*, but retains racialized stereotypes and gender binaries, privileges masculine behaviors, and both sexualizes and over-simplifies the professed feminist politics of its most powerful female lead.

The 100

Unlike *Into the Badlands*, which is set an unknown amount of time after a mysterious apocalyptic event, *The 100*'s setting is specific: ninety-seven years after the Earth's surface was ravaged by nuclear blasts, the descendants of an international group of survivors now reside in a connected group of 12 space stations collectively known as the Ark. When the Ark's life support systems begin to fail, a group of one hundred juvenile delinquents is unwittingly sent down to Earth to test the survivability of the surface. The teens quickly discover that they are not alone; they must learn to deal with "groundling" tribes, as well as the surface descendants of the U.S. government, and the remnants of an artificial intelligence now disguised as a god.

From a white feminist perspective, *The 100* is a groundbreaking post-apocalyptic series. It posits a future society where women are socially, politically and culturally equal to men, and both women and men may exhibit a variety of character traits without being shamed or singled out for challenging preconceived gender binaries. An initial analysis of gender roles—particularly the variety of roles open to female characters—explains why *The 100* has been critically received as a subversive example of feminist programming in articles like "*The 100* Is The Most Feminist Show on TV" (Zeidel), "5 Times *The 100* Totally Subverted (and Exceeded) Our Expectations" (Wilken), or "11 Times *The 100* Was More Progressive About Race, Gender, & Sexuality Than Many Shows Out There" (MacDonald). However, the series is also problematic on a racial level, and has undercut its own queer content with the use of troublesome tropes; a more reserved headline comes from *PopMatters*, "Why CW's *The 100* Is a Feminist Dream, Except for When It's Not" (Neumark). *The 100* is notable for its consistent breakdown of Othering tropes, and for its forays into diverse gender roles and performances, though it is more ambiguous with regard to both race and LGBTQ content.

Us vs. Them

The 100 works to subvert patterns common in other post-apocalyptic series by challenging notions of the alien Other. A primary theme of *The 100* is the breakdown in "us" vs. "them" mentalities that occurs when the Ark survivors encounter the humans ("grounders") still living on the Earth's surface. The grounders are initially positioned as nameless, faceless enemies— a jabbering and lethal horde that calls both to concepts of the alien Other and "savage" natives, both of which might be (and have been) used as metaphorical justification for aggression against a dehumanized foreign threat. However, the grounders soon gain distinct identities: Anya (Dichen Lachman), the local queen; Indra (Adina Porter), a senior warrior; Lincoln (Ricky Whittle), a warrior; and Lexa (Alycia Debnam-Carey), the Commander. When the grounders are revealed to speak English, it casts them as linguistically superior to the unilingual Ark survivors, and they are further able to voice their objections to the Ark group having invaded their territory. The Ark group transitions from being a band of survivors under siege by unknowable, hyperviolent "aliens" to realizing their own status as an unwelcome colonizing force. This both blurs the moral lines of the series and clears a path for the subsequent identity breakdown between groups, both of which are descended from old Earth. This is expressed in the grounder description of the Ark survivors as a clan, Skaikru ("Sky Crew"), in addition to their own Trikru ("Tree Crew"). This blurring is explicitly called out in the title of the season 1 finale, "We Are Grounders," and further complicated by Clarke's contradictory assertion to Anya, "We are *not* grounders" (1.13, "We Are Grounders, Part 2").

The clearest breakdown of identity comes via the romantic ties between Ark survivor Octavia (Marie Avergerpoulos) and grounder Lincoln, each of whom experiences identity tension as an adopted member of the "opposing" group. Early on, Octavia is kidnapped by Lincoln, who seeks to protect her from the members of his tribe who would kill her on sight; subsequently, Octavia must protect Lincoln from the Ark crew, who capture and torture him until Octavia helps him escape (1.08, "Day Trip"). Their entanglement is both a romantic union and a cultural exchange; Octavia learns the grounder language, adopts a grounder hair style, trains with Indra, and eventually claims her agency and identity as a grounder warrior, while Lincoln becomes an ally of the Ark survivors and eventually moves into their camp, wearing an Ark jacket as he joins the security forces. It is no coincidence that in the penultimate episode of season 2, Indra addresses Octavia as "Octavia of the Tree People," claiming her for the local tribe, while Clarke claims Lincoln as one of *her* people; the boundaries between the Ark and grounder groups fluctuate, then are re-drawn as Lexa betrays Clarke, Lincoln is dragged away by the grounders, and Octavia rebels against Indra, rejecting both her new identity and her old: "I have no home" (2.15, "Blood Must Have Blood, Part 1"). While Lincoln's involvement with the Ark camp eventually leads to his death, the identity tension originally created by the Lincoln/Octavia relationship is ongoing in Octavia's story. Octavia repeatedly disavows her Ark origins, embracing grounder culture and skills only to be drawn back to help the friends and brother who still have a claim on her.

Clarke also pursues close relationships with the grounders, which further serves to break down the us/them self/Other distinctions inherent in the series' pilot setup. As she establishes herself as the leader of the hundred and works to help her people survive the hostile planet, Clarke must gain the respect of the grounder leaders—first Anya, then Lexa. Their moral and ethical differences create the basis for exchange; initially, Clarke is despised by Anya as "weak," because Clarke shows mercy to defeated opponents. As Clarke fights Anya, the two going hand-to-hand to hand in the mud,[4] this is the first visual cue that Clarke and Anya are not so different: both end up filthy and bleeding, their previously distinct costuming now indistinguishable. Through such repeated—sometimes violent—interactions, Clarke both proves herself and begins to learn more about the grounders, including the death ritual she is able to perform for Anya when the queen is killed (2.04, "Many Happy Returns"). She must then learn to negotiate power with Lexa, the Commander of the grounder forces (and Anya's superior); here, mutual respect becomes mutual attraction, and the two share a kiss at the end of the second season (2.14, "Bodyguard of Lies"), again blurring us/them lines via romantic attraction and mutual cultural exchange. But Clark and Lexa's conflicting group loyalties produce an immediate schism in their budding relationship, as Lexa betrays their alliance in favor of preserving her own clans. Only after Clarke exiles herself from the Ark survivors, subsequently rejecting her identity and dressing as a grounder (3.01, "Wanheda, Part 1")—and only after Lexa abandons the grounder maxim, "blood must have blood," in favor of Clarke's more merciful approach—can Clarke and Lexa consummate their relationship. Both politically and romantically, Clarke and Lexa are established as equals. When Clarke pledges fealty to Lexa, positioning Skaikru as the thirteenth grounder clan under Lexa's command, Lexa reciprocates by vowing her own fealty to Clarke (3.03, "Ye Who Enter Here").

The relationships between Ark survivors and grounders are continually evolving, notably as expressed through Clarke, Octavia, Lexa, Lincoln, and their friendships and romantic entanglements; what *The 100* makes clear is that the boundaries between self and the perceived Other—as explored through Skaikru and Trikru—are porous and ever-fluctuating. This is particularly evident when the Ark survivors and grounders are revealed as historically linked, with the grounders unknowingly worshipping a version of the same artificial intelligence that started the nuclear launch which trapped the Ark station survivors in space. This, too, troubles the series' originally-established boundaries of Skaikru technology vs. Trikru primitivism, as artificial intelligence ALIE (Erica Cerra) infiltrates both groups—in the process, melding them into one force. The only solution to her Skaikru-triggered technological infection lies in Trikru bloodlines and religious tradition. In *The 100*, self and Other are intertwined and the distinctions between the Ark survivors and the grounders are constantly in flux.

Further, while Skaikru and Trikru first appear opposed but are gradually revealed as similar, the survivor group that initially presents as sympathetic is violently oppositional. Mount Weather hosts the descendants of the American government, who retained their sense of culture and history when they took shelter from radiation in the station below ground. At first, the Mount Weather group presents as familiar and "civilized": they are friendly and English-speaking. They provide clothing and food. Dante Wallace (Raymond J. Barry) is President, holding an office that has become passed down from father to son. He is also an elderly white man, literally the last embodiment of the American patriarchy. Despite the seemingly sympathetic compatibility of the Mount Weather survivors, however, Clarke is ill-fitting among them: though she briefly dresses in Mount Weather clothing, she is visibly uncomfortable. Sure enough, Wallace's authority and friendship prove untenable, as the medical "treatments" that sustain the station's inhabitants are revealed as blood transfusions from unwilling grounder prisoners. The relationship between Mount Weather and the grounders might be read as an extended demonstration of class privilege, in which those fortunate or politically important enough to gain shelter during nuclear holocaust continue to prey on the lower classes for generations; the arrival of the Ark group prompts a change in tactics, wherein full blood transfusions (and the death of the Ark "donor") might allow the Mount Weather people to walk on the surface again. The threat to both grounder allies and Ark survivors means that the hundred can maintain no relationship with the remnants of the American government; instead, Clarke joins in common cause with the grounders, and when that alliance fails, she irradiates the entire Mount Weather population in order to save her people. While *The 100* depicts a relationship between Ark survivors and the predominantly matriarchal grounders that is ongoing and increasingly reciprocal, Clarke's destruction of the Mount Weather colony illustrates the Ark survivors' split with historic American culture and the remnants of patriarchy.

The series thus challenges notions of self/Other, or us/them, by aligning the Ark survivors most closely with the grounders via the cultural exchanges that see Octavia and Clarke adopting (at various points in the narrative) grounder language, dress, and tradition, while grounder cooperation proves integral to "Skaikru"'s survival and grounder history proves rooted in the same series of events that led to the formation of the Ark. Certainly the relationships between Skaikru and Trikru are complex, and further inflected by Octavia's continued quest for identity and Clarke's reluctant positioning as Wanheda, the "Commander of Death." This ongoing negotiation between groups stands in stark contrast to Clarke's violent rejection of Mount Weather and its presentation of more familiar "American" culture; *The 100* inverts tropes regarding the "alien Other"—and the need to conquer it—by continually keeping the relationships and distinctions between Skaikru and Trikru in flux.

Gender

From the outset, *The 100* also challenges stereotypes about both gender binaries and the superiority of masculine behaviors. Clarke is first revealed as both a juvenile delinquent and an artist, drawing a vast mural on the wall of her containment cell. Throughout the series, she demonstrates a balance of aggression and compassion, maintaining this hybridity while also exhibiting intelligence, independence, and leadership. Clarke exhibits a blend of culturally gendered traits; she can be violent, empathetic, ruthless, and idealistic. When the hundred are first launched to the planet's surface, Clarke's control of the group is not established through force; rather, she is the leader who arranges shelter and food. She is also the de facto healer, but rather than assume a nurturing role and defer to the more aggressive Bellamy (Bob Morley), Clarke maintains attributes culturally coded as both masculine and feminine. While series such as *The Walking Dead* or *Revolution* might follow a formerly feminine character's "journey" into masculine power, illustrating the need to abandon compassion for ruthless aggression in post-apocalyptic chaos, *The 100* stresses Clarke's empathy as a necessary strength. Ostensibly, dialogue in the series might argue otherwise; Clarke has repeated conversations with Lexa about the presumed need to abandon emotion in favor of practical choices. But when Clarke holds a knife to Lexa's throat, on the verge of committing an assassination, Lexa apologizes: "I'm sorry. I never meant to turn you into this" (3.03, "Ye Who Enter Here"). In doing so, she acknowledges both the value of Clarke's nurturing emotionalism, and her own error in repeatedly encouraging Clarke toward detached, pragmatic violence. Clarke hesitates, rejecting aggression; as she does so, an alliance is mended.

This balance between violence and the desire for peace is evident as Clarke negotiates a series of increasingly dark moral choices; *The 100* allows her space in which to navigate complex issues. Clarke can sympathetically hum while she euthanizes a suffering and mortally wounded boy (1.03, "Earth Kills"); engage in a knock-down, drag-out fight with a grounder queen (2.04, "Many Happy Returns"); and commit genocide to save her own people (2.16, "Blood Must Have Blood, Part 2"). Most importantly, she can agonize over her decisions ("I tried. I tried to be the good guy"; 2.16, "Blood Must Have Blood, Part 2"); few of her actions are presented as unilaterally right or wrong. *The 100* is not a morally black-and-white tale like *Falling Skies* or *The Last Ship*, in which the heroes and villains are clear; neither does it demonstrate *The Walking Dead*'s slow descent into nihilism, wherein the protagonists become indistinguishable from those they are killing. Rather, its characters continually self-reflect, making violent choices but verbally regretting or doubting those choices as they seek to move forward. This is not to exonerate Clarke for genocide, but only to note that the series navigates a series of survival conflicts in which characters never cease to interrogate their own motivations and actions. One of *The 100*'s predominant themes is its constant moral struggle. Unlike *The Walking Dead*, it retains a sense of hope—"Maybe life should be about more than just surviving" (2.14, "Bodyguard of Lies"). Unlike *Falling Skies* or *The Last Ship*, it acknowledges its protagonists' flaws.

The 100 is also distinct from other contemporary post-apocalyptic series because it showcases a variety of female characters, rejecting repetitive archetypes and avoiding the "Smurfette principle" (Pollitt) trap of having one woman stand in for all. Clarke's mother Abby (Paige Turco) is a doctor on the Ark, eventually assuming the leadership role of Chancellor on the surface. Octavia becomes a fierce warrior and the primary liaison between two communities. Engineer Raven (Lindsey Morgan) is the group's primary communications and technology expert. Anya, Indra, and Lexa are all prominent grounder leaders. Even the artificial intelligence that launched the nuclear apocalypse, ALIE, projects a feminine image, modeled on the scientist who created her.

The closest *The 100* comes to a typical Hollywood "feminist" narrative—that is to say, a single female character's struggle to prove her masculinized talents versus men who openly deride her ability to do "man things"—is Octavia's early arc, in which she is a sheltered child who was raised in secrecy inside her mother and brother's living quarters. Octavia begins the series as the unwilling recipient of Bellamy's protection ("Anyone touches her, they answer to me"; 1.02, "Earth Skills"), but rebels against his monitoring and would-be control by kissing Atom (Rhys Ward; 1.02, "Earth Skills") and Jasper (Devon Bostick; 1.04, "Murphy's Law") and helping Lincoln. Only after Octavia has repeatedly claimed her own agency and developed the skills of a grounder warrior does Bellamy cease his attempts to monitor or regulate her activities. Taken alone, this plot thread might be considered another example of a woman adopting the masculine-coded skills that are the only possible route to survival in a hostile world; however, Octavia is only one of many women in *The 100*. Most importantly, in *The 100*, combat is not assumed to be a male domain or the only valuable skill type—combat skills are exhibited by both men and women, and pacifism, technical ability, empathy, nurturing, or other traits may also be exhibited by both genders, stripping Octavia's arc of some of the sexist implications it might hold in a different context. It might be easy to pick apart a single narrative—to criticize Octavia for her reliance on a romantic subplot or her embrace of increasingly violent skills and philosophies—but *The 100* stands out because it has so many women exhibiting different character traits in different roles, rather than a primarily male cast where individual women are presented as "the exception" worthy of note. *The 100* subverts gender binaries by featuring multiple women in leadership positions, and by advancing characters who demonstrate a variety of gendered traits.

The series' incorporation of a variety of male figures specifically rejects the hypermasculine, repeatedly punishing overly aggressive male characters. This is initially demonstrated through season 1's two male leads: Bellamy and Finn (Thomas McDonell). Bellamy poses the first threat to Clarke's leadership; particularly in the first season, he is aggressive and ruthless, torturing Lincoln, trying to control Octavia (and Octavia's sexuality), and advocating war. Finn, a pacifist and Clarke's initial love interest, is depicted as sensitive and desirable, while Bellamy's violent, competitive tendencies make him only a reluctant ally against the grounder threat. In the second season, these two roles are partially reversed. Finn, searching for a missing Clarke, becomes both a torturer, violently interrogating and executing a captive grounder, and a mass murderer, gunning down the unarmed population of a village. According to more typical action-movie trope progression, Finn's abandonment of his earlier "soft" ways in order to "save" the woman he loves would make him a hero. In *The 100*, his sudden bout of hypermasculine aggression makes him a war criminal and fails to help Clarke: "I found you," he proclaims, as she shakes her head in denial and dismay (2.05, "Human Trials"). In contrast, Bellamy becomes the voice of reason, advocating against torture and doubting the efficacy of information received under duress. Finn's excessive violence leads to his execution; Bellamy's change of heart saves him from the same.

This theme continues through the series. Throughout seasons 1 and 2, the Reapers represent the clearest exaggeration of hypermasculinity in *The 100*: they are all men, grounders captured and experimented on by Mount Weather, tortured into drug dependency and sent to attack their former people. The Reapers have lost the ability to communicate verbally; they are violent, hulking and unreasoning, as well as smeared in filth and gore. When Lincoln is captured and indoctrinated into the Reaper program, he must resist the drug addiction and fight his way back from nonverbal aggression in order to reclaim his position as an ally and romantic partner; here, hypermasculinity is a reversion to animalistic brutality and indiscriminate rage.

Season 3 presents a more nuanced dismissal of exaggerated masculinity and most specifically the stereotype of the soldier hero (à la *Falling Skies*, *The*

Last Ship, Revolution, Colony, or *Jericho*) whose skills and leadership are the only hope in post-apocalyptic chaos. Pike (Michael Beach), the leader of the Farm Station survivors, is a former "Earth skills" teacher but is immediately situated as a soldier by the military speech he and his people use: "watch our six"; "target engaged"; "ooh rah" (3.02, "Wanheda, Part 2"). His leadership is steeped in xenophobia and colonial aggression. He refuses to acknowledge the grounders as allies, locking those in camp (including Lincoln) in a cell. He leads the Ark security forces to massacre an army of grounders sent to protect Skaikru: "This land is ours now. Resist, and you will be met by force. Fight, and you will be greeted by death" (3.05, "Hakeldama"). While both Pike and Clarke commit war crimes, the series denies Pike the moral complexity ascribed to Clarke's decisions; Clarke is forced to choose between her people and the Mount Weather residents, while Pike's attack is an unnecessary aggression against unprepared and friendly forces. His approach is simplistic and short-sighted, illustrated by the naïve proclamations of his follower Hannah (Donna Yamamoto): "If something helps you survive, it's always the right thing. Pike taught me that" (3.08, "Terms and Conditions"). But Pike's actions rupture the alliance between Skaikru and Trikru. Pike is portrayed as racist, violent, and cruel; his "us or them" mentality is out of place in *The 100*'s complicated approach to survival and the Other, and his militarized tactics—though initially embraced by many of the Ark survivors—prove a short-sighted and bloody hindrance to the cooperation necessary for survival. This is a direct inversion of the more standard approach to soldier heroes of the post-apocalypse: Pike's xenophobic, violent rejection of the Other has no place in *The 100*'s future and presents a complication for the protagonists rather than the rescue implicitly promised by a macho man with a gun.

    The 100's characters continually struggle with violence and the morality of wartime conflict; combat is not always the correct or inevitable choice. Again, this is illustrated through Bellamy, whose somewhat erratic character arcs allow for multiple explorations of masculinity: from the overly aggressive bully who loses leadership to Clarke in the first season, to the calmer, more thoughtful fighter of season 2, to the would-be soldier who commits war crimes under Pike's guidance before repenting after his actions lead to Lincoln's death. Moreover, while conflicts between Bellamy and Clarke are not *explicitly* gendered, her capacity for empathy and mercy is depicted as a strength that makes her a better leader—for example, when she euthanizes Atom after Bellamy can't, when she mercy-kills a doomed Finn, and when she achieves *détente* with the grounders rather than mindlessly pursuing war. While Bellamy is coded as more traditionally masculine, Clarke's more gender-hybrid traits allow her to prevail—not using her femininity as a cloak or abandoning her more empathetic abilities, but taking advantage of all her skills and knowledges equally.

This is not to suggest that *The 100* is an unproblematic example of feminist gender performance; while there are multiple layered female roles, season 3 in particular shifts focus away from the women in order to concentrate on Pike's rise to power and his subsequent conflicts with Kane (Henry Ian Cusack), Jaha (Isaiah Washington), Lincoln, and Bellamy. The series is also not above using women's deaths as plot points, such as when Jasper's Mount Weather girlfriend Maya (Eve Harlow) is irradiated by Clarke's genocidal actions, triggering Jasper's psychological schism from the group. Likewise, Bellamy's girlfriend Gina (Leah Gibson) appears in all of two episodes before she is killed off to motivate his subsequent foray into violence; "Gina was real," a grieving Bellamy proclaims at the memorial service, and he may as well be trying to convince the viewing audience (3.04, "Watch the Thrones"). *The 100* also sexualizes women's bodies on more than one occasion. One moment from the pilot stands out, as Jasper watches Octavia strip down and jump into a river, and the camera lingers on Octavia's half-clothed figure: "Oh, damn," exclaims Jasper, staring, "I love Earth" (1.01, "Pilot"). Raven also strips for the camera, for little narrative reason (1.02, "Earth Skills"). As well, the extras in the grounder forces are generally male, meaning that female leaders like Anya, Lexa, or Indra are often foregrounded against all-male armies—visually portrayed as exceptions despite the apparently common dominance of women.

The 100 and Race

The 100's cast does incorporate significant racial diversity; the death of Finn in season 2 is also the death of the heterosexual white male romantic lead, leaving sometimes–Chancellor Kane, Jasper, and anti-hero Murphy (Richard Harmon) as the remaining recurring white male characters—only one of whom (Jasper) is a member of Clarke's group. Instead, non-white characters like Bellamy and Monty (Christopher Larkin) fill out the ranks of the hundred, with Lincoln and former Chancellor Jaha also appearing as series regulars. However, many of the central roles in *The 100* are reserved for white women; Eliza Taylor and Paige Turco receive top billing in the series, while Avgeropoulos is also a regular. With the exception of Lindsey Morgan as Raven, notable non-white female characters—Anya or Indra—are recurring; they receive less screen time and, in the case of Anya, are short-lived. Further, the white women's roles are inevitably privileged:

> *The 100* is guilty of perpetuating white feminism and presents its white female characters in ways that make it obvious just who is right and wrong within the context of the show. The white women are positioned as leaders and depicted as strong, righteous characters. This becomes problematic when we watch these same women treat other characters of color poorly, both women and men. They condescend and demean nonwhite characters in sometimes subtle, sometimes overt ways. Because they are women,

however, the show would have us believe that they are meant to be examples of "strong female characters," and so their treatment of non-white characters is never depicted as a flaw. It's merely depicted as what needs to be done in order for these white women to protect their people [Taub].

The 100 also aspires toward a particularly white American vision of a post-racial society wherein skin color no longer "matters" as long as everyone embraces the same culture and language. The Ark, as a meld of 12 separate stations, contains descendants of space refugees from multiple countries; however, judging by the flags on display, these were primarily Western English-speaking countries (e.g., the United States, Canada, the United Kingdom, New Zealand, and Australia). Flags from Japan and Russia are also visible, but no characters are shown speaking Russian or Japanese. Rather, on the Ark, American English is the common language, and the dream of the American "melting pot" has been achieved in its most problematic sense— one that suggests the only successful way to incorporate an immigrant population is for minority groups to be assimilated, sacrificing difference in favor of hegemonic, Western Anglo-Saxon harmony (e.g., Orosco 2).

When the hundred encounter English-speaking tribes and American Mount Weather survivors on what is formerly the continental United States, it only reinforces the pre-eminence of American culture onscreen. But *The 100*'s claim to a post-racial American future means that when the most dark-skinned member of the hundred, Jaha's son Wells (Eli Goree), dies within four episodes (1.04, "Murphy's Law"); when the supposedly-primitive grounders (who first appear as "tribal" figures wearing animal skins and war paint, shrieking in a foreign language) are initially represented by non-white characters Anya, Indra, and Lincoln; when Lincoln's kidnapping of Octavia at first appears to re-enact the pervasive and culturally damaging myth of an innocent white girl attacked by a sexually threatening Black man[5]; or when Lincoln is executed on his knees, surrounded by predominantly white soldiers, the connotations of such images are subsequently presented as free of any context of racism.

Pike is also a Black man, and the series rejects his aggressive militarized survival stance in favor of a white savior—here embodied by Kane, who is positioned as the diplomatic, idealistic, and noble alternative to Pike's dominance. Between them, Pike is the one depicted as racist:

KANE: Not all grounders are the same.
PIKE: They are to me [3.02, "Wanheda, Part 2"].

Again, *The 100*'s ostensible post-racialism works to disavow any troubling politics in casting Pike as the xenophobic villain to Kane's tolerant hero, even when Kane is literally crucified as he suffers, Jesus-like, for his convictions (3.13, "Join or Die"). Through characters like Kane, Clarke, Abby, Lexa, and even President Wallace, *The 100* includes a racially diverse cast but nevertheless normalizes white leadership.

Burying Its Gays

The 100 additionally proves complex with regard to its queer themes and content. To begin with, *The 100* again breaks from patterns set by other post-apocalyptic series when it features not just queer characters, but a bisexual protagonist; so far Clarke's onscreen sexual relationships include Finn, a briefly appearing trader named Niylah (Jessica Harmon), and Lexa. None of these encounters is presented as unusual or shocking, to Clarke or to anyone around her; *The 100* is not a coming-out story. This matter-of-fact approach to queer sexuality, particularly involving a series lead, marks *The 100* as groundbreaking in the genre—though, admittedly, there are limits. Two gay characters, Miller (Jarod Joseph) and Bryan (Jonathan Whitesell), are ostensibly in a relationship but seldom express physical affection, save for the occasional hug or quick kiss (e.g., 3.08, "Terms and Conditions"); all other characters are so far either canonically heterosexual or their sexuality is unaddressed. All characters are also cisgender.

Most dramatically, *The 100* becomes highly problematic mid-season 3, wherein Lexa is fatally shot moments (literally, in the next scene) after consummating her relationship with Clarke. This oft-recurring pop culture pattern has been defined as "Bury Your Gays," or "Dead Lesbian Syndrome," dating "back to 1976 on the soap opera *Executive Suite* when a lesbian character chases her love interest into the street only to be run over by a truck" (Snarker). Lexa's death created drama both onscreen and off; fan protest accused the series showrunner and writers of using tired, homophobic stereotypes, and of "queer baiting"—using the promise of a same-sex female relationship to draw in viewers, only to fail to deliver. Showrunner Jason Rothenberg defended the decision by noting that Alycia Debnam-Carey had been committed to *Fear the Walking Dead* and was unable to continue on *The 100* (Goldman); while this explains the need for the actor's absence, it is less defensible regarding the timing and nature of Lexa's being written out. Certainly, Lexa's death places an asterisk of significant size next to any claims that *The 100* constitutes a queer-friendly or inclusive series. Still, Clarke's easy acceptance and acknowledgment of her own bisexuality are a refreshing change from post-apocalyptic worlds in which queer characters, if they exist, are barely acknowledged.

Summary

The 100 questions easy xenophobic binaries and provides a variety of gender performing characters, as well as diverse roles for women. It further avoids denigrating feminine skills, instead ensuring that the strongest characters—like Clarke—are the ones who can demonstrate a wide range of abilities without regard for culturally entrenched gender roles. *The 100* strays from the pattern of the heterosexual white male lead, avoids glorifying hypermasculine violence or soldier/police training, and challenges heteronormativity.

Still, there are multiple qualifications to *The 100*'s positioning as a progressive series. It must be specified that the female characters who most benefit are white; while the series also features a significant number of non-white characters, it also presents a "post-racial" society that distinctly favors white America, and a future in which the descendants of multiple countries have banded together in English-speaking pseudo–American unity. Finally, *The 100* distinguishes itself with an openly bisexual lead, only to confine her same-sex encounters to one minor character and a recurring love interest who is immediately post-coitally killed. The series is still in production and some of these themes may eventually receive more attention; at the least, *The 100* suggests the *potential* for a televised post-apocalyptic series that imagines the possibility of an inclusive future.

Wayward Pines

While series like *Into the Badlands* and *The 100* explore the possibilities inherent in radical new futures, *Wayward Pines* does exactly the opposite, presenting Idaho in the year 4028, where the only traces of humanity remaining on Earth are located behind an electric fence. Outside the small American Midwestern town of Wayward Pines, the remnants of the human race (known as abberations, or "abbies") have become deadly, animalistic carnivores—the result of thousands of years of DNA mutation. For characters in the series, the change is instantaneous: abducted from their lives in the late twentieth and early twenty-first centuries, they have been cryogenically frozen. They each awaken after a "car accident," finding themselves in the hospital in a small town they are unable to leave. Cameras and microphones are everywhere. No one is allowed to talk about the past. Everyone is given a beautiful suburban home and a job, but misdemeanors are punished by public execution in the village square.

The series, based on novels by Blake Crouch, serves to a certain extent as thematic commentary on surveillance culture and fascist control, as one man—scientist David Pilcher (Toby Jones)—seeks to maintain control of the town at all costs, trying to preserve middle America by locking out the unknown and micromanaging the residents. The series' primary tensions are situated in paranoia and the uncanny; however, the setting's fundamental criticisms of the small-town Midwest American myth conflict with the fact that the town of Wayward Pines still remains the last hope for the survival of humanity.

The alien Other in *Wayward Pines* can be read as the threat of the violent unknown. In *Wayward Pines*, there literally is no civilization or society beyond the exceptionally white, English-speaking small town; David Pilcher, in attempting to save the human race, apparently chose to preserve an entirely American population—an interpretation of "American" that also clearly excludes non-white citizens. Though he laments the loss of "so much culture" (1.05, "The Truth"), Pilcher has done absolutely nothing to save the rest of the world, instead creating a future that is Wayward Pines, Idaho vs. an inhospitable, deadly planet. The text easily functions as an anti-immigration allegory; the future of humanity rests on maintaining the barrier between Wayward Pines citizens and the Others, no residents leaving and no monsters entering, while the town residents are pressured to have the children who will in turn propagate the (English-speaking, almost entirely white) human race.

White Saviors

The town's whiteness is most notable in the contrast between the tyrannical Black sheriff, Pope (Terrence Howard), and first-season protagonist Ethan Burke (Matt Dillon), who is abducted from his life in 2014 and brought to Wayward Pines as a counter to Pope's reign of terror. Pope publicly slits the throats of any residents who try to escape the town; Burke is meant as an antidote, to provide more "reasonable" forms of enforcement. Indeed, though Pope's executions are apparently in response to Pilcher's instructions, Pilcher still thaws Burke and introduces him to Wayward Pines in hopes that he will be better: "We need you. We need someone good" (1.03, "Our Town, Our Law").

Pope, as Burke's rival, is merciless, authoritarian, and cruel; he is corrupt and cannot be trusted with power. In contrast, Burke, a secret service agent haunted by the failures of the past, here fits the standard archetype of a law enforcement or military agent whose skills are ideal for post-apocalyptic leadership. He demonstrates this as he temporarily but successfully escapes the town's boundary fence, surviving for hours in the carnivore-infested jungle and persevering where others die almost instantly (1.02, "Do Not Discuss Your Life Before"). Burke's special status within the town is also apparent throughout the early episodes, as characters comment on the privileged treatment he receives—a "second chance" after an escape attempt, the best house in town, and the arrival of his wife Theresa (Shannyn Sossamon) and son Ben (Charlie Tahan) after everyone else in town has lost their previous family members (children, spouses, etc.) forever. Pilcher's insistence that Burke is "needed" cements Burke's status as a man with the potential to do important things.

Burke's early conflict with Pope ends in Pope's death, as Ben mows him down with a truck and then Burke shoots him in the head; this eliminates the only significant character of color in Wayward Pines. Since Pope, who toys with a terrified Ben and Theresa moments before he is killed, has been established as a villain, *Wayward Pines* frames his death as a victory for the "good" and "needed" Burke. The town, previously haunted by a Black man in a position of authority, can now escape its terrified inertia as Burke, a more typical white male hero, assumes office.

New Future, Old Stereotypes

In order to maintain its premise of perfect-town-in-which-something-is-uncannily-wrong, Wayward Pines must first be established as a "perfect" town, in the most classic American mythological sense. The town has a main street and a square; everyone knows each other's names. Burke evokes to the ghost of the wild west as he is made the "new sheriff"; this role, the pivotal and "selfless" man who brings "law and order to the wilderness" (O'Connor and Rollins 20), is key to the Wayward Pines presentation of the mythical imagery of rural, Midwest America—an America where men are unquestionably in charge (as the sheriff and the mayor, or more accurately behind the scenes, Pilcher).

The community demonstrates hegemonic gender norms. The women in the series are relegated to strict gender roles, though it may chafe at times—most particularly in the case of Burke's former partner Kate (Carla Gugino). Kate's struggle is detailed through flashbacks; having "arrived" in Wayward Pines twelve years earlier than Burke, she tried to escape, was committed and held in a padded room, and survived by complying with Wayward Pines' imposed happy narrative and marrying the local toy maker Frank (Reed Diamond). Kate, an experienced agent with the secret service, struggles most visibly against the confines of her enforced domesticity and her new role as cheerful toy shop cashier. More than any other character, Kate demonstrates the tension beneath the Wayward Pines hometown veneer: Kate, with Frank's assistance, presents as a model citizen but heads a terrorist group plotting to blow up the fence and escape to the outside world they do not realize no longer exists. But Kate's agency and professionalism are limited by her status as Burke's ex-lover as well as his ex-partner; as his former mistress, she is sexualized from her first appearance in the narrative, and her interactions with Burke and, most particularly, Theresa are a constant reminder of her status as the former "other woman." In this way, the most aggressive and combat-capable female character is constrained by reminders of her sexual past.

Still, Kate's position is less gendered than other women in the series. Burke's wife Theresa possesses no apparent background that merits her being cryogenically "saved" for the Wayward Pines future; she and son Ben are abducted as a preventative measure when they go to Idaho looking for Burke, then they are thawed in order to keep Burke happy. In Wayward Pines, Theresa is assigned the job of real estate agent, where she works in an office under the supervision of "Big Bill" (Michael McShane). Bill is an older white man, stereotypically sexist—calling Theresa "sweetheart" and "hon," and commenting on her appearance. Theresa's dislike of the situation is clear, and this is another method by which the "misfit" elements of the town are highlighted; Theresa is forced into a job for which she has no interest, working for a man she doesn't like, in an environment that actively offends her twenty-first-century sensibilities—and yet she must still maintain an awkward smile for the cameras. Conversely, however, there is no sense that *Bill* has any idea his approach is outdated. Instead, he is presented as a genial anachronism, whose banal yet overt sexism serves to normalize the behavior of others in the town as "not sexist" by comparison; that character trait is Bill's. Theresa's discomfort with Bill's overt, throwback sexism obscures the subtler sexist stereotyping of her 2014 role as Burke's long-suffering spouse, left out of his top-secret activities and caring for their child in his absence. When she is brought to Wayward Pines as Burke's wife and established as a working parent who still assumes primary responsibility for Ben—walking him to school or watching over him at the hospital while Burke leaves to take action—her supposedly post-feminist positioning is called into question.

Wayward Pines's gender binaries are also apparent when applied to first-season villains Pam (Melissa Leo) and Megan (Hope Davis), both of whom also occupy feminized roles: Pam as a nurse at the hospital and Megan as the head teacher at the local school. Each dominates through manipulation and, in Pam's case, intimidation; they do not participate in the violence that marks the men's actions. Pam—initially the most terrifying figure in Wayward Pines—is the one whose hidden compassion eventually leads her to help Theresa and Burke. Megan shows no such feminine softness, but her manipulation of the town's high school students is cast within the series as a conflict with Theresa, as they fight over the ability to "mother" Ben.

Dangerous Complicities

On one hand, it is significant that the villains in *Wayward Pines*—those who have abducted others without consent, and those who control the town infrastructure while imposing intrusive surveillance technologies and capital punishments—also actively perpetuate the town's faux American social structures. Nurse Pam, teacher Megan, sheriff Pope, and psychologist Pilcher all embrace their roles. The protagonists of the piece are the ones who rebel; they perceive the imposed artificiality of the town and its confining nature as a prison established through both authoritarian action and the literal presence of the giant electrified fence that circles Wayward Pines. This calls the myth of the American Midwest into question: here, the picturesque ideal of a small Idaho town is a Stepford-style facsimile of American nostalgia that imprisons protagonists seeking a return to their twenty-first-century urban lives.

However, it is also significant that once Burke learns the truth about the town—the fact that there is no "civilization" left outside the wall—he becomes partially complicit with Pilcher. Though he chooses to reveal the secret to the town residents, thus undermining the secretive control of Pilcher's people, he also works against Kate's terrorist group as he convinces her that bringing down the wall will only result in death. While *Wayward Pines* critiques the idyllic imagery associated with cultural notions of the American Midwest, it also fails to envision any alternative. When the world outside is filled with carnivorous, deadly enemies, the town—though it is flawed—is still the only viable solution for survival.

Summary

Wayward Pines posits a far-flung future in which the human race (as represented by white English-speaking Americans) still has one fragile chance to survive against the onslaught of the hostile, unknowable Other. The myth of small-town America is here presented as the last hope for humanity; while the town of Wayward Pines is inarguably depicted as both uncanny and dystopian, this is narratively blamed on Pilcher and his authoritarian surveillance techniques, as well as Pope's gleeful enforcement of public executions. The town's residents live in fear of monitoring by hidden cameras and microphones, and while they may remember their lives before Wayward Pines, they are unable to speak of their previous experiences, instead maintaining charades of smiling, folksy civility that hide their inner terror. *Wayward Pines* reiterates themes in other series; as in *Falling Skies*, it demonizes the Other, whereas like *Colony*, it criticizes the drastically authoritarian measures taken by authorities in the name of "safety."

If those elements are stripped away, the series presents us with a post-apocalyptic setting like many others: a small American community led by a white, heterosexual man with a history of patriarchal authority and combat experience, whose leadership is the only hope for keeping away the monsters at the gate. Wayward Pines's survival as a community rests on the actions of white men: Pilcher, leading the scientists whose experiments created and maintain the town; Burke, the secret service agent turned sheriff; and Ben, Burke's son and the leader of the First Generation children who are the pro-creative future of society. The town's routinely patriarchal structures and the white, heterosexual monoculture of its population go unaddressed; while it may be implied, through the experiences of characters like Kate or Theresa, that the town is a poor fit for twenty-first-century women, the gendering of their pre-apocalyptic (and now lingering) roles of illicit mistress or dutiful wife is unacknowledged. No one comments when the town's most prominent (and nearly only) Black character is killed, or when the "First Generation"'s assigned task of pairing off and procreating fails to account for the possibility of LGBTQ sexualities. There are children in Wayward Pines, but few elders (and no one old enough to need accommodation or care), and everyone is able-bodied. Little in the series challenges the hegemonic status quo.

Wayward Pines has a second season, which focuses on an almost entirely new cast of characters[6]; season 2 replaces the conflict between Ethan Burke and David Pilcher with the conflict between surgeon Theo Yedlin (Jason Patric) and new First Generation leader Jason Higgins (Tom Stevens). While an attempt is made to diversify the cast, adding Rebecca Yedlin (Nimrat Kaur) and C.J. Mitchum (Djimon Honsou) as regular characters, increasing the number of non-white recurring and background characters, and briefly exploring Frank Armstrong (Michael Gaza)'s position as a (presumably) queer teen, the renewed *Wayward Pines* never fully commits, instead retaining its focus on hetero white men like Theo, Jason, Xander Beck (Josh Helman), and Adam Hassler (Tim Griffin). The series further re-establishes a Black man, Mario (Christopher Meyer), as the face of a corrupt law enforcement system, and juxtaposes its increased character diversity against the onset of the town's inevitable demise. It also further incorporates questionable gender roles, adding Kerry Campbell (Kacey Rohl) as a victim of sexual abuse who unknowingly enters a romantic relationship with her own son, and "Margaret" (Rochelle Okoye), the nonverbal abbie leader, who is simultaneously a woman of color and a monstrous alien queen. Though *Wayward Pines* season 2 flirts with the radical realization that the abbies are intelligent beings—possibly humanity's rightful "replacements"—whose people and land have been vio-lated by the town's colonizing forces, it concludes with attempted biowarfare/genocide against the abbies as Theo and half the town members resume cryo-genic stasis, hoping for a better future under his leadership. The second verse reads, ultimately, much like the first—both morally ambiguous and unable to break from hegemonic norms.

Wayward Pines is fundamentally different from series like *Into the Bad-lands* or *The 100*, which attempt to posit future societies in which humanity has had a chance to regroup and restructure. The fact that Burke, Theresa,

Kate, Pilcher, Pope, and others are all transplants from the late twentieth or early twenty-first century means that they bring their contemporary culture with them; this preservation of current patriarchal systems is only reinforced by the small-town setting that forces those same characters to mimic archetypal roles associated with America's supposedly most wholesome, idyllic communities. The series presents a community infested with authoritarianism, in which intrusive surveillance, strict secrecy, propaganda, and disproportionate punishment all threaten both the nuclear (Burke) family and the small-town way of life; in this sense, it functions as a criticism of post–9/11 America and security precautions that routinely violate civil rights in the name of protection from outside forces. The basis of the myth, however—the notion of Midwestern America itself as the last bastion of human civilization—remains inviolate: Wayward Pines is situated as dystopian because of alterations that change the myth, and not because of the myth itself. The town as presented is a flawed mirror of the American dream, but it is still all that remains against a hostile outside world, and Burke must protect the populace (including his wife and child) from the danger of the vicious unknown.

Conclusion

If post-apocalyptic settings present the opportunity to build a new society on the ashes of the old—the opportunity to envision fictional environs wherein such new societies might flourish—then the moment directly post-catastrophe seems to be limited in our cultural imagination, as we fill such settings with characters who still remember their prior roles as soldiers, politicians, FBI agents, doctors, or stay-at-home spouses. These roles are too frequently used to define who these characters are in the post-apocalypse, how they relate to each other, and what sort of society they are interested in building. The character archetypes themselves restrict our post-apocalyptic imaginations; their too-familiar history—which is also ours—affects their perspectives and choices. *Wayward Pines* is emblematic of this; two thousand years in the future, the lives of its cryogenically-time-traveling characters are still inevitably structured according to the dictates of contemporary American patriarchy.

Series like *Into the Badlands* or *The 100* may have more potential for effectively challenging the status quo: they take place far enough in the future that Earth and the human race remain recognizable, but characters can be further removed from the societal trappings of the twenty-first century. Of course, they may ultimately still be hindered by the perspectives of the writers, directors, actors, and producers who are yet living there, and both *Into the Badlands* and *The 100* represent—to differing degrees—apparent attempts at diversity and inclusiveness that are undoubtedly problematic. Nevertheless, they both make initial strides toward "breaking the mold" of more common post-apocalyptic narratives. Some of this could be their post-post-apocalyptic settings; some could also be their status as more recent series, crafted within a context of increasingly-standard post-apocalyptic tropes and reading as clear attempts to stand out as new and different. While each series' break from such tropes may present with varying degrees of success, it seems heartening that they are trying—that in a sea of post-apocalyptic series that seem increasingly the same, there may yet be potential to break for shore.

Contexts and Conclusions

So many of our wastelands look the same.

Recent post-apocalyptic television has interrogated a variety of scenarios, from alien invasion to zombie uprising, sprinkled with looming pandemics and the constant shadow of nuclear Armageddon. Each scenario may be linked to contemporary events and fears: nuclear apocalypse has cast a shadow over our cultural psyches since World War II; aliens may represent concerns about immigration, invasion, and/or the war on terror; pandemics may evoke world news about bird flu or Ebola; zombies may stand in for any number of panics. It's no coincidence that the number of new Hollywood disaster movies doubled between the 1980s and 90s (Thompson 12); the world is becoming ever more globalized and more complex. Our apocalypses are a reflection of a current cultural vortex of fears (Berger 217), and "stories of the end of the world have never been more popular than they are today" (Garrett 184); their variety represents a multitude of threats (both real and perceived) in uncertain times.

However, the concept of apocalypse—dating back to Biblical interpretations—has also traditionally meant change rather than unrelenting catastrophe; an apocalypse is a time of renewal and even second chances (Thompson 3; Holba and Hart vii). Indeed, the Greek word "apokalyptein" means "to uncover/reveal"; destruction is followed by a new future (Knickerbocker 346). After the fall, what's left? According to much American television, after society crumbles, a white male hero is called to lead. He fits all hegemonic definitions of manhood; he is "a man in power, a man *with* power, and a man of power" (Kimmel 184). He is heterosexual and cisgender; he is skilled in combat and he knows how to shoot a gun. Maybe he's a war veteran or a police officer[1]; maybe he's just a guy with vast inner potential who was in the right (wrong) place at the right (wrong) time. Either way, there's a new sheriff in town—or a soldier, an ex–FBI agent, or just a cowboy wandering through. All of these are variations on the same wild west cowboy myth that has saturated post-colonial American discourse about masculinity, heroism, and survival on a frontier where the innocent must be protected against the savage Other. The case studies in this volume almost all follow variations on a pattern: a white man saving the last remnants of humanity in a post-apocalyptic war zone that has decimated the United States but also left the remainder of the American landscape as the broken playground for its new heroes.

Multiple other themes recur, broadly but consistently, across many of the series in this book. First, with the exceptions of *The Last Ship* and *Falling Skies*, most series register a strong distrust of the old American patriarchy, as evidenced by the inevitably complicating reappearance of a now-evil President of the United States, or the suspect authority of military forces claiming to be United States representatives. It seems clear that while the post-apocalypse offers an opportunity for white male heroes to reclaim authority, the tattered hegemonic systems that produced the disaster are also suspect; instead, the new and future wild west means the chance to rebuild, harking back to the days of colonial settlers and the nostalgic, mythological time when "real" men built America. *The Last Ship* and *Falling Skies* both offer American military forces as protection for the devastated masses, and explicitly seek the restoration of the American Presidency (and all of the historic trappings of patriarchy that such an office signifies); more common, however, are *Jericho*'s assertions that a homeland conspiracy created the nuclear apocalypse, or *Revolution*'s battles against "American" soldiers now cast as unwanted and unjust invaders. In these scenarios, America is lost, but America is also reborn, and the catastrophic event—whether explosion, disease, invasion, or risen dead—has cleared the way for a future that looks much like a mythologized white, patriarchal, heteronormative past.

Stories that emphasize fatherhood are also common—most particularly stories about fathers raising and protecting their sons, but also stories in which sons seek to reconnect with their lost fathers. We see father-son combinations foregrounded in *Jericho* (Jake Green's fraught relationship with his father Johnston), *Revolution* (Neville and son Jason; Monroe and Connor), *Jeremiah* (Jeremiah's search for his father Devon), *Falling Skies* (Tom and sons Hal, Ben, and Matt), *Colony* (Will has two sons and a daughter but is fixated on finding missing son Charlie), *The Walking Dead* (Rick and Carl), and *Fear the Walking Dead* (Travis and Chris). There are occasionally fathers and daughters, like Rick Grimes's toddler Judith in *The Walking Dead*, rarely seen onscreen, or Tom Chandler's son and daughter, seldom on board *The Last Ship*. Primarily, however, men in the post-apocalypse are concerned with preserving a line of heritage—genetic, cultural, familial—between fathers and sons. Girls are more frequently aliens or hybrids, like Tom's ill-fated alien child Lexi on *Falling Skies*, Nolan's adopted daughter Irisa in *Defiance*, or

Murphy's zombie child Lucy on *Z Nation*. For a meaningful parent relationship between a central character and a daughter, a mother is apparently required: *Revolution*'s Rachel and Charlie, *Fear the Walking Dead*'s Madison and Alicia (and Nick), or *The 100*'s Abby and Clarke.

But these stories about fathers most often go hand in hand with absent mothers; a disturbing number of post-apocalyptic heroes either begin the series with dead wives, or are soon widowed. These early victims of the apocalypse include Rebecca Mason (*Falling Skies*), Jenny Jones and Lori Grimes (*The Walking Dead*), and Darien Chandler (*The Last Ship*); Travis's ex-wife Liza also dies, leaving him with Chris (*Fear the Walking Dead*). This pattern of slaughtered women establishes heteronormativity and the fundamental threat to the nuclear family structure that has already been fractured (but can be re-established with the hero's new love interest, who is always female). Mom is replaceable; the children, specifically a man's sons, are not, as the hero must ensure his DNA is preserved for the future. He must also teach his child to be a "man" in a new, cruel world; if he fails, like *Fear the Walking Dead*'s Travis, he will lose his legacy.

The women who do survive in the post-apocalypse almost always occupy secondary roles. Burcar has described Western societies as "closed" systems in which "women are seen as deformities of a human race that is already male" (98); the women appearing on post-apocalyptic American television are generally young, slender, and entangled in romantic subplots. Many of them provide emotional and domestic support to male forces, and they are continually in need of protection. Women over the age of thirty, if they exist—Gail on *Jericho*, Carol from *The Walking Dead*, Rachel in *Revolution*—are mothers, often spurred to violence as an extreme manifestation of the care and nurturing they offer to those they love. Women are also frequently cast as medical specialists (*The Last Ship*'s Rachel, *Jericho*'s April, *Falling Skies*' Anne, *The 100*'s Abby, *Defiance*'s Yewll, *Into the Badlands*' Veil; *Revolution*'s Rachel is also a research scientist). This is a convenient way to professionalize female roles without casting prominent female characters in positions that would disrupt masculine hierarchies.[2] It also preserves gender binaries, continuing to associate women with nurturing; it is particularly notable in *Falling Skies*, where Anne is a pediatrician, or *The 100*, where Abby's desire to be a more effective doctor causes her to abdicate her leadership role as chancellor. Generally, doctor roles are almost exclusively taken by women, while men occupy top military positions or lead ragtag survivor groups; this is one way of ensuring that women are sidelined into advisory positions outside official chains of command. While they may occupy other roles as well (school teacher, bartender, prostitute, housewife), the association of women with medical science is a pervasive pattern extending through multiple series.

Women are also associated with sexual and biological vulnerability; no series unfolds without women being subject to sexual assault or its threat, to the point where a list of examples would include every case study in this volume. The most prominent rape victims might include *Defiance*'s Amanda and Kenya, but threats against women are commonplace whether they are throwaway comments or physical assaults, directed against offscreen communities, onscreen extras, guest stars, or series regulars. This repetitive trope of sexual violence is heteronormative—men's assault of women confusing sexual dominance with sexual desire and creating worlds where women are always and forever *extra* vulnerable, subject not only to alien attack, viral infection, or zombie bite, but also to the whims of marauding, brutal men. There are only two examples of men being threatened with rape: Aaron early in *Revolution* (1.01, "Pilot") and Carl in *The Walking Dead* (4.16, "A"). Here, a man and boy, both coded as "soft," are subject to the threat of sexual dominance (here separate from implications of desire); these examples both stand out as unusual and highlight how similar threats are never directed toward "hard" male series protagonists like Miles Matheson or Rick Grimes. The post-apocalypse is a place ruled by men, and women (and men) who survive must become more masculine. Still, women are forever subject to men's sexual dominance; even those women who master masculine combat or aggressiveness are subordinated through sexualization, both by costuming and camera angles that cater to the male gaze, and by the nigh-constant threat of assault. Post-apocalyptic television echoes post–9/11 anxieties about gender roles and the "softening" of twenty-first-century men (Faludi) by both doubling down on gender binaries and privileging abilities and behaviors perceived to be part of the masculine domain.

Post-apocalyptic series are also highly restrictive with regard to race. Non-white characters who survive the beginnings of the post-apocalypse often don't make it to the end—they more frequently die during the series' runs—and they often inhabit post-racial societies where their skin color or cultural background goes unacknowledged, or in which a survivalist premise demands that questions of racial or ethnic difference be set aside for unification against a common enemy. Post-racial themes are prevalent. This is not to argue that characters of color must always be tools in racial tension storylines, or that such characters, being "of color," are all the same and represent the same groups, interests, or struggles. The problem is that post-racial politics are a white fantasy of equality in which the specific distinctions between different non-white identity groups are erased, and white dominance still continues unremarked—an "illusion that racism has passed" that serves as "the ultimate realization of a hegemonic racial common sense—an inequality without descriptors, without sense, without presence" (Valluvan 2246; see also Warner xi). As Wright has argued, "American popular stories have generally portrayed white male superiority for more than two centuries" (159–60).

Post-apocalyptic television, by and large, continues this trend; its post-racial pretensions, symptomatic of popular post–9/11 texts, merely make the emphasis on white stories more covert (Alsultany 90).

Ultimately, many of the television series examined in this volume begin to overlap. Admittedly, part of this post-apocalyptic uniformity is a trick of casting, as the same actors (friendly to particular genres and/or filming locales) occupy multiple fictional landscapes. Examples include John Pyper-Ferguson's villainous appearance on *Jeremiah* followed a decade later by his heroics on *The Last Ship*, or Lennie James's shift from playing *Jericho*'s Hawkins to *The Walking Dead*'s Morgan. Sarah Wayne Callies dies as Lori Grimes on *The Walking Dead* but survives as Katie on *Colony*. Alycia Debnam-Carey dies as Lexa on *The 100* only to reappear months later playing Alicia in new episodes of *Fear the Walking Dead*. *Revolution*'s Billy Burke fights an animal uprising on *Zoo*. A wash of television series begins to blend together in a sea of broken cars, empty buildings, ragged clothing, and dangerous roads, with the same faces appearing, vanishing, and even perishing over and over again. These recurring faces may be the first visual cue that in watching today's post-apocalyptic television, we run the risk of watching the same stories ad nauseam.

But there is more to the uniformity of our post-apocalyptic visions than repetitive casting, shared directors and design crew members, or the same cities and fields that serve as common filming locations. Though it is, admittedly, "easy to overstate the uniformity of any genre category" (Mittell 238), and I have attempted to explore the distinct qualities of each series studied herein, I have also documented in detail the repetitive nature of wild west imagery, soldiers, secret agents, and manly men, as well as the ways in which twentieth-century American post-apocalyptic television concentrates on white male stories. There are exceptions, as series like *Fear the Walking Dead* or *The 100* strive—with varying degrees of success—to offer variations on an American future where women, non-white people, and LGBTQ people (and non-white queer people, and queer women, and all of those whose identities cross the nebulous boundaries of these groups) do more than occupy supporting roles in an all-too-familiar story. Even so, some tropes are repeated and some constrictions survive, whether through *Fear the Walking Dead*'s emphasis on the same nihilistic violence as its parent series, or *The 100*'s third-season divergence into dead lesbians and male-centered military and political conflict.

The post-apocalypse is a current and evolving part of the Western cultural zeitgeist; as Manjikian observes, "the 'privilege' of imagining the demise of the state is an exercise in arrogance and hubris available only to those in the developed world" (285). Vitally, we need to question not only gender and race roles as they appear in post-apocalyptic narratives, but also the overall privileging of culturally masculine traits and the suggestion that our future is an inevitably violent dystopia in which feminine "weakness" (traits such as empathy or pacifism) will only get someone killed. Post-apocalyptic fictions and their new societies have a rich potential to provoke "exploration and examination of all that we have taken for granted: political arrangements, gender norms, social practices" (Curtis 7); conversely, however, it is also true that our popular texts may promote fantasy escapism rather than truly addressing the social issues at the root of our cultural anxieties (Paik 55; Sontag 42). It is "necessary to examine the context that produces the crisis of masculinity as a symptom and to which narratives of hypermasculinity and paternalistic order are a solution" (Nilges 31–32). Our post-apocalyptic television is rife with the symptoms of white male anxiety and the paranoia of a patriarchy under threat.

These case studies have focused on a narrow sample of American series produced in the early twenty-first century; of course, television is only one strand in a much broader cultural tapestry. Moreover, we are entering a time when it becomes difficult to talk about television as a single medium—when the "collective" viewing experience has passed, as we watch television on our computers and phones and tablets, and when television series are produced for the internet in addition to cable and broadcast networks (H. Hendershot 204). It is difficult to separate television from the complex tangles of other media industries and cultural products (Meehan 122). It's difficult, also, to isolate "American television" as a particularly American phenomenon: American television reaches international audiences, is created by writers, actors, and producers from a variety of backgrounds, and may be co-produced by international partners, remade from prior international series, or filmed in international locations. Indeed, though this analysis is limited to programs at least co-produced by American television networks, many of the post-apocalyptic series herein are created across borders (and all are internationally accessible).

Though many series cover similar ground, questions also remain about how to interpret their successes or failures: "if a program raises important issues, but no one is watching, does it matter?" (H. Hendershot 210). At time of this writing, *The Walking Dead* is embarking on its eighth season[3] and *The Last Ship* is heading toward season 5, while *Revolution* and *Jericho* were each canceled after two years. Does this mean that the first two series are more culturally relevant? Certainly, the exact relationship between artists, producers, institutions, and "the larger patterns of social and cultural change is often obscure or problematic" (Slotkin 7). Sometimes audience reception is indeed a direct response to narrative: *The 100*'s angry fans may have negatively affected the show's ratings after they were enraged at Lexa's death in season 3 (Cranz). And sometimes networks, when making renewal decisions, do credit fan requests: at 29 episodes, *Jericho* is a much shorter series than many others in this analysis, but its 6-episode second season was the result of a fan campaign that had series supporters mailing more than 40,000 pounds of peanuts to CBS (McCullagh). However, it is difficult to make judgment solely based on ratings, as audience size and makeup varies between both years and networks. Further, ratings are not solely based on a series' perceived quality or resonance with the cultural zeitgeist; a series might also be boosted by a star cast member or additional advertising support, or hampered by a less desirable time slot or an uneven airing schedule. The potential for product placement deals, corporate sponsorship, merchandising, media tie-ins, or syndication may all dictate how much network support (and, subsequently, marketing) a series receives. Ratings and demographic information are difficult to track across series and networks, particularly as audience members discover programs over time and different platforms (H. Hendershot 210); a series' relative popularity may not be the most valuable tool used in its analysis.

It is also difficult to track who might take responsibility for any given series making it to air—or whether decisions made by writers, casting agents, network executives, producers, directors, actors, or distributors factor into a particular episode, character, or narrative arc. A surface scan of series writing credits indicates that many series are notably skewed to include male voices.[4] Such conjecture is severely limited: an IMDB credit list may give names, but these are distinctly unreliable indicators of gender that also give little to no indication of race, sexuality, and other demographic factors. We might list show creators: *The Walking Dead* is based on the comic series by Robert Kirkman, and was adapted for television by Frank Darabont. *Fear the Walking Dead* is credited to Kirkman and Dave Erickson. *The Last Ship* was created by Hank Steinberg and Steven Kane. Male showrunners have brought us *Jericho* (Stephen Chbosky, Josh Schaer, Jonathan E. Steinberg), *Jeremiah* (J. Michael Straczynski), *Revolution* (Eric Kripke), *Falling Skies* (Robert Rodat), *Into the Badlands* (Alfred Gough, Miles Millar), *Wayward Pines* (Chad Hodge), *Z Nation* (Craig Engler, Karl Schaefer). *The 100*, although based on novels by Kass Morgan, was adapted for television by Jason Rothenberg. There is little representation of women's voices.

While there is no "secret cabal of television executives planning to brainwash the masses" (Mittell 273), it is also no shock that we are seeing male fantasies fulfilled in a genre that is written and produced by men, within an overall industry governed by men (Writers Guild of America). Nor are these fantasies exclusive to post-apocalyptic television. It is striking, however, that this genre has achieved such ubiquity in the past fifteen years, and that—though such texts have existed before—the links it has to anxieties about contemporary issues like nuclear apocalypse, global pandemic, or immigration and war are so closely tied to much broader concerns about gender and race and sexuality, or the particularly Western and regressive dream of white male ascendance. And if "immense power and money await those who tap into our moral insecurities and supply us with symbolic substitutes" (Glassner xxviii), it is worth interrogating whose insecurities are being addressed in popular narratives, and by whom.

America's speculative futures need diversity, in terms of gender, ethnicity, sexuality, body type, and multiple other measurements. Some televised patterns have recently been altered slightly as twenty-first-century media tries to accommodate the demands of marginalized forces seeking inclusiveness and equality. More women are incorporated into these series, more non-white people, and more (at least a few more) LGBTQ characters appear. Each of these is limited by the prominence of the white male hero, who is almost inevitably—either through experience, natural ability, or both—the best and boldest leader with the vision to guide disparate people through these hard times. While this analysis has concentrated mainly on issues of gender, race, and sexuality, it should be noted that other marginalized groups are absent or almost wholly invisible; there are no transgender characters. Post-apocalyptic narratives are also, "by design, ableist in the extreme" (Kessock); characters with physical disabilities, if they do appear, occupy scattered supporting roles. *Jericho*'s Bonnie is Deaf, *The Walking Dead*'s Hershel survives a season and a half as an amputee, *Into the Badlands*'s Waldo occupies a wheelchair, and *The 100*'s Raven has a cybernetic leg brace; however, such characters are atypical and seldom central. An empty wheelchair in a *Fear the Walking Dead* refugee camp seems to suggest the most commonly presumed post-apocalyptic fate of someone who requires an assistive device—including glasses, as a general dearth of nearsighted characters (saving *Revolution*'s Aaron or *The Walking Dead*'s Denise [Merritt Wever]) suggests the same fate for any who lack 20/20 vision. Additionally, only one character—*The Last Man on Earth*'s Melissa—has a diagnosed mental illness. There is some variety in ages, with children appearing in multiple series and prominent characters over 50 including Hershel and Dale in *The Walking Dead*, Johnston and Gail Green in *Jericho*, Gail in *The Last Man on Earth*, and Dan Weaver in *Falling Skies*; for the most part, however, the faces and figures appearing and reappearing are homogenous, and men in their 30s and 40s take center stage. More research must (and, I am certain, will) be done in these areas. As well, some scholars have specifically related the rise of apocalyptic texts to the breakdown of neoliberal capitalist systems (Cunningham and Warwick; Hassler-Forest; Williams); certainly anxieties about class and wealth play a role and, though these issues have been briefly touched on at points in this text, such socio-economic analyses deserve further attention. Currently, new television episodes are being produced faster than I can write, and I anticipate a wealth of new academic work to fill the gaps.

This subject remains both topical and vital: if apocalyptic literature "has traditionally been written to comfort people whose lives are, or who perceive their lives to be, overwhelmed by historical or social disruption" (Rosen xii), then post-apocalyptic television seems geared as particular reassurance for white men who feel threatened by changes to twenty-first-century social relations. Television provides us with limited character roles that nevertheless act "to provide 'common-sense' understandings of gender and sexuality and to portray what is considered to be both 'appropriate' and 'inappropriate' social relations" (Feasey 155). Post-apocalyptic television is not the only television to offer socially conservative narratives; however, recent iterations of the genre are notable for the near uniformity of sexist, racist, and heteronormative elements. Such series address a variety of fears—nuclear war, cultural invasion, pandemic—but the most consistent fear is apparently the fear of a changing social status quo, as reflected by a repetitive desire to return to colonial narratives in which the white cowboy hero saves the town, or war stories where the (also white male) soldier has the skills, grit, and pluck necessary to survive. If contemporary post-apocalyptic television serves as a cultural reset button that posits the destruction of feminism, civil rights, queer rights, and other social movements whose advances in the twentieth century have begun to threaten heterosexual white male dominance (Nilges), it seems telling that *pre*-apocalyptic series like *Terminator: The Sarah Connor Chronicles* (Fox, 2008–09), *Extant* (CBS, 2014–15), or *V* (ABC, 2009–11) offer diverse female leads within settings that still include variations on current American infrastructures.

Mass media do not dictate ideology, but they are a part of a cyclical relationship between producers and consumers in which such ideologies are produced and reinforced (Slotkin 8); "television does not reflect as much as refract the world" (Mittell 270). Currently, the post-apocalyptic television genre serves as a microcosm demonstrating a particularly conservative viewpoint that has a significant foothold in American culture, as most recently expressed through Donald Trump's successful 2016 run for the presidency and his slogan, "Make America Great Again." Trump ran on a platform that evoked white nostalgia for a time when America was "great"; his popularity with former KKK leader David Duke and white supremacist groups is notable (Osnos). Such groups have patriarchal structures and frequently invoke cowboy myths; they have "spent a great deal of time creating an ideology about white male warriors battling nobly in the approaching apocalyptic encounter and working on pseudo-military maneuvers in isolate areas, many of which are in the West" (Schlatter 41). Series like *Jericho*, *Revolution*, and others in this volume romanticize variations of the same white Western mythology appropriated by radical white supremacist movements—and, further, incorporate the exaggerated gender binaries and militarized masculinities that Faludi links to post-9/11 panic in American media. Western culture seeks to define and redefine manhood in times of crisis (Kimmel 182); while some of the perspectives in post-apocalyptic television may well be the result of an industry seemingly perennially skewed toward white male creators (and the courting of male audiences), there can be no doubt that the dream of a return to some simpler, stronger myth of the American ideal is well rooted in a significant portion of the American population—and "in an effort to quell white American male fears, Hollywood has been enlisted time and again" (Pressley-Sanon 162). A few series, such as *The 100*, are working to break this mold, but unless radical change occurs in the future, this particular segment of American television may struggle with the political challenges of the present, condemned to rehash a forever sexist, racist, exclusionary past.

Chapter Notes

Chapter 1

1. With American president-elect Donald Trump calling for a renewed nuclear "arms race" (as of December 23, 2016), it seems possible that these anxieties will see a resurgence in American and world culture (Walsh).

2. This is not necessarily any attempt to explicitly align the series with truther explanations of 9/11; rather, these elements too are rooted in American culture that has long included a fascination with conspiracy theory. Rumors about a faked moon landing, the grassy knoll JFK shooter, or Roswell aliens all persist at the edges of American history, perhaps lent continuing life by conspiracies—such as Watergate, or cover-ups about cigarette health threats—that did prove to be true (Goldberg 32–34).

3. This is a defining moment in series narrative; when *Jericho* was canceled by the network after season 1, fans mailed packages of peanuts to convince executives to greenlight what became the shortened season 2.

4. For examples, see discussion board threads such as "'Revolution' New TV Series Comparisons to 'Jericho' (2006) Series" (http://www.trekbbs.com/threads/revolution-new-tv-series-comparisons-to-jericho-2006-series.185084/) or "New NBC Show: Revolution—Lost Meets Jericho—From Eric Kripke and JJ Abrams" (http://neogaf.com/forum/showthread.php?t=474030).

5. Cynthia is originally Aaron's "employer," which reads as either the barest nod to feminism or a note in the continued emasculation of Aaron's character, in which her superior social position is another hurdle of masculinity for him to overcome.

6. The series was canceled before this storyline could be resolved.

7. MILF is a colloquial North American acronym for "mother I'd like to fuck," denoting a sexually attractive woman with children.

8. The "previously on *Revolution*" segment that opens 1.20 ("The Dark Tower") explicitly conflates this; Miles goes directly from choking Rachel in one flashback to kissing her in the next.

9. Original promo posters in the series featured Charlie; by episode ten, this had changed, as the 2012 "fall finale" ads more prominently foregrounded Miles and Monroe with Charlie behind them in the middle.

10. This naming convention (first name "Miles" vs. surname "Monroe") is how the characters are addressed in the series.

11. As of January 28, 2018. http://archiveofourown.org/tags/Revolution%20(TV)/works.

12. In TVTropes terms, "Black Dude Dies First." http://tvtropes.org/pmwiki/pmwiki.php/Main/BlackDudeDiesFirst.

Chapter 2

1. Significant tension was documented between the network, the producer (MGM),

and showrunner J. Michael Straczynski, who left after season 2 (when the series was also canceled). For an example of the rumors surrounding the series, see http://www.mail-archive.com/brin-1%40mccmedia.com/msg20343.html.

2. This is also a theme in Straczynski's other work, such as *Babylon 5* (PTEN, 1994–97; TNT, 1998).

3. "Daniel" is represented almost exclusively by white male spokespeople with short brown hair and blue or brown eyes (e.g. Vincent, 2.04, "Deux Ex Machina"; Charlie, 2.05, "Rites of Passage"; Karl, 2.07, "Voices in the Dark"), leading soldiers who are also nearly exclusively white and male.

4. Interestingly, this narrative does not carry through; while Jeremiah is a father himself, he does not realize this, as his former partner Michelle (Sabrina Grdevich) raised his son in secret. When he discovers the truth, he makes peace with Michelle and begins forming a bond with Gabe (Spencer Achtymichuk), but only for a single episode, after which Michelle and Gabe vanish permanently from the screen.

5. By episode appearance, the most frequently appearing characters are Jeremiah and Kurdy (34 episodes), Markus (19 episodes), Erin (19 episodes), Lee Chen (18 episodes), Mr. Smith (15 episodes), and Libby (12). Theo and Elizabeth appear in 8 episodes each; Meaghan is in 7. http://www.imdb.com/title/tt0290966/?ref_=fn_al_tt_1.

6. She also briefly serves as a love interest for Jeremiah; she initially rejects his advances, but later poses as her twin sister in order to have sex with him. This both advances "no-means-yes" stereotypes, as Erin acts on her desires despite her vocal refusals, and skirts over issues of consent. By acting under a false identity, Erin rapes Jeremiah, and yet when she reveals the deception—alluding to it without directly confessing—he laughs it off. Erin is cast in a role that perennially nurtures a man, and then she is further sexualized and entangled in a complex mess of stereotypes regarding women's consent and the downplaying of sexual assault against men.

7. Considering Markus's characterization in season 1—his intellectual, diplomatic version of masculine leadership—it seems notable that his chaste relationship with Meaghan also emasculates him. He lacks the sexual virility of Jeremiah or Kurdy, both of whom have multiple onscreen sexual partners.

8. https://www.youtube.com/watch?v=SSS5sCSLwuE.

9. http://cdn2-www.comingsoon.net/assets/uploads/2015/04/thelastshiplarge.jpg.

10. For an example, see Brian Mitchell, *Women in the Military: Flirting with Disaster,* Regnery Publishing: 1997.

11. *The Last Ship* occupies a neutral position with regard to scientific institutions—something of a break from earlier pandemic narratives that reinforced the need for science and presented reassuring tales of crises averted at the last minute (Wald 268). Here, science—in the form of sociopathically irresponsible biochemist Niels (Ebon Moss-Bachrach)—is responsible for the pandemic in the first place, referencing cultural paranoia about bioengineering, biochemical warfare and experimentation. Rachel, however, is the face of science as savior, the science that can provide the only solution.

12. Notably, the women and girls endangered by Ruskov and El Toro have men who failed to protect them and are additionally emasculated: Quincy, a scientist with no combat training who cannot save his family himself, and Ervin Delgado (Alex Fernandez), the mayor who cooperates with El Toro rather than fighting back, and is subsequently forced to surrender his daughters. Both Quincy and Delgado represent "soft" men, unable to face off against terrorists and unable to protect their loved ones—who are, clearly, unable to protect themselves. This both lauds the actions of the heroic sailors and cautions against the familial tragedies that can result from male weakness. Indeed, Quincy's role as a traitor leads to his self-sacrifice and death (2.01, "Unreal City").

Chapter 3

1. http://www.imdb.com/title/tt1462059/?ref_=fn_al_tt_1.

2. Further, it's not clear why Ben retains his agency while Rick succumbs, though it may be read that Rick was abducted for longer. However, it is difficult to avoid reading racial implications here as well, since strong-willed Ben—as Tom's son—is a mem-

ber of the Mason family dynasty, while the psychologically weaker Rick—who appears in only 9 episodes—is Black, his father Mike (Martin Roach) preceding him in death.

3. Katie Marshall (Melora Hardin), the captain of the 14th Virginia, is already dead, and has been replaced by an alien replicant; she is another blonde white woman corrupted by alien influence. She is also an inept leader and Weaver's ex-lover; though she attempts to seduce him, her increasingly irrational commands lead to her death by mutiny (5.07, "Everybody Has Their Reasons"; 5.08, "Stalag 14th Virginia").

4. http://www.imdb.com/title/tt1462059/fullcredits?ref_=tt_ov_st_sm.

5. Moon Bloodgood's racial heritage is both white and Korean, as per her IMDB profile. http://www.imdb.com/name/nm1291227/bio?ref_=nm_ov_bio_sm.

6. *Falling Skies* does this very briefly, when Tom also compares the human resistance to Geronimo (4.03, "Exodus"); *Falling Skies* primarily projects a Native American "frontier" role onto the alien Volm, however, while *Colony* remains consistent in its appropriations.

7. In many ways, the series is reminiscent of the 1990s television program *Babylon 5*, which also required its human protagonist to navigate among a variety of alien races and customs.

8. The focus on Nolan-as-protagonist-lawkeeper also invites neoconservative narratives. At one point, Nolan shoots and kills a Castithan teenager who is holding a paintball gun—a plotline reminiscent of the same types of systemic police action that caused the rise of the Black Lives Matter movement. Nolan's actions are fully supported by the viewer's knowledge that Datak Tarr set him up, machinating the teen's death in order to score points in the mayoral race. Nolan is innocent within this framework, and his actions framed as certainly not racist (1.11, "Past is Prologue"). It is the same world in which Rafe McCawley, portrayed by Indigenous actor Graham Greene, finds he has been profiting from mining land illegally seized from Irathient settlers (1.03, "The Devil in the Dark").

9. Canonically, Nicky Riordan is revealed as an Indogene spy shortly before she is murdered (1.11, "The Bride Wore Black");

however, she is otherwise perceived as human and subsequently possesses human privilege for the duration of her time on the series.

10. The Brownstein article cited here profiles Rath's sister Meaghan.

11. Much as Nolan's promotion over Jessica (Berlin) Rainier at the beginning of season 3 is not presented as a question of sexism—and, furthermore, happens offscreen.

12. Amanda is also canonically heterosexual; Kenya's preferences are less clear. She may be bisexual, but she also seduces Stahma while working, and her only non-working relationships are with her ex-husband and Nolan.

Chapter 4

1. Glenn dies in the premiere episode of season 7.

2. Linneman, Wall, and Green have specifically linked racial panic and zombies in the 2012 Miami case of police fatally shooting Rudy Eugene while he ate a homeless man's face. Eugene was Black, of Haitian descent (507).

3. According to IMDB, Frank Dillane is biracial (his father is white and his mother is of Afro-Jamaican heritage). The character Nick is apparently white, as Nick and Alicia share the same father and the Nick role was originally cast with white actor Robert Sheehan before Dillane took over (Rowles). Multiple fan sites take issue with this. For an example, see "Why We Should Talk About Nick Being White," http://frank-d-makes-me-happy.tumblr.com/post/143518592392/why-we-should-talk-about-nick-being-white.

4. Cassandra is not given a pre-apocalypse back story. 10k's is limited, since he was a teenager camping with his father.

5. Vasquez returns for one episode in season 3 (3.09, "Heart of Darkness," where he dies) and Hector is also present as an antagonist in season 2 before he joins the survivors and is killed (by Vasquez) in 3.09.

Chapter 5

1. Steenbergen was in her sixties when filming began; she was born in 1953.

2. My reading of Todd as Latino is qualified; it is possible he is intended to be

perceived as a white man. Actor Mel Rodriguez is of Cuban American descent ("Little Havana"), and the narrative neither actively addresses nor disavows this ethnic heritage.

Chapter 6

1. Baron Chau (Eleanor Matsuura), an Asian woman, is added to the cast in season 2, possibly to counter any observation that other than Jacobee and the Widow, all other Barons were white men.

2. Baron Chau, as well as Jade's brief ascendancy.

3. 5 of 11 characters appearing in all 6 episodes of the first season are women.

4. This sounds like a sexy shot but it is in fact quite violent; one notable takeaway is that Clarke ends up with cuts on her face that last through the next episode. This small detail outlines one way in which the series resists sexualizing Clarke's body and features.

5. Octavia is small and white. Lincoln is tall, muscular, Black, and initially nonverbal; early episodes present the grounders as animalistic and unknowable jungle denizens.

6. Significant delays between the filming of the first and second seasons meant that many of the original actors had moved on to other projects (Anderton).

Contexts and Conclusions

1. This is not exclusive to the post-apocalyptic genre; men on television are frequently involved with law or crime, and "the prevailing depiction of male characters in the context of crime is of tough guys who frequently use aggression or violence" (Scharrer 163).

2. There is a marked contrast here with *Wayward Pines*'s Theo Yedlin, who uses his indispensability as a surgeon to assert political power (and who, it is implied, lets his rival die on the operating table). Yedlin's role suggests a tie between medicine and power and downplays any links between medicine and nurturing, thus masculinizing his position.

3. While embroiled in lawsuits (Bradley), which may conceivably affect the series' long-term future.

4. Choosing one illustrative example, the credits for *Defiance*, reveals a preponderance of male-coded credits: the series was created by Kevin Murphy, Rockne S. O'Bannon, and Michael Taylor, with additional writers Clark Perry, Todd Slavkin, Darren Swimmer, Kari Drake, Brian A. Alexander, Anupam Nigam, Bryan Q. Miller, Amanda Alpert Muscat, Bryan Garcia, Craig Gore, Bradley Thompson, Tim Walsh, David Weddle, Brusta Brown, Nevin Densham, Allison Miller, John Mitchell Todd, Phoef Sutton, Manuel Figueroa, Jordan Heimer, Nick Mueller, Geoffrey Tock, Gregory Weidman, and Paula Yoo; directors included Michael Nankin, Allan Kroeker, Andy Wolk, Allan Arkush, Larry Shaw, Omar Madha, Scott Stewart, Mairzee Almas, Félix Enríquez Alcalá, Todd Slavkin, and Thomas Burstyn. According to IMDB at http://www.imdb.com/title/tt2189221/fullcredits?ref_= tt_ov_st_sm.

Works Cited

Ahmad, Aalya. "Gray Is the New Black: Race, Class, and Zombies." *Generation Zombie: Essays on the Living Dead in Modern Culture.* Ed. Stephanie Boluk and Wylie Lenz. Jefferson: McFarland, 2011. 130–146.

Alsultany, Evelyn. "*24*: Challenging Stereotypes." *How to Watch Television.* Ed. Ethan Thompson and Jason Mittell. New York: New York University Press, 2013. 85–93.

Anderton, Ethan. "Second Season of 'Wayward Pines' May Have All-New Cast." */Film.* 28 June 2015. www.slashfilm.com/wayward-pines-season-two/.

Apuzzo, Matt, Sheri Fink, and James Risen. "How U.S. Torture Left a Legacy of Damaged Minds." *The New York Times.* 9 October 2016. www.nytimes.com/2016/10/09/world/cia-torture-guantanamo-bay.html.

Ausiello, Michael. "*Last Man on Earth*: Will Forte *Really* Didn't Want to Kill Off [Spoiler]." *TVLine.* 16 March 2017. tvline.com/2017/03/16/the-last-man-on-earth-season-3-lewis-dies-kenneth-choi/.

Badley, Linda. "Scully Hits the Glass Ceiling: Postmodernism, Postfeminism, Posthumanism, and the *X-Files*." *Fantasy Girls: Gender in the New Universe of Science Fiction and Fantasy Television.* Ed. Elyce Rae Helford. Lanham, MD: Rowman & Littlefield, 2000. 61–90.

Battistella, Edwin. "Girly Men and Girly Girls." *American Speech* 81.1 (2006): 100–110.

Berger, James. *After the End: Representations of Post-Apocalypse.* Minneapolis: University of Minnesota Press, 1999.

Bishop, Kyle William. *How Zombies Conquered Popular Culture: The Multifarious Walking Dead in the 21st Century.* Jefferson: McFarland, 2015.

Boluk, Stephanie, and Wylie Lenz. "Introduction: Generation Z, the Age of Apocalypse." *Generation Zombie: Essays on the Living Dead in Modern Culture.* Ed. Stephanie Boluk and Wylie Lenz. Jefferson: McFarland, 2011. 1–17.

Bradley, Laura. "*Walking Dead* Stuntman's Family Sues AMC for Wrongful Death." *Vanity Fair.* 24 January 2018. www.vanityfair.com/hollywood/2018/01/walking-dead-wrongful-death-lawsuit-frank-darabont-second-lawsuit-amc.

Braxton, Greg. "'The Last Ship' on TNT Is Packed with U.S. Navy Firepower." *Los Angeles Times.* 20 June 2014. www.latimes.com/entertainment/tv/la-et-st-last-ship-20140620-story.html.

Brownstein, Bill. "On the Scene of the Crime—And Comedy, Romance and Sci-Fi." *Montreal Gazette.* 5 February 2015. montrealgazette.com/entertainment/arts/on-the-scene-of-the-crime-and-comedy-romance-and-sci-fi.

Buchanan, Kyle. "Why Won't Hollywood Let Us See Our Best Black Actors?" *Vulture.* 27 April 2016. www.vulture.com/2016/04/hollywood-black-actors.html.

Burcar, Jillian. "Living Appendages of the Machine: Reproducing Sex and Gender in Cyborg and Zombie Narratives, from *Battlestar Galactica* to the *Walking Dead.*" *The Monster Imagined: Humanity's Re-Creation of Monsters and Monstrosity.* Ed. Laura K. Davis and Cristina Santos. Freeland: Inter-Disciplinary Press, 2010. 67–84.

Cady, Kathryn A., and Thomas Oates. "Family Splatters: Rescuing Heteronormativity from the Zombie Apocalypse." *Women's Studies in Communication* 39.3 (2016): 308–325.

Canavan, Gerry. "'We *Are* the Walking Dead': Race, Time, and Survival in Zombie Narrative." *Extrapolation* 51.3 (2010): 431–453.

Caputi, Jane. "Films of the Nuclear Age." *Journal of Popular Film and Culture* 16.3 (1998): 101–107.

CDC. "Zika Virus: Outcomes of Pregnancies with Laboratory Evidence of Possible Zika Virus Infection in the United States, 2016." 28 July 2016. www.cdc.gov/zika/geo/pregnancy-outcomes.html.

Cloud, Dana L. "'To Veil the Threat of Terror': Afghan Women and the <Clash of Civilizations> in the Imagery of the U.S. War on Terrorism." *Quarterly Journal of Speech* 90.3 (2004): 285–306.

Coleman, Lindsay Krishna. "The Whore with the Vampire Heart: Frontier Romanticism in John Carpenter's *Vampires.*" *Undead in the West: Vampires, Zombies, Mummies, and Ghosts on the Cinematic Frontier.* Ed. Cynthia J. Miller and A. Bowdoin Van Riper. Lanham: The Scarecrow Press, 2012. 33–44.

Cranz, Alex. "Angry Fans May Have Actually Driven Down the *100*'s Ratings." *Io9.* 11 March 2016. io9.gizmodo.com/angry-fans-may-have-actually-driven-down-the-100s-ratin-1764318782.

Crider, Michael. "CW Bites on Zombie Apocalypse Series 'Awakening.'" *ScreenRant.* 31 January 2011. screenrant.com/cw-zombie-tv-show-awakening/.

Cunningham, David, and Alexandra Warwick. "Unnoticed Apocalypse: The Science Fiction Politics of Urban Crisis." *City* 17.4 (2013): 433–448.

Curtis, Claire P. *Postapocalyptic Fiction and the Social Contract: "We'll Not Go Home Again."* Lanham, MD: Lexington Books, 2010.

"Defiance (Series)." *TV Tropes.* http://tvtropes.org/pmwiki/pmwiki.php/Series/Defiance.

Deutsch, Sarah. *No Separate Refuge: Culture, Class, and Gender on an Anglo-Hispanic Frontier in the American Southwest, 1880–1940.* New York: Oxford University Press, 1987.

Donovan, John. "Atomic Age Monsters: Radioactivity and Horror During the Early Cold War." *The Monster Imagined: Humanity's Re-Creation of Monsters and Monstrosity.* Ed. Laura K. Davis and Cristina Santos. Freeland: Inter-Disciplinary Press, 2010. 67–85.

Doyle, Don Harrison. *Faulkner's County: The Historic Roots of Yoknapatawpha.* UNC Press Books, 2001.

Droogsma, Rachel Anderson. "Redefining Hijab: American Muslim Women's Standpoints on Veiling." *Journal of Applied Communication Research* 35.3 (2007): 294–319.

Faludi, Susan. *The Terror Dream: Fear and Fantasy in Post-9/11 America.* New York: Metropolitan Books, 2007.

Fausset, Richard. "Refugee Crisis in Syria Raises Fears in South Carolina." *The New York Times.* 25 September 2015. www.nytimes.com/2015/09/26/us/refugee-crisis-in-syria-raises-fears-in-south-carolina.html.

Feasey, Rebecca. *Masculinity and Popular Television.* Edinburgh: Edinburgh University Press, 2008.

Feshami, Kevan A. "Death Is Only the Beginning: George A. Romero's Model of the Zombie and Its Threat to Identity." *The Monster Imagined: Humanity's Re-Creation of Monsters and Monstrosity.* Ed. Laura K. Davis and Cristina Santos. Freeland: Inter-Disciplinary Press, 2010. 85–96.

Garrett, Greg. *Living with the Living Dead: The Wisdom of the Zombie Apocalypse.* New York: Oxford University Press, 2017.

Glassner, Barry. *The Culture of Fear: Why Americans Are Afraid of the Wrong Things.* New York: Basic Books, 1999.

Goldberg, Robert Allan. *Enemies Within: The Culture of Conspiracy in Modern America.* New Haven: Yale University, 2001.

Goldman, Eric. "The 100 Showrunner on

the Huge Lexa Reveals and Shocks in 'Thirteen.'" *IGN.* 3 March 2016. www.ign. com/articles/2016/03/04/the-100-show runner-on-the-huge-lexa-reveals-and-shocks-in-thirteen.

Greene, John, and Michaela D.E. Meyer. "The Walking (Gendered) Dead: A Feminist Rhetorical Critique of Zombie Apocalypse Television Narrative." *Ohio Communication Journal* 52 (2014): 64–74.

Hantke, Steffen. "Bush's America and the Return of Cold War Science Fiction: Alien Invasion in *Invasion, Threshold* and *Surface.*" *Journal of Popular Film and Television* 38.3 (2010): 143–151.

Hassler-Forest, Dan. "Cowboys and Zombies: Destabilizing Patriarchal Discourse in the *Walking Dead.*" *Studies in Comics* 2.2 (2011): 339–355.

Helford, Elyce Rae. "Introduction." *Fantasy Girls: Gender in the New Universe of Science Fiction and Fantasy Television*. Ed. Elyce Rae Helford. Lanham, MD: Rowman & Littlefield, 2000. 1–12.

Hendershot, Cyndy. "Vampire and Replicant: The One-Sex Body in a Two-Sex World." *Science Fiction Studies* 22 (1995): 373–398.

Hendershot, Heather. "*Parks and Recreation*: The Cultural Forum." *How to Watch Television*. Ed. Ethan Thompson and Jason Mittell. New York: New York University Press, 2013. 204–212.

Hewitson, James. "Undead and Un-American: The Zombified Other in Weird Western Films." *Undead in the West: Vampires, Zombies, Mummies, and Ghosts on the Cinematic Frontier*. Ed. Cynthia J. Miller and A. Bowdoin Van Riper. Lanham: The Scarecrow Press, 2012. 166–181.

Hibberd, James. "Comic-Con Reviews NBC'S 'Revolution': Fans Say..." *Entertainment Weekly*. 12 July 2012. www.ew. com/article/2012/07/12/comic-con-revolution.

Ho, Helen K. "The Model Minority in the Zombie Apocalypse: Asian-American Manhood on AMC'S the *Walking Dead.*" *The Journal of Popular Culture* 49.1 (2016): 57–76.

Hoffstadt, Christian, and Dominik Schrez. "Aftermath: Post-Apocalyptic Imagery." *British Science Fiction Film and Television: Critical Essays*. Ed. Tobias Hochscherf

and James Leggott. Jefferson: McFarland, 2011. 28–39.

Holba, Annette M., and Kylo-Patrick R. Hart. "Introduction." *Media and the Apocalypse*. Ed. Kylo-Patrick R. Hart and Annette M. Holba. New York: Peter Lang, 2009. vii–xiv.

Holmlund, Christine. "A Decade of Deadly Dolls: Hollywood and the Woman Killer." *Moving Targets: Women, Murder and Representation*. Ed. Helen Birch. Berkeley: University of California Press, 1993. 127–151.

hooks, bell. *Black Looks: Race and Representation*. Boston: South End Press, 1992.

Hubner, Laura, Marcus Leaning and Paul Manning, "Introduction." *The Zombie Renaissance in Popular Culture*. Ed. Laura Hubner, Marcus Leaning and Paul Manning. New York: Palgrave Macmillan, 2015. 3–14.

Huddy, Leonie, and Stanley Feldman. "Americans Respond Politically to 9/11: Understanding the Impact of the Terrorist Attacks and Their Aftermath." *American Psychologist* 66.6 (2011): 455–467.

Inness, Sherrie A. *Tough Girls: Women Warriors and Wonder Women in Popular Culture*. Philadelphia: University of Pennsylvania Press, 1999.

Kakoudaki, Despina. "Spectacles of History: Race Relations, Melodrama, and the Science Fiction/Disaster Film." *Camera Obscura* 50.17, no. 2 (2002): 109–153.

Keetley, Dawn. "Introduction: 'We're All Infected.'" *We're All Infected: Essays on AMC'S The Walking Dead And the Fate of the Human*. Ed. Dawn Keetley. Jefferson, NC: McFarland, 2014. 3–25.

Kelly, Mary Louise. "Even with Failures, North Korea's Nuclear Program Races Ahead." *NPR*. 25 October 2016. www.npr. org/sections/parallels/2016/10/25/ 499321245/even-with-failures-north-koreas-nuclear-program-races-ahead.

Kennedy, Randall. "Racial Passing." *Ohio State Law Journal* 63.3 (2001): 1145–1193.

Keränen, Lisa. "Concocting Viral Apocalypse: Catastrophic Risk and the Production of Bio(In)Security." *Western Journal of Communication* 75.5 (2011): 451–472.

Kessock, Shoshana. "Disability Erasure and the Apocalyptic Narrative." 28 August 2017. shoshanakessock.com/2017/08/28/

disability-erasure-and-the-apocalyptic-narrative/.

Kimmel, Michael S. "Masculinity as Homophobia: Fear, Shame and Silence in the Constitution of Gender Identity." *Feminism and Masculinities*. Ed. Peter F. Murphy. Oxford: Oxford University Press, 2004. 182–199.

Knickerbocker, Dale. "Apocalypse, Utopia, and Dystopia: Old Paradigms Meet a New Millennium." *Extrapolation* 51.3 (2010): 345–357.

Koblin, John. "How Much Do We Love TV? Let Us Count the Ways." *The New York Times*. 30 June 2016. www.nytimes.com/2016/07/01/business/media/nielsen-survey-media-viewing.html.

Kordas, Ann. "New South, New Immigrants, New Women, New Zombies." *Race, Oppression, and the Zombie: Essays on Cross-Cultural Appropriations of the Caribbean Tradition*. Ed. Corey James Rushton and Christopher Moreman. Jefferson: McFarland, 2011. 15–30.

Kremmel, Laura. "Rest in Pieces: Violence in Mourning the (Un)Dead." *We're All Infected: Essays on AMC'S The Walking Dead And the Fate of the Human*. Ed. Dawn Keetley. Jefferson: McFarland, 2014. 80–94.

Lauro, Sarah Juliet. "The Eco-Zombie: Environmental Critique in Zombie Fiction." *Generation Zombie: Essays on the Living Dead in Modern Culture*. Ed. Stephanie Boluk and Wylie Lenz. Jefferson: McFarland, 2011. 54–66.

Lilley, Terry G., Joel Best, Benigno E. Aguirre, and Kathleen S. Lowney. "Magnetic Imagery: War-Related Ribbons as a Collective Display." *Sociological Inquiry* 80.2 (2010): 313–321.

Limerick, Patricia Nelson. "The Adventures of the Frontier in the Twentieth Century." *The Frontier in American Cinema: An Exhibition at the Newberry Library, August 26, 1994–January 7, 1995*. Ed. James R. Grossman. Berkeley: University of California Press, 1994. 67–102.

Linneman, Travis, Tyler Wall, and Edward Green. "The Walking Dead and Killing State: Zombification and the Normalization of Police Violence." *Theoretical Criminology* 18.4 (2014): 506–527.

Little, Judith A. "Introduction." *Feminist Philosophy and Science Fiction: Utopias and Dystopias*. Ed. Judith A. Little. New York: Prometheus Books, 2007.

"Little Havana to Hollywood: 5 Questions for 'Getting On's' Mel Rodriguez." *NBC News*. 17 November 2014. www.nbcnews.com/news/latino/little-havana-hollywood-5-questions-getting-ons-mel-rodriguez-n250036.

Lucanio, Patrick. *Them or Us: Archetypal Interpretations of Fifties Alien Invasion Films*. Bloomington: Indiana University Press, 1987.

MacDonald, Lindsay. "11 Times the *100* Was More Progressive About Race, Gender, & Sexuality than Many Shows Out There." *Bustle*. 4 February 2016. www.bustle.com/articles/138293-11-times-the-100-was-more-progressive-about-race-gender-sexuality-than-many-shows-out.

Manjikian, Mary. *Apocalypse and Post-Politics: The Romance of the End*. Lanham, MD: Lexington, 2012.

Manning, Paul. "Zombies, Zomedies, Digital Fan Cultures and the Politics of Taste." *The Zombie Renaissance in Popular Culture*. Ed. Laura Hubner, Marcus Leaning and Paul Manning. New York: Palgrave Macmillan, 2015. 160–173.

Martin, Geoff, and Erin Steuter. *Pop Culture Goes to War: Enlisting and Resisting Militarism in the War on Terror*. Lanham: Lexington Books, 2010.

McCullagh, Declan. "Deluge of Peanuts Brings Back 'Jericho' TV Show." *CNet*. 6 June 2007. www.cnet.com/news/deluge-of-peanuts-brings-back-jericho-tv-show/.

McIntosh, Jonathan. "Military Recruitment and Science Fiction Movies." 28 September 2016. www.youtube.com/watch?v=N5xfBtD6rLY.

McRobbie, Angela. "Postfeminism and Popular Culture: Bridget Jones and the New Gender Regime." *Interrogating Postfeminism: Gender and the Politics of Popular Culture*. Ed. Yvonne Tasker and Diane Negra. Durham: Duke University Press, 2007. 27–39.

Meehan, Eileen R. *Why TV Is Not Our Fault: Television Programming, Viewers, and Who's Really in Control*. New York: Rowman & Littlefield, 2005.

Michaela. "Z Nation Exclusive: Anastasia Baranova Talks the Man, Bisexuality, and

Addy's Revenant." *OMFGTV*. 4 November 2016. http://omfgtv.com/syfy-anastasia-baranova-addy-season-3-preview-bisexual-sex-dana-kiss-sun-mei/.

Mikkelson, David. "Feminist Bra Burning." *Snopes*. 7 October 2007. www.snopes.com/history/american/burnbra.asp.

Miller, Cynthia J. "'So This Zombie Walks into a Bar...': The Living, the Undead, and the Western Saloon." *Undead in the West: Vampires, Zombies, Mummies, and Ghosts on the Cinematic Frontier*. Ed. Cynthia J. Miller and A. Bowdoin Van Riper. Lanham: The Scarecrow Press, 2012. 3–18.

Miller, Cynthia J., and A. Bowdoin Van Riper. "Introduction." *Undead in the West: Vampires, Zombies, Mummies, and Ghosts on the Cinematic Frontier*. Ed. Cynthia J. Miller and A. Bowdoin Van Riper. Lanham: The Scarecrow Press, 2012. xi–xxvi.

Miller, Liz Shannon. "'Into the Badlands': The Hong Kong Secret That Makes the Show's Amazing Martial Arts Possible." *IndieWire*. 25 March 2017. www.indiewire.com/2017/03/amc-into-the-badlands-season-2-martial-arts-daniel-wu-1201796263/.

Mitovich, Matt Webb. "*The Last Ship* EPs Talk Rachel Scott Decision, 'Ferocious' Slattery Situation." *TVLine*. 19 June 2016. tvline.com/2016/06/19/the-last-ship-season-3-premiere-rachel-scott-died/.

Mittell, Jason. *Television and American Culture*. Oxford: Oxford University Press, 2010.

Moreland, Sean. "Shambling Towards Mount Improbable to Be Born: American Evolutionary Anxiety and the Hopeful Monsters of Matheson's *I Am Legend* and Romero's *Dead* Films." *Generation Zombie: Essays on the Living Dead in Modern Culture*. Ed. Stephanie Boluk and Wylie Lenz. Jefferson: McFarland, 2011. 77–89.

Nail, Paul R., and Ian McGregor. "Conservative Shift Among Liberals and Conservatives Following 9/11/01." *Social Justice Research* 22 (2009): 231–240.

Neumark, Selena. "Why CW'S the *100* Is a Feminist Dream, Except for When It's Not." *PopMatters*. 28 October 2015. www.popmatters.com/feature/why-cws-the-100-is-a-feminist-dream-except-for-when-its-not/.

Nilges, Mathias. "The Aesthetics of Destruction: Contemporary US Cinema and TV Culture." *Reframing 9/11: Film, Popular Culture and the "War on Terror."* Ed. Jeff Birkenstein, Anna Froula and Karen Randell. London: Continuum International Publishing, 2010. 1–10.

Nurse, Angus. "Asserting Law and Order Over the Mindless." *We're All Infected: Essays on AMC'S The Walking Dead And the Fate of the Human*. Ed. Dawn Keetley. Jefferson: McFarland, 2014. 68–79.

O'Connor, John E., and Peter C. Rollins. "Introduction: The West, Westerns, and American Character." *Hollywood's West: The American Frontier in Film, Television, and History*. Ed. Peter C. Rollins and John E. O'Connor. Lexington: The University Press of Kentucky, 2005. 1–34.

Oldring, Amanda. "The Culture Apocalypse: Hegemony and the Frontier at the End of the World." *Stream: Culture/Politics/Technology* 5.1 (2013): 8–20.

Olsen, Douglas P., and Anne Gallagher. "Ethical Issues for Nurses in Force-Feeding Guantánamo Bay Detainees." *American Journal of Nursing* 114.11 (2014): 47–50.

Orosco, José-Antonio. *Toppling the Melting Pot: Immigration and Multiculturalism in American Pragmatism*. Indiana University Press, 2016.

Osnos, Evan. "Donald Trump and the Ku Klux Klan: A History." *The New Yorker*. 29 February 2016. www.newyorker.com/news/news-desk/donald-trump-and-the-ku-klux-klan-a-history.

Otterson, Joe. "'Walking Dead' Posts Lowest Midseason Finale Ratings Since Season 2." *Variety*. 12 December 2017. https://variety.com/2017/tv/news/walking-dead-season-8-midseason-finale-ratings-1202637454/.

Paffenroth, Kim. "Zombies as Internal Fear or Threat." *Generation Zombie: Essays on the Living Dead in Modern Culture*. Ed. Stephanie Boluk and Wylie Lenz. Jefferson: McFarland, 2011. 18–26.

Paik, Peter Y. "Apocalypse by Subtraction: Late Capitalism and the Trauma of Scarcity." *Beyond Globalization: Making New Worlds in Media, Art and Social Practices*. Ed. A. Aneesh, Lane Hall, and Patrice Petro. New Jersey: Rutgers University Press, 2012. 49–71.

Works Cited

Pallotta, Frank. "'Walking Dead' Rises Again with Record High Ratings." *CNNMoney.* 14 October 2014. money.cnn.com/2014/10/13/media/walking-dead-ratings/index.html.

Parks, Rita. *The Western Hero in Film and Television: Mass Media Mythology.* Ann Arbor: UMI Research Press, 1982.

Petersen, Anne Helen. "'Whores and Other Feminists': Recovering *Deadwood*'s Unlikely Feminisms." *Great Plains Quarterly* 27 (2007): 267–282.

Pfitzer, Gregory M. "The Only Good Alien Is a Dead Alien: Science Fiction and the Metaphysics of Indian-Hating on the High Frontier." *Journal of American Culture* 18.1 (1995): 51–67.

Pokornowski, Steven. "Burying the Living with the Dead: Security, Survival and the Sanction of Violence." *We're All Infected: Essays on AMC'S* The Walking Dead *And the Fate of the Human.* Ed. Dawn Keetley. Jefferson: McFarland, 2014. 41–55.

Pollitt, Katha. "Hers; the Smurfette Principle." *The New York Times.* 7 April 1991. www.nytimes.com/1991/04/07/magazine/hers-the-smurfette-principle.html.

Pressley-Sanon, Toni. *Zombifying a Nation: Race, Gender, and the Haitian* Loas *On Screen.* Jefferson: McFarland, 2016.

Proctor, William. "Interrogating the *Walking Dead*: Adaptation, Transmediality, and the Zombie Matrix." *Remake Television: Reboot, Re-Use, Recycle.* Ed. Carlen Lavigne. Lanham: Lexington Books, 2014. 5–20.

"Ramona Young." *Naluda.* n.d. naluda.com/interviews/ramona-young/.

Rees, Shelley S. "Frontier Values Meet Big-City Zombies: The Old West in AMC'S the *Walking Dead.*" *Undead in the West: Vampires, Zombies, Mummies, and Ghosts on the Cinematic Frontier.* Ed. Cynthia J. Miller and A. Bowdoin Van Riper. Lanham: The Scarecrow Press, 2012. 80–96.

Rosen, Elizabeth K. "Introduction." *Apocalyptic Transformation: Apocalypse and the Postmodern Imagination.* Ed. Elizabeth K. Rosen. Lanham, MD: Lexington Books, 2008. xi–xxxiv.

Rosenberg, Alyssa. "Check Out Syfy's New Show *Defiance* for the Women." *Slate.* 17 April 2013. www.slate.com/blogs/xx_factor/2013/04/17/syfy_defiance_has_promising_female_characters_like_stahma_irisa_and_amanda.html.

Rowles, Dustin. "Meet the Irish Actor Who Says His Agent Cost Him a Lead Role on the 'Walking Dead' Spinoff." *Uproxx.* 24 March 2015. uproxx.com/tv/meet-the-irish-actor-who-says-his-agent-cost-him-a-lead-role-on-the-walking-dead-spin-off/.

Rubio, Marco. "Iran Nuclear Deal an Unfolding Disaster." *CNN.* 18 October 2016. www.cnn.com/2016/10/17/opinions/iran-nuclear-deal-disaster-rubio/.

Rushton, Cory James, and Christopher Moreman. "Introduction: Race, Colonialism, and the Evolution of the 'Zombie.'" *Race, Oppression and the Zombie: Essays on Cross-Cultural Appropriations of the Caribbean Tradition.* Ed. Cory James Rushton and Christopher Moreman. Jefferson: McFarland, 2011. 1–14.

Scharrer, Erica. "The Man in the Box: Masculinity and Race in Popular Television." *Communicating Marginalized Masculinities: Identity Politics in TV, Film, and New Media.* Ed. Ronald L. Jackson II and Jamie E. Moshin. New York: Routledge, 2013. 159–173.

Schlatter, Evelyn A. *Aryan Cowboys: White Supremacists and the Search for a New Frontier, 1970–2000.* Austin: University of Texas Press, 2006.

Sharon. "What Shipping Richonne Taught Me About Racism." *Black Girl Nerds.* 22 February 2016. blackgirlnerds.com/what-shipping-richonne-taught-me-about-racism/.

Sharp, Patrick B. *Savage Perils: Racial Frontiers and Nuclear Apocalypse in American Culture.* Norman: University of Oklahoma Press, 2007.

Sharp, Patrick B. "Space, Future War, and the Frontier in American Nuclear Apocalypse Narrative." *Space and Beyond: The Frontier Theme in Science Fiction.* Ed. Gary Westfahl. Westport, CT: Greenwood Press, 2000. 151–156.

Sifferlin, Alexandra. "4 Diseases Making a Comeback Thanks to Anti-Vaxxers." *Time.* 17 March 2014. time.com/27308/4-diseases-making-a-comeback-thanks-to-anti-vaxxers/.

Simone, Gail. *Women in Refrigerators.* March 1999. lby3.com/wir/.

Simpson, Philip L. "The Zombie Apocalypse Is Upon Us! Homeland Insecurity." *We're All Infected: Essays on AMC'S* The Walking Dead *And the Fate of the Human.* Ed. Dawn Keetley. Jefferson: McFarland, 2014. 28–40.

Singer, Peter. "Meet the Sims … and Shoot Them." *Brookings.* 22 February 2010. www. brookings.edu/articles/meet-the-sims-and-shoot-them/.

Slotkin, Richard. *Gunfighter Nation: The Myth of the Frontier in Twentieth-Century America.* New York: Atheneum, 1992.

Snarker, Dorothy. "Bury Your Gays: Why 'The 100,' 'Walking Dead' Deaths Are Problematic (Guest Column)." *The Hollywood Reporter.* 21 March 2016. www. hollywoodreporter.com/live-feed/bury-your-gays-why-100-877176.

Sontag, Susan. "The Imagination of Disaster." *Commentary* (Oct. 1965): 42–48.

Sponsler, Claire. "The Geopolitics of Urban Decay and Cybernetic Play." *Science Fiction Studies* 20 (1993): 251–265.

"Stahma Tarr." Accessed April 2015. www. defiance.com/en/series/cast/stahma-tarr.

Sullivan, Tom R. *Cowboys and Caudillos: Frontier Ideology of the Americas.* Bowling Green: Bowling Green State University Popular Press, 1990.

Surette, Tim. "Exploring *Revolution*'s Homoerotic Subtext: Why Miles and Monroe's Relationship Is More Interesting than the Blackout." *Tv.com.* 7 June 2013. www.tv. com/news/exploring-revolutions-homoerotic-subtext-why-miles-and-monroes-relationship-is-more-interesting-than-the-blackout-137036218721/.

Takacs, Stacy. "Monsters, Monsters Everywhere: Spooky TV and the Politics of Fear in Post-9/11 America." *Science Fiction Studies* 36.1 (2009): 1–20.

Tasker, Yvonne, and Diane Negra, "Introduction: Feminist Politics and Postfeminist Culture." *Interrogating Postfeminism: Gender and the Politics of Popular Culture.* Ed. Yvonne Tasker and Diane Negra. Durham: Duke University Press, 2007. 1–26.

Taub, Gabby. "The 100 Has a White Feminism Problem." *Women Write About Comics.* 21 March 2017. womenwriteaboutcomics.com/2017/03/21/the-100-has-a-white-feminism-problem/.

Thomas, Anne-Marie. "To Devour and Transform: Viral Metaphors in Science Fiction by Women." *Extrapolation* 41.2 (2000): 143–160.

Thompson, Ethan, and Jason Mittell. "Introduction: An Owner's Manual for Television." *How to Watch Television.* Ed. Ethan Thompson and Jason Mittell. New York: New York University Press, 2013. 1–9.

Thompson, Kirsten Moana. *Apocalyptic Dread: American Film at the Turn of the Millennium.* Albany: State University of New York Press, 2007.

Tomes, Nancy. "Epidemic Entertainments: Disease and Popular Culture in Early–Twentieth-Century America." *American Literary History* 14.1 (2002): 625–652.

Turner, Matthew R. "Cowboys and Comedy: The Simultaneous Deconstruction and Reinforcement of Generic Conventions in the Western Parody." *Hollywood's West: The American Frontier in Film, Television, and History.* Ed. Peter C. Rollins and John E. O'Connor. Lexington: The University Press of Kentucky, 2005. 218–239.

Urbanski, Heather. *Plagues, Apocalypses and Bug-Eyed Monsters: How Speculative Fiction Shows Us Our Nightmares.* Jefferson: McFarland, 2007.

USAID. "Emerging Pandemic Threats." Last updated 18 July 2016. www.usaid.gov/ what-we-do/global-health/pandemic-influenza-and-other-emerging-threats.

Valluvan, Sivamohan. "What Is 'Post-Race' and What Does It Reveal About Contemporary Racism?" *Ethnic and Racial Studies* 39.1.3 (2016): 2241–2251.

Vernon, JoEtta A., J. Allen Williams, Jr., Terri Phillips, and Janet Wilson. "Media Stereotyping: A Comparison of the Way Elderly Women and Men Are Portrayed on Prime-Time Television." *Sociology Department, Faculty Publications.* University of Nebraska, 1990. digitalcommons. unl.edu/sociologyfacpub/5.

Vials, Chris. "The Origin of the Zombie in American Radio and Film: B-Horror, U.S. Empire, and the Politics of Disavowal." *Generation Zombie: Essays on the Living Dead in Modern Culture.* Ed. Stephanie Boluk and Wylie Lenz. Jefferson: McFarland, 2011. 41–53.

Wald, Priscilla. *Contagious: Cultures, Carri-*

ers, and the Outbreak Narrative. Durham: Duke University Press, 2008.

Walliss, John, and James Aston. "Doomsday America: The Pessimistic Turn of Post-9/11 Apocalyptic Cinema." Journal of Religion and Popular Culture 23.1 (2011): 53–64.

Walsh, Michael. "'Let It Be an Arms Race': Trump Doubles Down on Nuclear Proliferation." Yahoo News. 23 December 2016. www.yahoo.com/news/let-it-be-an-arms-race-trump-doubles-down-on-nuclear-proliferation-153229263.html.

Warner, Kristen J. The Cultural Politics of Colorblind TV Casting. New York: Routledge, 2015.

Weart, Spencer R. Nuclear Fear: A History of Images. Cambridge: Harvard University Press, 1988.

Westfahl, Gary. "Introduction: Frontiers Old and New." Space and Beyond: The Frontier Theme in Science Fiction. Ed. Gary Westfahl. Westport, CT: Greenwood Press, 2000. 1–8.

Whitten, Chris. "Gadsden Flag History." Gadsden.Info. 2009. www.gadsden.info/history.html.

Wilken, Selina. "5 Times the 100 Totally Subverted (And Exceeded) Our Expectations." Hypable. 3 August 2015. www.hypable.com/the-100-review-sexuality-female-characters/.

Williams, Evan Calder. Combined and Uneven Apocalypse. Hants: Zero Books, 2011.

Woolf, Nicky. "Ebola Isn't the Big One. So What Is? And Are We Ready for It?." The Guardian. 3 October 2014. www.theguardian.com/world/2014/oct/03/-sp-ebola-outbreak-risk-global-pandemic-next.

Worland, Justin. "American Tourism Might Be Helping North Korea's Weapons Program." Time. 10 November 2016. time.com/4566405/north-korea-us-tourism/.

Wright, Will. The Wild West: The Mythical Cowboy and Social Theory. London: Sage Publications, 2001.

Writers Guild of America. WGAW 2015 TV Staffing Brief. documents.latimes.com/writers-guild-america-west-tv-staffing-brief/.

Yang, Jeff. "Into the Badlands' Daniel Wu Is the Asian American Action Hero That Bruce Lee Should've Been." Slate. 23 November 2015. www.slate.com/blogs/browbeat/2015/11/23/into_the_badlands_daniel_wu_interview_he_s_the_asian_action_hero_that_bruce.html.

Young, P. Ivan. "Walking Tall or Walking Dead? The American Cowboy in the Zombie Apocalypse." We're All Infected: Essays on AMC'S The Walking Dead and the Fate of the Human. Ed. Dawn Keetley. Jefferson: McFarland, 2014. 56–67.

Zeidel, Alex. "The 100 Is the Most Feminist Show on TV." Previously.Tv. 17 December 2014. previously.tv/the-100/the-100-is-the-most-feminist-show-on-tv/.

Index

183

www.ingramcontent.com/pod-product-compliance
Lightning Source LLC
Chambersburg PA
CBHW031136270326
41929CB00011B/1640